PEOPLE, POLITICS AND COMMUNITY IN THE LATER MIDDLE AGES

PEOPLE, POLITICS AND COMMUNITY IN THE LATER MIDDLE AGES

Edited by
JOEL ROSENTHAL AND COLIN RICHMOND

ALAN SUTTON · Gloucester

ST. MARTIN'S PRESS · New York
1987

942.03
P39

First published in Great Britain in 1987
Alan Sutton Publishing Limited
30 Brunswick Road
Gloucester GL1 1JJ

British Library Cataloguing in Publication Data

People, politics and community in the later Middle Ages.
  1. Great Britain—History—Lancaster and York, 1399–1485
  2. Great Britain—History—Henry VII, 1485–1509
  I. Rosenthal, Joel T.   II. Richmond, Colin
  942.04   DA245

  ISBN 0-86299-359-8

First published in the United States of America in 1984
St. Martin's Press, Inc.
175 Fifth Avenue
New York, NY 10010

Library of Congress Cataloging in Publication Data

People, politics and community in the later Middle Ages.
Includes bibliographies and index.
  1. Great Britain—Politics and government—1154–1399—Congresses.
  2. Great Britain—Politics and government.—1399–1485—Congresses.
  3. England—Social conditions—Medieval period, 1066–1485—
  Congresses. I. Rosenthal, Joel Thomas, 1934– . II. Richmond.
  Colin. III. International Congress on Medieval Studies (20th : 1985 :
  Western Michigan University)
  JN137.P46   1987   942.03—dc19   87–21173

  ISBN 0-312-01220-9

Typesetting and origination by Alan Sutton Publishing, Gloucester
Printed in Great Britain

Contents

Introduction

These papers comprise an international collection of work focusing on fifteenth century England. Some of them were presented at the XX International Congress on Medieval Studies at Western Michigan University, May 1985. Others were presented at the fourth symposium on fifteenth-century English history at Keele University, July 1985. A few were gathered from other sources and efforts.

The papers that we offer here were not commissioned to deal with any particular theme or set of problems. Rather, each represents an individualized contribution. In some cases the paper is drawn from a dissertation or a portion of a larger work-in-progress, while in others it is a detached or an *ad hoc* essay. Thus, apart from their inherent merit and interest – and the readers, not the editors, must be the final judges in that court – we can address ourselves to the issue of a unity or coherence for the collection that was not consciously imposed by the editors or acknowledged by the authors.

In this discussion we must beware of simply falling on our knees before the idol of 'the common theme'. It is tempting to offer a title or subtitle that blankets a useful miscellany and that then appears to convert the entire endeavour into an aggregation of related essays on some issue that we declare, *ex-post facto*, as being of paramount importance. From this sort of editorial largesse we may sometimes derive such a useful (and now conventional) package as 'the general crisis of the seventeenth century', or, we imagine, 'the industrial revolution' itself. But on the other hand, we can wind up with a group of papers that have been pushed into a procrustean bed perhaps never occupied by any of the inhabitants of the place or time actually under examination, nor, consciously, by any of our contributors. Part of our task as historians is to impose meaning and order upon the multiplicity of past action, and to show causal chains and some suggestions for a rank ordering of significance, aetiology, and teleology. But part of our task is to recognize diversity and eccentricity; to find some comfortable interpretation that accounts for both trees and forests.

When we talk of the fifteenth century there is a great temptation to speak of a 'general crisis of law and order' and to discourse sagely about the collapse of the social synthesis or symbiosis that had once given rise to powerful central institutions and a strong, if fluctuating, continental presence. But before we embrace such themes, along with their implications for social change and for historiographical interpretation, we should pause to ask how much of that very crisis was perceived and noted by men and women of the time. The answer, as we well know, is partially dependent upon what we choose to look at and whose words we choose to take most seriously. The Pastons and the Celys and their ilk lived and worked through the worst days of this general crisis, but for the most part they were too concerned with short term fortunes and vicissitudes to have much interest in conjuncture, let alone in the long durée and menalité. So much for myopia and our inclination to set today's table with yesterday's dishes. The world of these families on the make was no less important or real than that of Justice Fortescue, and a good deal more vivid to follow in detail. *The Chronicles of London* saw change and crisis, and there is a lesson for us in their resolve not to err on the side of verbosity: 'And the said Duke (of Gloucester) was with quene Anne his wif at and in Westmynster Chirch crowned wt greate solempnyte of many states and gentilmen, the vjth day of July'.[1]

On the other hand, we hardly wish to iron out all the wrinkles of the fifteenth century. There is no question that someone looking backwards in the year 1500 could well reflect upon a number of unusual features in the century that had just come to its end. Including the hapless Edward V there had been seven kings between 1400 and 1500. This was about double the number the English had been called upon to endure in the thirteenth or fourteenth century; the calculus of royal succession had indeed speeded up. How clear was it to our observer of 1500 that England's days as the owner-occupier of considerable portions of France were now over? This is not so easy to answer; we are all wise about foreign affairs, but our wisdom varies considerably with our identification with our rulers and their policies. And lastly, to what extent were the breakdowns of law and order and the tally of battles fought upon home soil to be interpreted (in 1500) as but rather strong reactions to ephemeral problems, to what extent had they pleaded a case for basic flaws in the social fabric? Again, we can probably put our money on either runner at about the same odds. If we wish we can see Edward IV and Henry VII as presiding over a 'new monarchy', just as we can choose to see them merely driving along in a late medieval state coach. Are we perceptibly lurching into a new era, or are we sitting around with varying degrees of patience, awaiting the arrival of Thomas Cromwell, or – of considerably greater interest – of Oliver?

Reflections of these sorts are meant to open questions and issues, not to close them. One point served by this collection of papers is to demonstrate once more how current interest in the last medieval century still continues in full spate. Our search for a common theme in the papers is partially an intellectual challenge, partially a delight in our excess of riches. The floodgates that K. B. McFarlane long controlled and that he slowly began to open before his death in 1966 now serve to guide a steady flow of work about society and politics. There is one particular way in which we continue to stand as his heirs.[2] Through his own work he seemed to posit the idea that the best way to crack the code of the fifteenth century was by working from small groups outward. He never tried his hand at a total or a synthetic explanation: his approach was too austere, his horizons deliberately kept too limited. A comprehensive view would only emerge from the disciplined treatment of carefully circum-scribed problems and topics. He may also have felt that a century was really but a short span and that the intellectual challenges lay in studying the particular. Certainly the years between 1399 and 1509 are an uncertain period that lends itself neither to the broad brush nor to the cult of the individual. After Henry V died in 1422 the century is largely devoid of heroes. Though this is not much loss, it does affect the nature of biographical and political studies, and it fuels our propensity to look away from the great white fathers towards various social groups of relatively handy size – be they rural or urban, great or petty in stature, secular or spiritual.

Editors would be remiss if they did not offer some guidance – by which is meant, impose some unity – regarding that which they edit. In so far as the papers we offer here do have a common theme, it would seem to be concerned with the attempt to identify and situate self within the context of group or community and then to formulate membership within that community so as to delineate the boundaries between 'us' and 'them'. Such a thesis is striking neither for its novelty nor for any special applicability to the fifteenth century. If it is not quite a universal explanation for innumerable forms of social action, it is hardly a mere result of a 'general crisis' within our period. Rather, the papers offer a series of case studies examining how fifteenth century men and women – though almost always men, as we come to the issue – in the midst of crises and of calm patches can be seen to move along what were to them particularized lines of force and which to us are simultaneously comprehensible as fitting into a general field theory. Individuals lived lives that were some mixture of the forces over which they had control and those which they did not. We see, in the instances below, how they tried to use their share of the first side to buffer the ways in which their share of the second would bounce them around.

We must not become antinomians. For all our reluctance to allow a 'general crisis' explanation to take the reins, there were real anomalies in

England in these years. A century that opens with a parliament-kissed usurper on the throne and that ends with a battlefield victor as his ultimate successor did pose certain genuine problems regarding stability and continuity. No wonder, we are prone to assert, people sought to belong, to find groups, communities, and social units into which they could fit, into which they could climb as chance offered. However, the particular and unique events and circumstances of fifteenth century England were the context, the occasion, for the desire to belong to community; they were not the cause. That lies far deeper in us all. The forces that shape the segmentation of a traditional or tribal society into age sets and totemic and secret bands are akin to those that led an American historian to characterize the people of the United States as a nation of joiners. Most of us, it seems, want to belong – even if it is only to the aggregation of eremetic brothers and sisters who used to be so prevalent in the deserts of Egypt and Syria.

Seen in this perspective, the papers below do present many variations on a common theme. We see tales of personal and group integration – some more successful than others – and we see elaborate efforts to build individual and collective identities, as well as historical myths constructed so as to lend security and credibility to all sorts of enterprises. Such psycho-social devices are in no way the special property of the people of the century under discussion. But each tale is worked out as a case study, a small segment of 'the total' history of the fifteenth century: careers, institutions, ideas, social interaction, and self consciousness all have their parts upon the stage. The universal quest – along with the search for sex, money, and domination – was to be enough like other people so as to be accepted, enough ahead of the others to be first in the queue. Some tension between competition and co-operation, some uneasy stasis between belonging and not-belonging helped drive the social machine (along with its separate human components).

The study of the life of a successful individual is likely to conclude with more credits on that side of the ledger reserved for balance and co-operation than on that marked imbalance and competition. Of course, the subjects of success stories can well afford to try to look like everyone else; their race was mostly a winning one and they had no trouble joining and belonging. Thus the two bishops whose lives and res qestae are treated below are readily seen as end results of harmonious careerism, even if they took an occasional knock along the way. William Alnwick is one of those bishops who emerged from an unknown background and who then climbed a long way, most of it upwards. Rosemary Hayes' verdict, that he was 'a natural candidate for promotion,' seems eminently convincing, especially as we can study in detail how he went up and up the ladder. His legal training and his contacts in what we can think of as keeper of the privy seal are all benchmarks that we expect to attend the long and profitable episcopal career. Alnwick is typical of the service-oriented prince of the church, just as he is of the reticent and rather private individuals who filled so many of the realm's higher positions while keeping an eye upon their main chance.

William Waynflete followed a different route. He rose to prominence and fame through service to and within the educational network, though we must remember how heavily that network depended upon royal endorsement and endowment. The great founder-bishop (of Magdalen College, Oxford, and of grammar schools at Oxford and Wainfleet, Lincolnshire) rose by dint of service at Winchester College and Eton, and by catching (and holding) the royal eye. Such service impressed upon Waynflete himself the possibilities of benefaction and foundation – if sufficient support were forthcoming. He combined educational vision, the ability to attract support, traditional obeisance to philanthropy and alms giving, and canny administrative skills. Virginia Davis gives us as rounded a picture of such a man as we are likely to get; such a tough, ambitious, and yet visionary man is not often an easy cypher to solve.

A few significant individuals clearly stand at the top, the brightest examples of careerism. But the process itself is also worth attention simply as a process. As men rose they had also to seek acceptance in their new roles and by their new colleagues. As such, careerism was a complex and never static endeavor, and its structural–functional rhythms had to accomodate the demands of society's rulers, of the supply of and the demand for personnel, of the institutions needed to train and funnel those personnel, and of the incessant call for rewards and promotions (along with punishments and demotions). Though at first glance we might assume a simple link between upward mobility and social (and personal) integration, they can be uneasy companions. Michael Bennett's essay draws upon a large canvas, and by no means the least compelling part of his picture is the chiaroscuro between some general and long term patterns and the quick vignettes provided by such as the Finchams of Norfolk or a number of the archbishops of York. A perennial problem for students of English society centers on the question of its 'openness', and we like to think that we are helping cultivate a landscape of opportunity that runs from the civil servants and new men of Henry I through the Labour leaders of the day before yesterday. We can also pause for a moment to reflect on the other dynamic – of downward mobility, of the lack of sons, of debt and lost law suits, of mistaken speculations, even of death and execution. However, it was the potential of successful careerism, not the grimmer odds against success, that helped hold 'the system' together; those 'innumerable strands of enterprise and careerism', as Bennett sums it up. Each careerist presumably assumed that for him, at least, there would always be an open door and a welcome into the club.

For a few years, in the late fourteenth and early fifteenth century chancery clerks and peers with large bureaucracies thought they had found a course of mutual advantage. This door, until the accession of Henry V, opened either way, and Charles Smith is able to trace both chancery careers and the composition of aristocratic councils and general staffs as the strands of membership and service intertwined. But reaction followed: it was decreed that a man could not serve two masters, or rather, that he could not belong in two places at once. What is of interest is that it was not the masters or their versatile servants who chafed at this law of the conservation of self interest, but rather those who were being excluded from or by the new set of links. All parties consenting, loyalty could be considered as a tamed animal, quite happy on a long and a flexible lead.

Other types of organizations and other communities – large and small, localized or geographically catholic – had their own priorities as they too chased that elusive oracular spot at which social management and external approval became as one. Urban gilds are a prime example of inclusiveness, whereby the behavior of members, their concerted social action, and their collective image and prestige merged. Ben McCree's discussion of internal gild behavior, especially touching members' morals and the level and style of social intercourse between gild members, illustrates the extent to which the perception of others affects how we behave, or how we wish to be seen to behave: 'a game of appearances', and a well understood game at that. Few may have been fooled by the creation of an elaborate facade of manners and regulations, but all were socialized to be respectful regarding the emperor's wardrobe and the washing of the linen.

The aristocratic or great bourgeois household, like the gilds, was both a nurturing and a manipulative institution, R.G.K.A. Mertes discusses how it could offer cohesion and common purpose as it simultaneously served its lord, its constituent members, and its surrounding neighbours and dependants. 'Good governaunce' meant the socialization of household personnel, the support of upper class philanthropic and elemosinary activities, and the creation of a social unit within which labor and discipline were supposedly balanced by rewards and a sense of community. What is of special interest is the way in which the household of an absent master might continue to serve many of the same purposes. It existed for its own members and residents, at all social levels, as well as for him who ultimately called its tunes: a 'familye (that) may live together in love and kindnesse', as those in positions of power liked to put the matter.

The realm, at least through the seventeenth century, can easily be seen as an aggregation of localized communities, each with its own variation of a hierarchical social structure and provincial loyalty and identity. We are much better informed, of course, about such phenomena in Tudor and

Stuart times than we are for the later middle ages, though some recent work has begun to correct the imbalance.[3] Three papers in this collection examine some segment of the kingdom, and each paper pays due attention to how local problem solving and local loyalty smoothed over some problems, though often at the cost of raising others. Simon Payling examines the correlation between the strength of the king's arm and the local inclination to resort to some form of self help. However, local self help was not necessarily anarchy or a Hobbesian free-for-all, and when lord Cromwell wanted to preserve local stability and to maintain a balance between various factions in the area he dominated, he could enlist the gentry and the legally adroit for his purposes. On the other hand, fifteenth century Nottinghamshire was not a pastoral utopia of shepherds and amorous pipers, and when the same lord Cromwell chose to crush his opposition and over-awe the uncommitted, he likewise was able to enlist the (same) upper middle class landholders and the white collar professionals.

Often conflict resolution just means conflict. When serious fighting occurred, men tended to fight in units that relied heavily upon their local bonds, as they continued to do until the carnage of the Western Front in the First World War ended the territorial organization of the English army. At Blore Heath on 22 September 1459 the men of Cheshire stood together and fell together. Or so, James Gillespie tells us, has the myth run for almost 500 years. A more detailed analysis of the combatants and the resulting casualty lists makes the matter less dramatic and more checkered; local ties may have drawn the men together into lord Audley's ranks, but such ties were invariably not strong enough to hold them together against either the charge of Yorkist cavalry or a keen scrutiny of the extant sources and family histories. To the losers stone dead may have had no fellow, but to the community of Cheshire gentry it was not necessarily the only alternative.

Against a more determined ruler the men of Cornwall and the southwest had less flexibility after the risings of 1497. In this remote corner of the realm, social bonds and regional identity bound minor peers, gentry, and ecclesiatical and urban leaders, though hardly to their profit or advantage after the fall of Perkin Warbeck. Ian Arthurson argues that regional prosperity helped bind men to a common cause, and that Henry VII correctly realized that he had to deal with – and eventually to isolate and humble – not just a few malcontents or cranks or social deviants, but a community. And the early Tudor mix of the carrot and the stick, of the axe, the bond, and the recognisance, was specially orchestrated towards this end. The southwest was made to realize how close to the edge it had walked, and it would be 'almost fifty years before any westerners dared raise their heads again in the political arena of the realm'.

Not all communities were tied by the immediate bonds of self interest and reciprocity. An historical myth that not only justified Scotland's separatism and independent status but that give her seniority and perhaps ideological primacy over England was worth more to people north of the border than a mere bedside tale. Nor is it a surprise that Scottish historians phantisized their past and sought to transmute moonbeams into noonday sunshine. We have no trouble following how or why, in Marjorie Drexler's exposition, the pseudo-historical package of Grecian origins and Celtic migration was accepted as the genuine article with so little dissent. In a world order where origins counted for so much more than subsequent evolution, it was a fortunate community that could compensate for some of its beleagured past by forging a useful view of national and royal cosmology. Every people should have at least one set of tales of an Alfred and his cakes, one Geoffrey of Monmouth.

Nor were the king's subjects the only ones who searched for legitimation in mythopaeic activities. Even kings themselves wanted to belong, to be seen to be an even more integral part of their own proper group. In their case membership was in the most exclusive club of all – that which only admitted those who wore a crown. But for those who qualified, Joel Rosenthal argues, there were still types of behavior and activity that served to demonstrate first class membership, that exalted the lord's anointed above and beyond other applicants and would-be-brothers, and that linked members across the span of the years. The quest for belonging is an endless one; neither sight of the grail nor safe return to home and hearth serve to mark its logical terminus.

For all our generalizing, variety of approach has to be intrinsic to any useful and suggestive collection of papers. We have argued here for a way of linking these essays, but we are in no position to insist that this reading be accepted – by authors or by readers – in whole or necessarily even in large part. This collection follows on the heels of similar volumes edited in recent years by the late Charles Ross, Ralph A. Griffiths, R. B. Dobson, and Tony Pollard. In his own introduction Professor Dobson spoke of these volumes as 'an experiment well worth continuing,'[4] and we can only hope that this present contribution causes no one to change his or her mind on that sanguine suggestion.

As well as those whose names appear in the table of contents, many others have contributed to the enterprise which now bears fruit: Bernard Finnemore, Ralph A. Griffiths, DeLloyd J. Guth, A. Compton Reeves, Marjorie McIntosh, Edwin B. DeWindt, Tony Pollard, John Theilemann.

NOTES

1 Kingsford, C.L. (ed.), *The Chronicles of London*, Oxford, 1905: reprinted, Gloucester, 1977, p. 191.
2 For other assessments of McFarlane's legacy, Colin Richmond, 'Review Article: After McFarlane', *History* 68(1983), 46–60; G. L. Harriss, Introduction to K.B. McFarlane, *England in the Fifteenth Century: Collected Essays*, London, 1981, ix–xxvii.
3 Michael Bennett, *Community, Class, and Careerism: Cheshire and Lancashire Society in the Age of Sir Gawain and the Green Knight*, Cambridge, 1983.
4 R. B. Dobson (ed.), *The Church, Politics and Patronage in the Fifteenth Century*, Gloucester, 1984, p. 9.

The Rising of 1497: A Revolt of the Peasantry?

I. ARTHURSON

I

On 30th September, 1497, Henry VII entered the town of Wells in Somerset. Mounted on a warhorse he was fully clothed in armour. At his back he had a force of over 10,000 men, and this included most, if not all, of the noblemen of England, probably his son, Prince Arthur, and certainly over half the government of England.[1]

At this stage Wells did not interest the King very much. It was simply a convenient resting place on the road to Exeter. Things were to change very much within a couple of years, but at that moment the King's thoughts were of Exeter: Exeter, the town which during the recent rebellion had stayed loyal to the King, and was now in the hands of the Earl of Devon. The Earl himself could not meet Henry at Wells because he had been wounded in the recent fighting. So he had sent a number of his lieutenants to meet the King and reassure him that Exeter was a royal stronghold, that Daubney, his Chamberlain, held the county of Somerset, and that Robert, Lord Willoughby de Broke held Portsmouth and Dorset. Perkin Warbeck, the begetter of the whole affair, had fled from Taunton to Beaulieu, first looking for sanctuary and then for surrender. Only Cornwall remained in open rebellion against its King; but soon it too would be reduced to obedience by de Broke, Daubney and the Earl.[2]

When Henry entered Wells he bore in his wake a large artillery train, and a body of Dutch gunners who exercised frightening rituals, and had unpronounceable names. It was, as he himself said, 'an armee royall of peuple soo furnisshed with artilleryes and ordeinices for the felde as shalbe hable to defende any prince christian With goddes fauour'.[3] Faced with this obvious manifestation of Henry's power the small time oligarchs who ruled Wells could hardly have remained sanguine. Not only were they visited by their Monarch, but behind the King's train came that of his secretary, Oliver King – the Bishop of Bath and Wells, their Bishop. It must have been an awesome occasion.

The names of those who greeted their King were not recorded. But we do know that Henry was welcomed to the town by its Mayor, Nicholas Trappe.

Nicholas presumably made a fulsome speech of loyalty to the King, applauded, not to say egged on, by his fellow burgesses. For the moment they pleased Henry. Three years later they were nowhere near as fortunate. Then, they were called before the King's Commissioners, twice, and asked to explain their behaviour and actions during June of '97.[4] Alas, they could not satisfy the King's men. Had they ever really satisfied the King? The group who had stood to welcome Henry VII were royally fined:—

> Nicholas Trappe – £10.
> John Smith – Mayor during the insurrection – £40.
> The two Town Constables – £10 and £6 – and the Town's Auditors – that is the clique which ruled Wells, and always provided its mayors – were massively fined.

Nonetheless, in the Autumn of '97 Henry did not bother them for long. He stayed only one night and was gone, via Taunton and Tiverton, to Exeter, which he reached on 7th October. Of all the towns in the west, Exeter had been most loyal during the risings. It had done its best to stop Michael Joseph, though it had failed: and it had fought off Perkin Warbeck. Other towns told different stories and paid for them, but Exeter, said Henry, to his Earl of Devon, made him 'right glad and pleased'. When the King got there after his long journey he presented the city with a sword and a ceremonial cap of maintenance. Then he settled into his temporary accommodation near St. Peter's Close and called the rulers of the west before him. He did not pull his punches. He placed the blame for the success of the first rising on the gentry and charged them with breach of duty. More than this he did not do. And, indeed, in the one month he spent at Exeter he could do very little. He did what was normal for a King to do in such circumstances. He weeded out the chief rebels and executed the most obviously guilty. The less guilty he first terrified, with threats of hanging, and then pardoned.[5]

One thing the King was prepared to do. He used his knowledge of finance to reward and, simultaneously, to punish those he suspected of treachery. The Abbot of Tavistock, for example, had lent the King £60 for his war against Scotland. Henry repaid this immediately, and then placed the Abbot under a bond in 500 marks to be loyal for the rest of his life or suffer the consequences.[6]

Yet, in the end, Henry could do little more than restore order to the west, and to give it back to its proper governors, the Earl of Devon, Lord Daubney, Lord de Broke, men whose absence had allowed the rebellion to develop. Having done this, he did no more. After an enormous feast, the like of which Exeter could not have seen in twenty years, the King left his loyal city on 2nd November.[7] However, if Henry had not been completely ruthless while he was in the west, he had divined that there was more to the rising of June than had met his eye. There had been an uncomfortable number of gentlemen, churchmen and burgesses caught up in the affair who had unctuously sued for mercy. However, before we look at these people we must ask why it was that they, and the rest of the western community, should have become involved in this massive upheaval? In other words, we must return to the days immediately before the rebellion erupted on 14th May.

II

On the 14th May, 1497 the whole resources of the realm of England were being marshalled to deliver a crippling blow against the kingdom of Scotland and Perkin Warbeck. By land an army of 20,000 men, or more, was to be sent against the Scots. By sea over 70 ships, and 5,000 men, were to attack Aberdeen and Edinburgh. No part of England, and no part of the community was unaware of these facts, and very few people escaped some responsibility for seeing that this happened. Everyone was to provision, pay for, or fight in the King's armies. And the armies were to be equipped with the very best and most expensive of weapons. No one could escape the consequences of the war with Scotland.[8]

In all this the talents of the west of England were indispensable. The west is, as it was then, a maritime region, and Cornwall especially had skill in the crafts needed in time of war. To undermine Scottish castles experts were needed. Henry called for 96 miners, presumably tinners, to be provided from the Duchy of Cornwall and kitted out with Tudor livery and mining gear.[9] From Cornwall too came his Commander in Chief of the Navy, Lord de Broke. He was Lord Steward of the Duchy of Cornwall. De Broke was to gather ships from all the western shires, including Cornwall, and assemble them at Portsmouth. From Cornwall he took the *Anne of Fowey* and others, from Devon two ships, from Bristol one ship, belonging to Sir Robert Pointz, as well as three others. So it went on round the region. These ships were, let us remember, to carry an army. Cornwall and Devon were not called on to provide men, but counties further north did not escape. Somerset, Wiltshire and Gloucestershire had to raise 2,000 soldiers, and at least another 2,000 men were expected from further afield. This meant that when the rebellion broke out, and the rebels reached Somerset, there were no soldiers between Taunton and Guildford with which to oppose them. Nor were there any loyal commanders for the King to fall back on. They were at sea with their ships.[10]

So much for the King's navy. It was substantially a western force. What of the armies by land? The army to attack Edinburgh was to be of two parts. One part, the vanguard, was to muster at Berwick by mid-June, and the other part was to begin mustering after mid-summer, probably in July. This second 'ward' was to have been commanded by the King. The vanguard was to be led by the King's Lord Chamberlain, Giles Daubney. Daubney was a Somerset man, and, like de Broke, a veteran of the campaigns of '83, '85, '87 and '92. It was expected that Daubney would lead a van of over 10,000 men into Scotland.[11] Personally speaking Daubney would have led his Somerset tenants against the Scots, and he would have done so in the company of near neighbours of his. From Somerset James, Lord Audley, was to lead 100 men, and Roger Twynhoo was to lead 20 men. In fact, both these men became rebels. Nearby Wiltshire was to send 100 men with Sir Walter Hungerford.[12]

This, then, was the west's contribution, more, not less, than other parts of the realm: two commanders, a navy and many soldiers. Other parts of the country were expected to make contributions too, of course. In the north of England, wagons to transport supplies. Vast numbers of bows and arrows made in the Midlands. Beer, and beer barrels came from Kent, grain from the South Midlands and Yorkshire.[13] All this cost a great deal of money. Parliament granted Henry £120,000. The King also took large grants from the Church, and from the border areas normally exempt from taxation, Wales and the marches. To cap it all, there had also been a forced loan levied in the six months between December, 1496, and May of 1497. The point here is not so much the amount of money being asked for, which was colossal, but that very few individuals, even if they escaped enrollment in their Lord's retinue, or avoided contributing to the material preparations for the campaign, escaped paying. Everyone was expected to pay; churchmen, merchants, gentry, royal administrators, nobility and peasantry. And the Parliamentary Acts by which Henry raised his tax, the old fifteenth and tenth as well as the new fangled subsidy, dug deep into the recent wealth of the south west. Worse was the thought that even those whose purses could bear such a strain might find themselves assessing taxes, gathering them, paying their own, and fighting for the King.[14]

Small wonder then that many rebels were men who loaned the King money, and helped to gather his taxes as well. They would have come under tremendous pressure from their neighbours to join the rebellion. The logic of the situation, perhaps illogic would be a better word, was inescapable – something had to give. Too much was being expected in return for too little. England was not seriously threatened by Scotland. But Henry VII's policy, and Henry VII's claim to the throne, that motor of his policy, were being probed. Henry's reaction to this probing was in inverse relation to the impact of the feeble raid by James IV and Perkin Warbeck. Questions were also being asked of Henry's political ability. Could he (did he ever) carry the realm into successful outward war? There was, after all, in June, 1497, a strange implosion, a reversion, almost, to civil war, in answer to this question. It only needed one show of defiance from the west and the whole pretentious edifice of Tudor dynasticism would crumble. When Michael Joseph An Gof, the smith, objected to the assessment of taxes at St. Keverne the wonder is not that he and his rebels were able to march to Blackheath and fight the King, but that the King found the political will in the rest of the community to resist them.

In fact, in the west of England, the showing made by Tudor loyalists was pathetic. They let the rebels pass through Devon to reach Somerset. Here the rebels launched a savage and audacious pincer attack across country, against London. Could they have managed this if they had not had either the outright support of the community, or if the community – gentry, clergy and towns – had not connived with them? This seems to me as doubtful a proposition as it did to Henry VII. As early as three days after the battle of Blackheath, the King had proclaimed that his rebels had 'levied war. . .through the counties of Somerset, Dorset, Wiltshire, Sussex and Surrey . . . so that many of the King's subjects of the same counties to them resorted, repaired and greatly increased their number . . . to fight against the King's highness'.[15] Parts of this proclamation presaged the huge enquiry of later years, when Henry spent almost a decade rooting out 'his' rebels. The fact that today we know that the entire community of the west was involved in insurrection is testimony to the King's realisation that at Blackheath he had faced deposition not by peasants but by the political nation of the west.

III

There can have been very few rebellions, ever, which have been levied exclusively by one class upon another. Most rebellions have involved oddities of one sort or another – the romantic, the renegade lord, the poor gentleman, the religious fanatic, successful, even unsuccessful, rebellion in the middle ages was inconceivable without the support of the politically important. This is seen as much in the sixteenth century as it is in the almost classical case of the Peasants' Revolt of 1381. The so-called Cornish Rising has always been a widely touted exception to this rule, with its amalgam of peasant discontent, aristocratic stupidity, legalistic protest and Perkin Warbeck.[16]

Why 1497 should stand as the exception to the rule is difficult to see. The chronicle sources have been available for many years and have always suggested what the King knew, wide support for the rebels. In any case, to suggest that those who fought at Blackheath were *only* peasants suggests absurd naivety about peasant abilities; either that or a wilful ignorance about rebellions and the communities from which rebels come.

We cannot and do not know the exact composition of the army which fought at Blackheath. We do, however, know some of the names and fortunes of those Henry considered rebel, and these come from every position in the community. No rebellion which developed as this one did, into a sophisticated campaign, could have escaped from its own county without the collusion of the gentry. Regardless of the actual circumstances which allowed the rebels to cross the Tamar, had the Cornish gentry mobilised their following for the King, there might have been a static rising but not a campaign. Instead of opposing the rebels the gentry of western Cornwall threw in their lot with them (I would state it positively) and marched out of Cornwall. In 1498 and '99 they were the first to be punished by the King. Some rather unimportant gentlemen had been executed in '97, but a larger and more influential group was dealt with two years later. Their names form a continuum of Cornish history from the middle ages to the present – the Godolphin family, the Trefusis family, the Trewynnard family, the Bevil family, the Durant family, the Bere family, Nans of Kerrier; and their punishments, bonds of loyalty, involved them with others of the same class. These were, in fact, families who, in happier times, served the King; and even in less happy times, for, in 1499, they were obliged to collect the fines from their own villages.[17]

The idea that the rebellion of '97 was exlusively Cornish has been challenged before, although this happened a long time ago in a rather obscure article. The author of that article pointed out that the King paid a great deal of attention to Somerset after the rebellion, and proceeded to show that some Somerset gentry families were treated exactly as their Cornish counterparts had been. He showed that Thomas Malet, Alexander Pym and John St. Aubyn were placed under multiple bonds and heavily fined as well.[18] Unfortunately he did not go on to examine the lists of fines, for had he done so he would have made an interesting discovery. He would have found that in Somerset alone twenty-two gentlemen were fined. This was a prestigious group. It included four sheriffs, three M.P.'s and James Daubney, the brother of the King's Chamberlain. These families were the most eminent the County could boast. The Lutterels, for example, still own Dunster Castle. Sir Hugh was fined £200. Sir John Speke, who was the Earl of Devon's Steward, was fined £200 before he obtained a pardon.[19] And let us not, at this juncture, paint Henry VII, in 1497 and after, in the colours of Henry VI, dolling out pardons to the fortunate culpable. Behind this punishment was real knowledge and discrimination, and many hours of personal interrogation by the King. The fines were real fines; they were collected, not merely assessed, and the punishment was real punishment. After all, there were many gentry who were never fined. Somerset was gone through with a fine tooth comb, and perhaps as much as half the county establishment was found wanting. In Dorset that old fool Sir Nicholas Latimer once again backed the wrong horse, and once again was fined, bound over and lost control of his estates. In Devon loss of manorial rights and a perpetual annuity to the Tudors, was the preferred method of punishment.[20] However, let us turn to the partners in crime of the gentry, the clergy.

The Peasants' Revolt and the Pilgrimage of Grace have received much attention, and one prime group which has emerged in the forefront of rebellion, either because of belief, or for social reasons, is the clergy.[21] Ostensibly they, like the gentry, had a duty to their patrons, to say nothing of the medieval God, to ensure order. And, following the A.L. Rowse of *Tudor Cornwall*, we know that the Abbots of Ford, Cleeve, Muchelney and Athelney were fined by the King. But this is as far as we have got. E. Chisolm-Batten, unnoticed by Rowse, had pointed the way, earlier and further.[22] Following him we find clergy of all descriptions up to their necks in rebellion. The Abbot of Tavistock we have seen in trouble with the King. To him can be added monks of Glastonbury Abbey, venerable doctors and canons from Wells Cathedral, and forty-four parish clergy from the region between Lands End and Chippenham. Their punishments were precisely those of their flock. They were bound under recogniances for loyalty, fined, and they bought pardons at high prices. No wonder. At St. Erth (in Cornwall) the constellation of Thomas Polstrong, its vicar, and the Trewynnards, gentry, father and son led their village into rebellion. Subsequently all three suffered the full rigour and variety of Henry's financial punishments. Indeed, so troubled by clerical involvement was Henry that, for several years after the rising, he had clergy brought to court so he himself could question them. At the time one observer even went so far as suggesting that the clergy had stimulated the rebellion. They certainly bore an unenviable burden of taxation that year. And, as in Ireland in 1798, the parish priest militant led his flock into battle and rebellion.[23]

The natural leaders of the community, the gentry and the clergy, cannot automatically be called the leaders of the risings. These would have emerged as the rebellion developed. But, what can we say if not of the led, at least of the others involved? We must dispose of one myth. The army which fought at Blackheath was not just a Cornish army. Its soldiers came from all six shires of the west. Nonetheless, what sort of Cornishman was there? This is not a very easy question to answer. Rather negatively we can say that we know of few or no tin miners involved. In fact, the only known 'tinner' was a man from Devon. He was attainted. From Devon and Cornwall came a variety of types – mariners, shipmen, yeomen, barbers, franklins, saddlemakers – as well as the gentlemen already named.[24] However, because of the way the rebels were punished we know more about Somerset than any other county. The fines in Somerset account for almost 4,000 names and raised just over eleven and a half thousand pounds. Most of the people on the fine rolls were merely recorded, not described, and that very absence of a label suggests their status: they were peasants. But there were a few the King's commissioners described. The lowest form of social life is there, still, in 1497, the serf: the bondman from the Abbot of Glastonbury's estates. And, indeed, we see a nice mirror to rural life held up by these rolls. Here are the millers, blacksmiths and farmers of Somerset. There from the towns are pewterers, goldsmiths, carpenters, arras makers, butchers and bakers.[25]

We can go further and ask of those obvious peasants: whose peasants were they? Whose tenants? We know that Lord Audley's Somerset tenants followed him. He would have been a poor Lord if he could not have required that. We know also that when he got near to London Audley called for money from his lands in Surrey, and one of his servants from Shere near Dorking delivered it to him at Blackheath.[26] At Taunton the bishop of Winchester's tenants, and his officers were rebels. Giles Daubney, the King's Chamberlain, who fought against men from Somerset at Blackheath, was lucky. None of his tenants joined with Audley. On the other hand, Lord Willoughby de Broke was not so fortunate. At the time he was fighting for Henry VII in Scotland, his Somerset tenants were fighting against Henry.[27] A rebellion of this sort, one which involved a forced march and a pitched battle at the end of it, is, by and large, the work of men. I say by and large, because we know from Somerset, Dorset, Wiltshire and Hampshire the names of forty-six women punished in their own right. We might choose to construe this as punishment for their husbands' crimes; but the most recent work on early modern insurrections suggests a rising of our sort will have a quota of female rebels – precursors of Rosa Luxemburg perhaps?[28] Clearly there is no way of knowing if these women stood cheek by jowl with their menfolk at Blackheath; but in 1572 the Countess of Northumberland was described as stout-hearted compared to her weak and vacillating husband. She egged him on into rebellion. Was this true in the case of Margaret Vowell of Wells? She found that just when her husband died, and left her all his wealth, the King's Commissioners visited Wells. She immediately lost what she had inherited when the Commissioners fined her £10.[29] The experience of the ladies of Somerset says much for their fortitude, and their opinions, presumably. Anna Burton paid the most – £40 – and every graduation of class and fine is found between herself and Alice Shepard, widow, who forfeited goods worth £1.[30]

Margaret Vowell brings us back to where we began – the town of Wells. We have seen the involvement, largely, of the rural community. It was no light matter to leave lands unattended for two mid-summer months, June and July, even less so in September, just on harvest time. Indeed, the intercession of the harvest, rather than his loyal forces, may have saved Henry Tudor from a more turbulent upheaval than that which attended Perkin Warbeck on his arrival in Cornwall. Still, it would be unwise in the England of the fifteenth century to make much of a town–country divide. Small towns with mud roads, lacking walls, had few defences against a rebel army, and they needed none from men whose eyes were fixed firmly on that better defended sister city – London. The towns of Somerset were punished thus:[31]

Bridgwater	£172.	10.0.
Taunton	£499.	5.8.
Wells	£356.	6.8.
Bruton	£302.	0.0.

What had they done? Individual merchants could doubtless tell individual stories; but we have only their names and their fines. We do not know what they sold or gave to rebels. The towns themselves are another matter. Bridgwater had ominous connections with Lord Audley and his gentry associates. It was at Wells that Audley sacked the Bishop's gaol, was acclaimed leader, and then launched his attack on London. it was in Taunton, in September, that the Provost of Glasney College, the extortioner credited with causing the May rising, was rent limb from limb, and left for dead in the market place.[32] What did Bruton do? Nothing we can know of: but in 1500 Henry's Commissioners paid special attention to this small south Somerset town. Once again, discrimination was the watchword. Devon, that most loyal of shires, found its towns barely touched. Exeter was rewarded. Plymouth was pardoned after a mayoral visit to the King and the work of the Commissioners had cleared it of rebel infection. Barnstaple was left in quiet somnolence.[33]

IV

Where does all this get us? Most writers on 1497 are baffled. Why the west? And why Cornwall, they ask? Then they give up, and resort to the oldest cliché of a cliché ridden reign. The west was poor and, being so poor, it must have objected to paying taxes for war on the Scottish border.[34] Polydore Vergil maintains this. And what Vergil wrote Bacon blessed.

It seems to me high time this explanation was stood on its head. To begin with several more modern commentators than Polydore Vergil suggest that neither the west, nor Cornwall, was particularly poor.[35] Indeed, some areas of the west appear to have been rather well off. The rebels from Somerset, many of them, were those who could, and did, make substantial loans to Henry VII, in the six months before May, 1497. These were rich men from a rich county.[36] So for that matter was Devon rich and it, in case determinism of one kind or another is raising its nose to sniff the air, did not throw itself into rebellion.[37]

The war against Perkin Warbeck interested the west far more, not far less, than other parts of the country. After all, much of the navy, many of the men, and half the King's ships, were provided by the region: and both Henry's principal commanders were westerners. In short, power politics interested these men as much if not more than money. And the west had played not a small part in the political establishment of Henry VII.[38] It was the southern, western and Cornish gentry who had supported him in 1483. Richard Edgcombe, whose feeble son Piers, was trounced by Perkin Warbeck, was involved in Buckingham's rebellion. He created more trouble for Richard III a year later, and returned to his native Cornwall, triumphant, in 1485. Thereafter, he rose to become Controller of Henry's household, a busy soldier-diplomat; and died in harness during the Breton Campaign in 1489. He was its commanding officer. This was the calibre of Henry's westerners, repeatedly: Tuberville, Daubney, De Broke.[39] By removing his two most able commanders from the mid-west, Henry created the pre-condition for a successful rising. By removing manpower, in the form of 4,000 soldiers, he compounded the condition. Devon was the only county in the west where the King had any depth of support – if deep is not a misnomer for the Earl of Devon. One may even wonder if Henry knew the risk he was taking. He spent the late summer of 1496 on a tell-tale progress through Hampshire, Dorset, Somerset and Wiltshire, at the end of which he bound together major western families for the allegiance of Thomas, Marquis of Dorset. Every one of the principals was later engulfed by rebellion: Lord Audley (£200) in leading it.[40]

The taxation of 1497 was the link which joined otherwise obstinately disparate social groups. It gave coherence to a rising which has more to do with politics than profound, or even superficial, socio-economic forces. Through the lives of the more politically important rebels runs a strand which gave the lie to pure economic grievance as the motive force of the rising. Not everyone, after 1487, had accepted with alacrity the reign of Henry Tudor. Some people's loyalties were deeper, blood deep, than those of the majority of trimmers we have come to know as the English governing classes. In 1497 Henry VII had planned to attack Perkin Warbeck's masters, a group of ex-Plantagenet – Neville servants ensconced in Scotland. His war was against this mongrel group, and few, in normal circumstances, would have cared much for their particular master, Edward, Earl of Warwick. But these were not normal circumstances. The demand for taxes saw to that. At the head of the rebels we see Lord

Audley: son of a father who had risen to eminence under Edward IV and Richard III. Unearthed among the guilty, at Exeter, we find John Hayes, a man repeatedly punished by Richard III and Henry VII for his adherence to the Earl of Warwick. Supporting Audley we find a Twynhoo; part of a family bound to the Plantagenets by murder and mischance as well as fees.[41] These men were not rebel by accident. They rode a wave which Henry had generated, and it almost drowned him.

That they nearly succeeded in removing him from his throne seems to me a good illustration of the words of Miss Margaret Condon. Of the reign as a whole she says, there was 'a certain superficiality of achievement despite all the augeries of change: an impermanence, a fragility in part caused by the tensions which Henry VII himself created'.[42] On the other hand, such were the qualities of the man that in '97 he was able, if only just, to contain these tensions. The westerners who had sought to dissipate them paid dearly, not with their actual lives, but with the economic life of the region.

It was almost fifty years before any westerners dared raise their heads again in the political arena of the realm.

AFTERWORD

This paper proposes that the rising of 1497 was not wholly Cornish nor entirely peasant. That proposition rests on the evidence of punishments made, in most cases, several years after the rising. This occasioned some debate when the paper was discussed.

Henry VII's retribution left its mark in four ways: pardons, bonds for future loyalty, fines, and in the attainder of 1504. Pardons and the meaning of pardons is an intractable region: fools rush in where angels fear to tread. No pardons for rebellion *per se* are recorded on the Patent Rolls. Pardons which do exist, and which can be connected with the rising, are in the main Cornish, twenty out of a possible thirty-eight. Two appear so early, 3 July 1497, that they can be nothing other than a form of fire insurance, proof againt the flames of royal prosecution, taken out by a saddler and a mercer of Bodmin. The rest, eighteen more, are a different matter. They appear in three groups; five in 1500; nine between 1501 and 1503, and three at the end of the reign. Only the first group of five pardons, six if we include a stray of the year 1498, cannot be connected in positive fashion with further punishment for rebellion. I will not here engage in a piece of spurious historical analysis over these six pardons. One observation will suffice. Henry VII took such close and personal control of the punishment of rebels that to obtain a pardon was the necessary adjunct to survival. That being the case these Cornish pardons give us the names and status of active rebels.[43]

Of the king's sustained scrutiny of rebels we are in no doubt. Firstly
there is the character of the man: thorough to a fault. Secondly there is
the evidence of this in form of his Chamber books, both books of Issue and
of Receipt. The books of Receipt show that those fines which were
assessed, between 1498 and 1500, were collected.[44] The books of Issue are
important because of their memoranda sections. Margaret Condon has
shown us that on occasion memoranda were dictated by the king himself.
Here we find notes concerning payments, duplicate lists of rebels kept by
Henry, and informal aggreements between Henry and his commissioners.[45] Finally there is the king's endorsement, printed by James
Gairdner in 1863, of the roll now known as the British Library's Royal
Roll 14 B vii' 'Fynes off the counties of Somerset, Dorset, Wiltes and
Hampshire, wherof William Hatteclyff is receyvor and must answere the
mony'.[46]

The first commission to fine rebels (ultimately there were three) was
issued on 13 September 1498. It was directed to Cornwall and Devon
alone. Henry's commissioners possessed powers to cite rebels before them,
take bonds, fix punishments in accordance with crimes, and to issue
pardons to those communities which sued to the commission for them.
The work of the commission has left us with an incomplete set of bonds,
two fine rolls, and a series of marginalia which suggest that previous
commentators, notably A.L. Rowse, seriously underestimated the
commissioners' powers. The original bonds, taken in the winter of 1498,
still survive. They can be seen in the Public Record Office in Class E114,
King's Remembrancer Bonds and Obligations. Where the original is
deficient, or missing, we also possess, from a stock-taking exercise of 1505,
a list of these unexpired bonds for good behaviour and future loyalty.[47]
The fines purged the counties of the contempt of rebellion. This is stated
at the head of the Devon roll; that for Cornwall is damaged. The fines, of
three sorts (on communities, on individuals, and for the bail of
individuals) were assessed on mainpernors who took it upon themselves
to make payment for their inferiors. The amount assessed, and gathered in
by August 1499, was £1148.13.4. But if the memoranda of the Issue books
is consulted then we should read the true fine of Cornwall and Devon as
nearer to £1500 than £1200. In relation to what was to succeed them these
assessments are simple affairs; and they produced simple records, rolls of no
more than six membranes each, lists of places and names, mainpernors
and amounts.[48] Only after payment of these fines do we find any
Cornishman, other than the fat merchants of Bodmin, pardoned.

In all Somerset only seven people were pardoned; that is to say had
pardons recorded on the patent roll. Those thus pardoned were four
gentlemen, among whom two recorded the heaviest fine made in
Somerset, £200 each; an ex-bailiff of Wells; and John Audley, James, lord

Audley's brother, a man who paid for his pardon by turning informer and sending Warbeck and the Earl of Warwick to death in 1499.[49] But for Somerset, between 1500 and 1506, fining was to become a way of life. The second commission to fine rebels – directed to Somerset, Dorset, Hampshire and Wiltshire – was appointed on 10 March 1500. The commission worked for four and a half months in Somerset and Dorset. While there it hired spies, *exploratori*, whose job it was to unearth the guilty in their communities. Whole townships were examined.[50] In August of 1500 the commisioners reported to Henry at Woodstock, but the king was not satisfied. After discussion, therefore, he directed a third commission to the same counties, and this was appointed on 6 August 1500. We know little of its work, but it seems to have operated in much the same way as its immediate predecessor.[51]

These two commissions produced two rolls of assessments, the first being the British Library's Royal Roll, the second being the Public Record Office's Roll E101/516/24. The Royal Roll begins with the names of four highly placed western clerics. Each hundredal name is given and then, within tithings, individual assessments are recorded. At the end of this roll of 3329 names are found the names of four people whose fines were fixed at Greenwich, as well as thirty-two whose goods were forfeited as fines. The roll is forty-four membranes of vellum, and the fine assessed was £9,572.10.0. The Record Office Roll is not one document but five. That is five smaller rolls, possibly separate assessments, have been bound into one roll. Each roll is arranged, geographically, in identical manner to the Royal Roll; but with an ever diminishing number of membranes as the roll is read. In the case of the Record Office Roll the names of persons are found opposite their assessments, and the amount payable as portions of that assessment. There are, thus, four columns; a fine and three instalments. This roll records persons and communities. In this respect it is unlike the Royal Roll which deals with individuals alone. The assessment of this Record Office Roll was £4,624.8.8. It consists of thirty-three membranes of vellum. Between them the two rolls assessed 4541 people, and villages beyond that, to pay £14,153.2.0.

Unlike the rolls from Cornwall and Devon which talk of an unnamed 'contempt' against the king these later rolls are explicit. The Royal Roll says that it is a list of fines taken from the king's 'rebelles et transgressores in comitatibus Somerset, Dorset, Wiltes et Suthamptonaie, pro suis contemptibus et offensis aliquibus suis favoribus sive assistentiis cuidam rebelli Michaeli Joseph aut suo adhaerenti Jacobo nuper domino Audley, et cuidam idolo sive simulacro Petro Warbec Flandrae nato, factis sive perpetratis; qui cum debita satisfacione se submittere voluerint at gratiam et pardonationem domini regis, eos et quemlibet eorum ad eandem admittere et recipere'[52] This way the West bought its pardon. And, notwithstanding two commissions, two assessments, two sets of receivers and much confusion, every fine was paid.[53]

Only at the end of this elaborate process of punishment was an act of attainder passed against the rebels of '97. In this there is something unique. There is nothing unique in the methods by which Henry VII punished the rebels. Fines had been used by Edward IV. Bonds had been used by Richard III. Attainder had been used, since 1453, by each succeeding victorious party in the civil wars. Few, however, between 1453 and 1497, waited, as did the rebels of '97, for seven years before attainder.[54] During the wait, we know, certain names were considered for attainder, but did not appear in the bill. And when the act was passed it contained some striking omissions. No reference is found to Thomas Flamank, the man credited with colouring the rebellion with legality, nor to Michael Joseph An Gof, the Great Captain of Cornwall who led it from St. Keverne to Blackheath. In their stead the blame for rebellion was laid at the feet of Lord Audley and an assortment of minor gentlemen and yeomen.[55]

Significance here is to be found in the date of the attainder, 1504. By this time Henry VII knew better than anyone else who had supported the rebellion: they had paid him their compositions, either for fighting at Blackheath or giving food and money to the rebels. By 1504, though, Henry faced one of those periodic tests of authority which dogged his political life. His first born son was dead. His wife was dead. He was in ill health. Another pretender had sprung up, and his heir, Henry of York, was but 13 years old. Men talked of a revival of civil war; and none vouched for Henry Tudor's son. The act of 1504 aimed at decapitating noble support for Yorkism and attainted the already dead Earl of Warwick. But to the rebels of 1497 it clearly did not do justice. With no sense of historical irony it attributed an event essentially stirred up by Tudor dynasticism to the yeomanry and peasantry of the west. Why? The answer lies in the political conditions of the year 1504. Could a king caught like Henry VII by a recurrent political paradox begin a wholesale, or even partial, attainder of his ruling classes in the west of England? This would merely have exacerbated his already awkward situation. Far better create a Parliamentary fiction, by finding culprits of a low status, than point accusingly at the political nation. To stir up old enmities and indecisions would be counterproductive to political survival. In any case the western gentry (and clergy) were buying themselves back to grace. Henry VII had their money. What more did he need?

To begin to examine the events of 1497 from the attainder outwards, as has been done in the past, is to misunderstand Henry VII's government and the nature of the revolt.[56] Certainly the act of attainder dealt with those, though only some, who began the rebellion. But perhaps in looking at origins we neglect actuality. A recent article by John Walter has demonstrated convincingly what happened to rebels who could attract no support. They could create no rebellion. When we lift our eyes from the act of attainder we see that apart from sparks all fires have flames as well.[57]

NOTES

1   Wells Town Hall, Acts of the Corporation 1450–1553, pp. 201–202. *PRO* E36/126 ff22r–36r.
2   I. Arthurson, '1497 and the Western Rising', unpublished PhD thesis, University of Keele (1981). Chapter 6, 'The suppression of the West', narrates this.
3   Spiro Collection New York, Signet Letter of Henry VII, 16 September 1497. This manuscript is cited by kind permission of its owners Mr and Mrs H. Spiro.
4   Wells Town Hall, Acts of the Corporation 1450–1553, pp. 197 and 201. BL Royal Roll 14 Bvii mm31v–32r. *PRO* E101/516/24 m13v. The foliation on these two manuscripts is derived by counting. They are not numbered.
5   Arthurson, *loc. cit.* The king's expression comes from his Signet Letter in the Spiro Collection, New York. His remarks on the gentry are to be found in John Hooker's Commonplace Book. This is unpublished and is found in Devon Record Office, Exeter City Archives Book 51 f328v.
6   Abbot Richard Banham of Tavistock's dealings with the king are found at *PRO* E404/82, unnumbered Warrant for Issue, dated 23 October 1497. The bond is listed *PRO* E101/517/11 f12r.
7   *PRO* E101/414 14 f7r. Diurnal expenses of the Household normally ran between £30 and £40. On 2 November they were £140.10.7.
8   *PRO* E34/2 is a file of Privy Seals, etc., for loans for the 1497 campaign. These letters were written at the beginning of December 1496, *PRO* E405/79 m15r. Printed texts may be found in A.F. Pollard, *The Reign of Henry VII from Contemporary Sources* (1913) Vol 2, p. 45 and E.C. Patten, 'Letters Missive to John Calycote of Shepton Mallet', *SAS*, Vol 30 (1894), pp. 159–165. Figures for shipping derive from known accounts and commissions, cf. Arthurson, *op. cit.*, pp. 572–585, Appendix C, Shipping Utilized by Henry VII: 1496–1497.
9   *PRO* E405/79 m23v.
10   Shipping, Arthurson, *loc. cit.* 2000 soldiers to be raised by commission *CPR 1494–1509*, p. 93. *PRO* E405/79 mm16r and 23v records £8,186.12.11 to be spent on 4000 soldiers and 49 vessels in De Broke's force.
11   J. Hunter, *South Yorkshire* (1831), Vol 2, p. 313 for directions to muster to Daubney's vanguard. Also Arthurson, *op. cit.*, pp. 121–122. On a Royal Ward, Arthurson, *op. cit.*, p.156.
12   Daubney's retinues may be found at *PRO* E405/79 mm35v–37v.
13   This statement is a formulation of 'War with Scotland', chapter 2 of Arthurson, *op. cit.*
14   A discussion of Parliamentary Taxation is found in R.S. Schofield, 'Parliamentary Lay Taxation 1485–1547', unpublished Ph. D. thesis, University of Cambridge (1963), esp. pp. 184–192. The legislation is found in *Rot. Parl.* Vol 6, pp. 514–517. On clerical taxation see D. Wilkins, *Concilia Magnae Britannae et Hibernia* (etc.), Vol 3 London (1737), p. 645. *CFR 1485–1509*, p. 253. On the loan in advance of taxation, A. H. Thomas and I. D. Thornley eds., *The Great Chronicle of London* (1938), p. 275 and C. L. Kingsford ed., *Chronicles of London* (1905), p. 213. On patterns of wealth, R. S. Schofield, 'The Distribution of Wealth in England 1334–1649', *EcHR*, Second Series, Vol 18 (1965), pp. 483–510.
15   P. L. Hughes and J. F. Larkin, *Tudor Royal Proclamations*, Volume One *The Early Tudors 1485–1533* (1964), p. 39.
16   Thus A. L. Rowse, *Tudor Cornwall* (new edition 1969), chapter VI.

17   Act of attainder 1504, *Rot. Parl.* Vol 6, pp. 544–545. For attempts to deduce the numbers executed following the battle of Blackheath see Arthurson, *op. cit.*, pp. 367–369. This attempt seems to me rather less conclusive than when it was written first, in 1979. For bonds see the Afterword to this piece. Gentry names are found on the fine roll for Cornwall *PRO* E101/516/27.

18   E. C. Batten, 'Henry VII in Somersetshire', *SAS*, Vol. 25 (1879), pp. 49–79.

19   E. Green, 'Wayford Church and Manor House', *SAS*, Vol. 28 (1882), p. 63 cites James Daubney as Giles, Lord Daubney, the king's chamberlain's brother. On Sir John Speke, J. C. Wedgwood, *History of Parliament. Biographies of the Members of the Commons House 1439–1509* (1936), p. 785. As the earl of Devon's steward 1488–1489 see BL Add Ch 68411. He was an assessor of the subsidy of 1497: *Rot. Parl.* Vol. 6, p. 517. Their fines, Daubney (£100), Lutterel (£200), and Speke (£200), are found *PRO* E101/516/24 m3r and BL Royal Roll 14 Bvii m14v. Speke's pardon, *CPR 1494–1509*, p. 197.

20   Sir Nicholas Latimer of Duntish, Dorset, is identified from the Chamber Issue book *PRO* IE101/413/5 f292v. Pardoned 1501, *CPR 1494–1509*, p. 281. Bonds, *CCR 1500–1509*, pp 13, 41–42, 86. Reference to Devon is to the cases of Thomas Worth of Worth and Robert Batyn of Donsland who were obliged to pay annuities to the king. Their sons continued this after the deaths of their fathers. Arthurson, *op. cit.*, pp. 381–382.

21   R. Hilton, *Bondmen Made Free* (1973), pp. 207–210. M. Bowker, 'Lincolnshire 1536: heresy, schism or religious discontent?', in D. Baker, ed., *Schism Heresy and Religious Protest*, Studies in Church History Vol 9 (1972), pp. 194–212. See also, T. Pakenham, *The Year of Liberty. The Great Irish Rebellion of 1798* (first published 1969).

22   Rowse, *op. cit.*, pp. 317–318. Batten, *op. cit.*, pp. 71–72.

23   Arthurson, *op. cit.*, pp. 467–472, Table 18 Clergy Punished: Cornwall, Devon, Somerset, Dorset, Wiltshire. The example of St. Erth is from *PRO* E101/516/27 and *PRO* E114/91/1. On Henry's interrogation of clergy; BL Royal Roll 14 Bvii m42v, *PRO* E101/415/3 f33r, and *PRO* E101/517/20.

24   See Afterword and note 43.

25   Arthurson, *op. cit.*, pp. 459–461.

26   BL Royal Roll 14 Bvii mm15v, 20r, 21v, 33v, 34r membrane 1, 43r. *PRO* E101/516/24 mmlv, 13v, 16r. *PRO* SC 11/828. SC 6/Henry VII 1065. *Ibid* 1067. SC 2/200/59.

27   J. Gairdner, *Letters and Papers Illustrative of the Reigns of Richard III and Henry VII*, Rolls Series, Vol 2 (1863), pp. 76–78. BL Royal Roll 14 Bvii m15r/v. *PRO* E101/516/24 mm4dr/v, 11v. The reference to de Broke's manor is to Castle Cary, Somerset.

28   Arthurson, *op. cit.*, pp. 456–458. J. Walter, 'A Rising of the People? The Oxfordshire Rising of 1596', *Past and Present*, No. 107 (May 1985), pp. 90–143.

29   For the countess, A. Fletcher, *Tudor Rebellions* (1968 edition), p. 102. F. W. Weaver, *Somerset Medieval Wills 1383–1500*, *SRS*, Vol 16 (1901), pp. 368–370 for will of Richard Vowell. His wife's loss of goods is found BL Royal Roll 14 Bvii m43r.

30   BL Royal Roll 14 Bvii m2r, Anna Burton of Taunton; m25r Alice Shepard, widow of Banwell.

31   Extracted from Arthurson, *op. cit.*, pp. 439–450, Table 16 Hundredal fine of Somerset, Dorset, Wiltshire and Hampshire, composite fine. Bridgwater p. 439, Taunton p. 442, Wells p. 442, Bruton p. 439.

32   On Bridgwater, Somerset Record Office D/B/bw 61 *passim*, especially 61/101 and 61/1364. The Audleys had a house in Bridgwater in 1381. It was burnt during the Peasants' Revolt. R.B. Dobson, *The Peasants' Revolt of 1381* (1970), p. 281. On Wells, *PRO* C1/217/20. On Taunton, *The Great Chronicle op. cit.*, p. 282, *Chronicles of London op. cit.*, p. 218.

33   On Bruton, *PRO* E101/517/20. On Exeter, Devon Record Office, Exeter City Archives Book 51 f329v. On Plymouth, West Devon Record Office Ms W130 ff42v–43r.

34   Rowse, *op. cit.*, p121. Those who followed him, for example Anthony Fletcher *Tudor Rebellions*, p. 13.

35   J. Hatcher, *Rural Economy and Society in the Duchy of Cornwall 1300–1500* (1970). J. Hatcher,

English Tin Production and Trade before 1550 (1973). J Hatcher, 'A Diversified Economy: Later Medieval Cornwall', *EcHR*, Second Series, Vol 22, pp. 208–227.

36 See, for example, the list of loans made to Henry VII in 1496–7. Arthurson, *op. cit.*, pp. 657–663 Appendix F Loans in anticipation of Taxation compared to punishment for rebellion.

37 W. Hoskins, 'The Wealth of Medieval Devon', in W. G. Hoskins and H. P. R. Finberg eds., *Devonshire Studies* (1952), pp. 212–249.

38 Paper presented by N. Kingwell at the Keele Conference.

39 Wedgwood, *Biographies of the Members of the Commons House*, pp. 259–260, 884–885. G. E. Cokayne, *The Complete Peerage* (1910–1959) Vol 12, part 2, pp. 683–686, on de Broke.

40 For progress see Household accounts PRO E101/414/6 ff34r–45r and Warrants for the Great Seal PRO C82/149, 150. For bond, CCR *1485–1500* p. 289.

41 The career of James Tuchet, lord Audley's father John, sixth lord Audley, receives attention in every book touching politics between 1459 and 1485. See for example C. D. Ross, *Edward IV* (1974) pp. 26, 31, 34n, 80, 82, 83n, 97, 118, 121, 123, 130, 157n, 214, 221n, 223. C. D. Ross, *Richard III* (1981) pp. 12, 42, 66n, 160–162. For John Hayes' punishment see B. P. Wolffe, *The Royal Demesne in English History* (1971), p. 182. *Rot. Parl.* Vol 6, pp. 454–456. CCR *1485–1500*, pp. 200–201. For the Twynhoo family, Wedgwood, *Biographies of the Members of the Commons House*, pp 886–888. Hayes, Twynhoo and the previously mentioned Sir Nicholas Latimer have in common their earlier attatchment to George Plantaganet, duke of Clarence. They were members of his affinity. Sir Hugh Lutterel of Dunster was connected tangentially to Clarence. Their master's son, Edward, earl of Warwick, was Henry VII's prisoner. M. A. Hicks, 'The Career of George Plantagenet, Duke of Clarence, 1449–1477', unpublished D Phil thesis, university of Oxford (1976), pp. 374–378.

42 M. M. Condon, 'Ruling Elites in the Reign of Henry VII', in C. D. Ross, ed., *Patronage, Pedigree and Power in Later Medieval England* (1979) p. 134.

43 CPR *1494–1509* pp. 109, 136, 214, 215, 217, 219, 237, 239, 244, 266, 285, 318, 341, 509, 526, 572. Individuals attainted, and subsequently pardoned, are not included in this list.

44 Chamber Receipt book PRO E101/413/2 iii pp. 9, 13, 20, 25, 64, 131, 192. Chamber Issue books PRO E101/414/3 f247v, E101/414/16 ff88r, 120v, 121v, E101/415/3 f248v E36/123 pp. 6, 7, 9, 43, E36/214 p. 380, BL Add Ms 21840 f43r.

45 Condon in Ross, *op. cit.*, p. 127.

46 J. Gairdner, *Letters and Papers Illustrative of the Reigns of Richard III and Henry VII*, Rolls Series, Vol 2 (1863), p. 336.

47 The text of the commission is given in toto, A. F. Pollard, *op. cit.*, p. 111–114. Bonds are found PRO E114/1/2 and E114/91/1. The supplementary list is at PRO E101/517/11 ff 10r–12r, dated 1st February the twentieth year of Henry VII's reign, i.e. 1505.

48 Rolls are found: Cornwall, PRO E101/516/27, and Devon, *ibid.*, 28. Date of account PRO E101/414/3 f161v. Also Arthurson, *op. cit.*, p. 402.

49 CPR *1494–1509*, pp. 123, 188, 197, 218, 392.

50 CPR *1494–1509*, pp. 202. Reference to *exploratori* is made in the commissioners' accounts. PRO E101/517/20. Gairdner, *op. cit.*, pp. 75–76.

51 CPR *1494–1509*, p 203.

52 Gairdner, *op. cit.*, p. 335.

53 Gairdner, *op. cit.*, pp. 76–77. Arthurson, *op. cit.*, pp. 422, 433.

54 For Edward IV see C. F. Richmond, 'Fauconberg's Kentish Rising of May 1471', *EHR* Vol 75 (1971), pp. 673–693. For Richard III see C.D. Ross, *Richard III* (1981), pp. 180–181. On attainder see J.R. Lander, 'Attainder and Forfeiture 1453–1509', in his *Crown and Nobility* (1976), pp. 127–158, and also, Appendix C, Attainders and Reversals, 1453–1509, pp. 307–308.

55 *Rot. Parl.* Vol 6 p. 544. Richard Pendyne of St. Just in Pendeen, West Cornwall, was said to have lain under a 'pretensyd attaynder . . . after the fild Callid blak heth'. His name is not found in the act. Royal Institution of Cornwall Ms BB/1/1 is an indenture in which we are told

this. The sense of the document is that the Pendyne family were excluded from their lands because of the father's involvement at Blackheath, and his expected attainder.

56 Rowse, *op. cit.*, pp. 122, 123, 130, in ignorance of the earlier work of E.C. Batten, *op. cit.*, on Somerset.

57 J. Walter, *op. cit.*, p. 120. Walter gives as the major reason for the failure of the Oxfordshire Rising, 1596, its limited social and geographic base. This limitation was located ultimately in its leadership. Walter says that 'Despite Authority's fears, there was no gentry leadership. Nor was there any clerical involvement . . .More surprising was the absence of the middling sort, a group otherwise prominent in the early modern agrarian crowd and backbone of earlier rebellions.'

I should like to thank Mr George Coombs who invited me to give a shorter version of this paper at the Nottinghamshire Local History Association Sixth Form Conference, at the University of Nottingham, in 1983.

Careerism in Late Medieval England

MICHAEL BENNETT

In the evolution of English society in the centuries before the Industrial Revolution three features are often noted as distinguishing the English from the continental experience. First, there is the precocious growth of a strong, centralised nation state; second, there is the steady economic integration of the nation; and third, there is increasing evidence of social mobility. All three developments have their roots in Anglo-Saxon times, and reach a stage of maturity in the seventeenth century best exemplified in the prodigious growth of London as the hub of power, the engine of economic growth and the clearing-house of social status.[1] Nevertheless it is the intervening period, especially the hundred or so years before and after the Black Death, that seem to have been crucial. Even as early as the fourteenth century England was highly integrated politically and economically, and in the fifteenth century Italian observers were noting its relative social fluidity.[2] All three features have had their share of attention from historians, but rarely has their dynamic interrelation been the focus of interest.[3] In this paper it is intended to link them together in a sketch of the history of what can be termed 'careerism' in late medieval England.

The focus on 'careerism' perhaps needs some justification. In the first place it usefully reverses the perspective adopted in most histories of medieval England. Instead of the traditional story of the triumph of the crown and the bureaucracy at Westminster over a recalcitrant baronage and other particularist forces, and of the progressive penetration by market forces from London of the economic backwaters of provincial England, what can be emphasised here is the vital role played in the integration of the national polity and economy by men from outlying regions. At the same time it makes it possible to transcend some of the problems associated with the study of social mobility. The concern of this paper is with the experience of careerism rather than its fruits. Its interest is in the movement of men from their ascribed place on the land, in their response to opportunities presented by trades and professions, and in their purposeful application to advancement. The experience of careerism, in this general sense, was undoubtedly more common than successful social climbing. It has a significance far greater than the sum of all the individual success-stories.

I

There is no obvious starting-point in the history of careerism in medieval England. Even in the Dark Ages the production and exchange of specialised commodities never entirely ceased, and long before the Norman Conquest groups of craftsmen and traders had secured freedom from the constraints of the agricultural regime and were enjoying corporate immunities in boroughs and enjoying the freedom of movement so vital to their enterprises. The coming of Christianity likewise added to the complexity of English society, providing opportunities for education as well as a vocation for certain sections of the population. With its growing consciousness of its own identity and its relative openness to all talents clerisy was the archetypal profession. Alongside salvation in the next life, protection in this world also generated specialisation within society. Prowess in arms was always a significant avenue of advancement, particularly as it was difficult to deny promotion to men who displaying their mettle on the battlefield usurped the functions of the landed aristocracy. A final broad area of careerism, which in various respects drew on the expertise of commerce, the church and chivalry, was government. As the English state developed ever more elaborate and extensive functions from the eleventh century onwards, it required more and more men who had the merchant's skills of literacy and numeracy, the educated clerk's facility with speechifying, letter-writing and legal reasoning, and the successful soldier's flair for decision-making and leadership.

However far back its roots can be traced, English careerism developed apace in the twelfth and thirteenth centuries. The considerable advance in population, perhaps trebling between 1086 and 1272, the prodigious increase in the intensity, and for a time the efficiency of cultivation, the proliferation of markets and towns all signal the development of an increasingly rich and complex society. Needless to say, the opportunities in manufacturing and trade increased substantially, though since the world of high finance and *grand commerce* was dominated by Jews and other aliens there seems to have been correspondingly less room for the emergence of an assertive *haute bourgeoisie*. Since for most of the thirteenth century England was immune from sustained warfare, and since military functions remained to some degree a preserve of the feudal classes, soldiering was also less evident as a means of social climbing. In other fields of endeavour, however, it was an age of unparalleled expansion. The growing wealth, power and institutional complexity of the church attracted large numbers of men of talent and ambition, and from the twelfth century promotion was increasingly predicated on education. Even before 1200, hundreds of English clerks thronged the schools of northern France, and the emergence in the early thirteenth century of reputable *studia* at Oxford and Cambridge brought university study within the reach of many more native scholars.[4] Though most information is available regarding the progress of higher education, there can be no doubt that the scholastic achievement of Oxford in the age of Grosseteste was built upon a massive groundswell of basic educational provision in the provinces.[5] Certainly the growth of towns and trade, and the increasing interest in efficient estate-management, set up a wholly unprecedented demand for literate and numerate officials. As the crown continually added to its rights and responsibilities, not least during the reign of Henry II, the royal administration emerged to rival the church as a major employer of clerical talent. The nascent bureaucracy at Westminster required its own well-trained staff, while the rapid development of the legal system demanded its own specialised body of operatives, not only in the king's employment but also to service the needs of a wider community which was becoming increasingly enmeshed in an all-embracing system of national justice.

The reigns of the three Edwards brought further development. While the pace of economic expansion began to slacken, there was sufficient momentum in the system between the 1270s and 1340s to allow further growth and differentiation in occupational structures. In the countryside land shortage and the commutation of rents forced the peasantry to resort to the market, whether to sell their labour or their produce. Small towns proliferated, facilitating seignorial exploitation but also in important ways adding to the store of local opportunities. Fuller record-keeping and more efficient exaction of rents, tithes and taxes added to the burdens of the peasantry, but also provided employment of a new kind. Throughout this era the seemingly inexorable logic of institutionalisation and specialisation added to the range of openings in all walks of life. War and politics, however, were the real motors in the dramatic expansion of career activity under the three Edwards. The conquest of Wales, the struggle with Scotland, and above all the wars in France mobilised the manpower of the nation on a scale inconceivable before and rarely matched since. Soldiering resumed its role as the most celebrated form of social advancement. Military activity also stimulated other sectors of careerism. It enlarged the royal household and the retinues of magnates, it increased the number of bureaucrats, set up a demand for civil lawyers to staff embassies, it created a new class of government creditors and war-contractors. In some measure it broadened the geographical range of English enterprise, through more determined control of Ireland and Aquitaine, the annexation of Wales and Calais, and through short-term adventurism in Scotland, Flanders and further afield.

Between the twelfth and early fourteenth centuries English society grew in complexity, spawning opportunities for employment and enterprise in the interstices of an essentially rural economy. Since the general context of this development was population growth and economic expansion, however, the increase in the numbers of tradesmen and professionals might well have been more impressive in absolute than relative terms. More remarkable perhaps is the degree to which this progess was maintained, even in some respects accelerated in the later middle ages. The role of the Black Death and subsequent plague epidemics in opening up, at least in the short term, career opportunities to new men is well known. It even seems likely that it altered the balance of English society in the longer term. While the overall population was dramatically reduced, perhaps by over a third, the number of openings in trade and professional life seems not to have been affected to anywhere near the same degree. Even though many towns languished in the later middle age, the urban sector probably increased as a proportion of the population until the early sixteenth century, with London as the chief beneficiary of this expansion. While the large-scale mobilisation of manpower seen in the first phase of the Hundred Years War was not repeated, the level of military operations maintained by the depleted population in later phases was impressive enough to embark on a systematic settlement of Normandy. Despite some moves towards rationalisation, the numbers of benefices in the church and posts in the royal administration remained fairly constant. The later middle ages indeed saw further differentiation within the ecclesiastical hierarchy and the emergence of lay professionalism in government and law.[6] There might even have been some increase in the demand for priestly and administrative services in less formalised capacities. To the extent to which war and politics extended the horizons of English careerists at foreign expense, and that institutional development led to more elaborate career-structures, there may even have been real as well as relative growth.

The rapid expansion of career opportunities was not an unmixed blessing for the lower orders. There were general benefits to be derived from the growth of towns, the church, and government, but for the majority of the population few could have been immediately apparent. To the degree to which the nobles used the market to exploit their lands more efficiently, the church to endow their younger sons, the law-courts and the state itself to advance their class-interests, such developments added substantially to the burdens of the peasant class. Needless to say, such a model of the operations of the system would be far too crude. In terms of career opportunities, for example, it is clear that men of humble origins were able to advance themselves materially, often to the vocal dismay of the magnates. The basic problem, of course, is to know how deeply and widely through the population the connections necessary for careerism penetrated, and whether there was any expansion, or contraction, over time. Unfortunately the backgrounds, social and regional, of even quite distinguished careerists can be surprisingly obscure, itself perhaps a significant point.[7] Starting from the premise that in the twelfth and early thirteenth centuries career opportunities diminished as one moved down the social scale or as one moved north of a line between the Trent and Severn, however, it is certainly possible to detect, from the late thirteenth century onwards, unmistakable signs of expansion in both directions.

In the circumstances of the thirteenth century the growth in the trades and professions need not have led to a deeper penetration of career opportunities. Early in the reign of Henry III it might have seemed that England would succumb to the forces of economic and cultural imperialism, as foreign merchants, churchmen and adventurers found the realm a field of enterprise. Moreover, in an age of population expansion, all ranks of society, not least the nobles, had to find places for more sons, which might well have left no openings for newcomers. Yet for a variety of reasons the competitive position of the best placed and most advantaged groups was being undermined. Foreigners were denied positions in the royal administration from the reign of Henry III, somewhat frozen out of the church, and (where not expelled like the Jews) increasingly penalised in their commercial operations. More to the point perhaps, the nobility did not take full advantage of the new opportunities. As regards the English upper classes, both the crown and the church looked for commitment and merit, and many baronial and knightly families seem to have been unprepared to offer either. Far from monopolising the highest offices in church and state, the rich and well-born, for all their advantages, often found themselves displaced in the race for preferment by men of obscure and presumably humble background.[8] According to K. Edwards's study of the origins of the fifty-five members of the episcopate under Edward II, only one was connected with royal or comital families, five were from the baronial class, and fourteen more from knightly families, leaving over half from (presumably) burgess and freeholding backgrounds.[9]

The widening of the community of English careerism can be readily demonstrated. For most of the thirteenth century it is possible to discern a 'charmed circle' of recruitment centred on the Home Counties, but with important advance-posts in East Anglia, the Midlands and the West Country. From the reign of Edward I, however, elite groups began to acquire a more decidedly backwoods flavour.[10] The Welsh marcher counties produced their first crop of distinguished careerists around this time: Robert Burnel, chancellor of the realm, Walter Hopton, justice of king's bench, and Walter Wenlock, abbot of Westminster were all from

Shropshire. Around the same time a remarkable coterie of clerks from Yorkshire and south Humberside were establishing themselves in the royal administration. According to J.L. Grassi, William Hambleton, chancellor at the end of Edward I's reign, was almost unique as a northerner when he joined chancery in the 1260s, but by the close of his career he was the senior member of an affinity several dozen strong, including William Melton, archbishop of York (1316–40) and three others who were promoted to the episcopate in the reign of Edward II. Among other offices, the keepership of the rolls was monopolised by this group for fifty years from 1295 to 1345, and by their proteges from 1371 to 1397.[11] Between the forward positions in Shropshire and south Yorkshire traditions of careerism were being consolidated in the north Midlands. Staffordshire spawned three puissant judges: Ralph Basset, Roger Hillary and William Shareshull. Even the remote and hitherto marginal counties of the Northwest began to join the national mainstream. With footholds in the chancery and privy seal offices from the 1330s Lancashire clerks consolidated their position in the royal administration with the promotion of John Winwick (d. 1360) to the keepership of both seals.[12] On a smaller scale, Cumberland men also made their mark: Adam Eglesfield and his more illustrious nephew, Robert Eglesfield, were prominent king's clerks, while Robert Parving, a lawyer-knight rose to the king's bench and, for a time, the chancellorship.[13]

Both trends continued in some measure in the aftermath of the Black Death. The natural assumption that the demographic collapse of the late middle ages fostered unprecedented mobility, as men (and women) from lower down the social scale or from more distant regions began to benefit from the new opportunities, finds some confirmation in the evidence. Judging from debate in London and elsewhere over the exclusion of the sons of villeins and poorer freeholders from apprenticeships, it must be supposed that young men of mean birth were not only swelling the ranks of the proletariat but also working their way into the gilds. It is certainly the case that London was recruiting its population from a much wider geographical pool from the late fourteenth century onwards, with the Home Counties and East Anglia losing their earlier stranglehold. Over forty per cent of new apprentices in the Tailors' and Skinners' companies in the last decades of the fifteenth century were from north of the Trent.[14] Even the mayoralty of London itself lay under siege: the twenty-three worthies in the Yorkist period included only two native Londoners and nine others from the Home Counties and East Anglia, but a goodly assortment from provincial towns like Bristol and Coventry, a number of Midland counties and, quite remarkably, three from Cheshire.[15] Recruitment into the church followed a similar pattern. While there is only impressionistic evidence for changes in the social origins of priests, there is firm evidence of changing regional patterns of recruitment, with the northern dioceses contributing a higher proportion as the fifteenth century wore on. It is instructive that over sixty per cent of English bishops in the Lancastrian and Yorkist periods were drawn from classes below that of the squirearchy, while forty-three per cent hailed from six northern shires.[16]

Needless to say, opportunities could not expand as rapidly as expectations. The high mortality in the third quarter of the fourteenth century seems to have created a sudden upturn in demand for qualified craftsmen and trained professionals which after a generation or so returned to more modest levels. At the same time the scaling down of military activities after the Treaty of Bretigny in 1360, and again after the reign of Henry V, reduced opportunities in that sphere. In many fields of endeavour there is evidence of new barriers to mobility, whether through attempts to restrict opportunities for female employment, to exclude the low born from gilds and associations, to hold men to the trades of their fathers, or to check immigration from the Celtic fringe. Above all there is interesting evidence of increasingly keen competition for advancement in church and state through an escalation of credentialism. By the end of the fourteenth century a 'crisis in patronage' can be observed in the church, as new cohorts of graduates sought placements.[17] It might even be the case that the upper classes, themselves squeezed by falling levels of rent, began to show more interest in education and its fruits. Yet conditions of high mortality and high real wage-rates continued to favour lower class and backwoods careerism throughout most of the later middle ages, a point perhaps best illustrated by Welsh enterprise in this era. The Black Death created openings for Welsh labourers; the French wars drew heavily on the man-power of the hills and valleys; a series of clerks from south Wales found high preferment in the English church;[18] in spite of legal obstacles Welsh adventurers achieved signal successes in all fields long before their triumph at Bosworth. By the beginning of the Tudor era traditions of careerism were both deeply rooted and widely diffused.

II

From this sort of evidence, limited though it might be, it is at least apparent that career opportunities in late medieval England were not structured in quite the fashion that might at first be supposed. Proportionate to its size in the total population, the peerage was better represented than other social classes in such elite groups as the bishops, but the provision of places for younger sons of noble families seems never to have been part of the role of the royal administration, perhaps quite the reverse. Similarly, while it seems that at first London, the Home Counties and southern England were best placed to benefit from the expansion of education and employment, it is clear that very rapidly, certainly by the reign of Edward I, opportunities became more widely available, with some provincial communities contributing disproportionately. Of course, what needs to be discovered are the channels along which men from lower social strata and backwoods areas could be drawn into national life. At this stage all that it is possible to do is to point to a number of significant networks.

In medieval England it did not require an introduction at court to enter the royal service. The king's household was largely peripatetic, gathering on its progress a fluctuating body of temporary servitors, some of whom at least found permanent positions. Judging from their surnames, the body of men known as the king's messengers were recruited widely from the main staging-posts and favoured halts in royal itineraries.[19] In most districts there were lordships or villages which were either anciently royal demesne, or otherwise in the hands of the king, queen or a prince of the blood. A large number of royal clerks and retainers were indeed home-grown on royal manors. Then again, England was a unitary state with a well-developed system of local administration, and from the thirteenth century the crown increasingly drew on the services of men with roots in their bailiwicks. The sheriffs and other office-holders hired their own assistants, who might then be introduced into royal service. The church was likewise a ubiquitous institution. With its apex in the see of St Peter, and its roots in countless parishes, the ecclesiastical hierarchy provided a viable career structure for men from the furthest outposts and the lowest ranks of Christian society. Personal connection was often important: curates seeking altar-boys from among their kinsmen and parishioners; bishops recruiting their teams from their friends and university connections. Promotion often required movement, and new appointments to bishoprics would usually take kinsmen and colleagues with them, thus establishing in the chapter a whole coterie of clerks from another diocese. The monasteries, likewise, had long traditions of seeking out and nurturing local talent, and within their organisation promising youths could progress from serfdom to song-school, from house to house in the pursuit of learning, and from provincial obscurity to national eminence. The landed wealth and secular interests of the great ecclesiastical lordships drew into harness an array of lay officials from reeves and bailiffs to estate-managers and lawyers.[20] Though disavowing property and career activity, the mendicant orders were notoriously successful in recruiting and nurturing talent, and in nosing out opportunities for influence and power. Nor must it be forgotten that the leading members of the aristocracy, and indeed even many mere knightly houses had estates in different parts of the country. It was to their tenantry that magnates looked first to staff their households and military retinues, thus sometimes bringing together men from far-flung manors in regional or even national networks of patronage. The diffuse pattern of landholding, rooted in some respects in the circumstances of the Norman settlement, not only explains their precocious commitment to the unitrary state, but also directed them towards a distinctive form of brokerage, trading on influence at court to add to their local following, and securing good will in the royal administration by having helped the careers of rising bureaucrats.

The dramatic expansion in the community of careerism around the reign of Edward I can in some measure be explained in terms of these networks. The king's vigorous campaigning in Wales and Scotland not only made him keen to draw into his service the fighting men of the Welsh and Scottish marches, but also to spend time in those areas, where he necessarily had to make use of, and perhaps came to appreciate local talent. Robert Burnel, the Shropshire clerk, was already in the royal service in the 1260s, but it was his master's interest in Wales that probably gave him his greatest opportunities. Meanwhile, since such sees as York and Lichfield regularly served as the prizes of prominent royal servants, it is no hard matter to explain the processes by which clerical career opportunities came to be seeded in the north midlands and Yorkshire. J.L. Grassi has pointed to the influence at York of archbishops like Walter Giffard and William Greenfield, who though from the Southwest played such an important role in drawing northern clerks into the royal service, and to the siting of key government offices at York from 1298 to 1304 and at various other times during the reigns of Edward I and his son.[21] Finally, there can be no doubt that the geographical spread of career opportunities was also a function of the growing political influence of a number of magnates with power-bases in the west and north. The ambition and affluence of Thomas of Lancaster and his successors ensured that the Lancastrian connection would be distinguished by its size and sophistication, and serve as a passport to advancement in the realm at large. It was a pattern followed in some measure by princes of the blood, like the Black Prince in his lordships of Cornwall and Chester, and eventually adopted by kings themselves. Appropriately enough, the development of chamber government as a means by which monarchs like Edward II and Richard II sought to circumvent an increasingly independent bureaucracy was linked to the deployment of men from areas with strong royal connections, most spectacularly the palatinate of Chester.

Alongside the needs of crown, church and aristocracy for able and loyal servitors, however, the activism and ambition of the lower orders need acknowledgment. It would certainly be unwise to under-estimate the scale of geographical mobility in the middle ages. Young men and women sought service; labourers moved with the harvest; some craftsmen such as builders were necessarily itinerant; pedlars moved from market to market; all kept a watch for the main chance. Even in more exalted forms of careerism there was always an element of wander lust, and popular literature is replete with tales of men who left their native homes to seek an education, to live on their wits in the towns, to find military adventure, or simply to acquire worldly wisdom. Sadly, the sources provide only occasional glimpses of the enterprise and mobility of individuals. Hugh the Barber, apparently from Ely, was plying his trade among the students of the University of Paris, when he was drawn into the service of Thomas Cantilupe, the future bishop of Hereford. In later years he worked at Hereford, travelled to Rome, and settled as a married man in London.[22] The paths which led the scholar William of Ockham to the imperial court and the soldier Sir John Hawkwood to fame and fortune in northern Italy are tantalising. For men whose sights did not extend so far, careerism became less and less dependent on reckless commitment. The tracks pioneered by one generation of adventurers, became well-marked roads for their younger kinsmen. Even before the Black Death many fairly humble provincial families must have had at least one possible contact in London or some other major centre, whose household might provide temporary shelter and employment. Few could have been so well placed as the Shropshire kinsmen of Walter Wenlock, abbot of Westminster, who were accommodated in the royal abbey on their arrival in the capital.[23] A century and a half later, a London merchant not only left £20 to give his Shropshire nephews a start in life, but also £10 for the repair of roads westwards to Shrewsbury.[24]

For a variety of reasons, careerism bred careerism. The pattern by which successful men, most notoriously high government officials and churchmen, took into their service young people of their kin and ken is well documented. In this fashion whole networks of clerks linked by blood, affinity and locality can be traced in the writing offices at Westminster, in the cathedral chapters, and so on. It took the combined resources of T.F. Tout and A.H. Thompson to trace the main ramifications of the Thoresby–Waltham–Ravenser affinity so prominent in chancery in the fourteenth century.[25] Yet it is misleading to talk too glibly in terms of dynasticism and nepotism. Given the wide circle of potential claimants to their favour, patrons had perforce to be selective in their sponsorship, no doubt singling out the most suitable of the country cousins. Moreover, in an age in which the master's household was in many fields the main source of technical training and accreditation, the principles of promotion through connection and promotion through merit are hard to unravel. This point is underlined by the manner in which households were the repositories of books and other tools of trade. It is interesting to see such items handed down in wills through kin and locality-based networks of careerism. John Fairfax, who enjoyed some worldly success without being either a graduate or a royal clerk, left his books on canon and civil law to his nephew Brian Fairfax, who in fact already had them on loan at Cambridge. Another member of this career-minded Yorkshire family, several generations on, was a worthy beneficiary of a similar gift. The register of legal precedents and forms compiled by the Yorkshire chief justice, Sir William Gascoigne, passed into the hands of another Yorkshire lawyer, John Dautrey, who then bequeathed it to Guy Fairfax, subsequently justice of the king's bench.[26]

The support that aspiring careerists derived from their sponsors extended beyond the confines of the household. A merchant of London might have no place for a nephew in his own service, but through business contacts could find him a place with another master. Even Robert Wycliffe, a Yorkshire clerk, was expected to be able to arrange an apprenticeship with a London tailor for a boy from his native village.[27] Churchmen were especially well-placed to support their proteges in education. As part of the extensive patronage extended to his Kentish kinsmen, Richard Swinfield, bishop of Hereford, provided allowances or benefices for several nephews to study at Oxford. John Swinfield, archdeacon of Shrewsbury, was able to progress to the University of Paris.[28] Walter Wenlock, abbot of Westminster, helped to support a nephew, a cousin and even a poor scholar who had attached himself to his nephew in their studies at Oxford. He even made a gift to one of Bishop Swinfield's nephews.[29] At their death-beds many successful men left money to assist deserving young men of their kin or ken who were struggling to follow in their foot-steps, or embarking on other careers. Thomas Tildesley, a serjeant of law from south Lancashire, and a brother of Christopher Tildesley, goldsmith of London, left money to endow apprenticeships in London for other kinsmen.[30] Bequests to provide exhibitions for favoured individuals at school or university were quite common. The colleges and fellowships established at Oxford and Cambridge from the late thirteenth century onwards, besides being works of piety and generalised philanthropy, tended to perpetuate the founder's concern for scholars of his kin, connection and 'country'. Exeter College and Queen's College founded at Oxford by the royal clerks Walter Stapledon and Robert Eglesfield in the early fourteenth century were intended to enhance opportunities for scholars from the far Southwest and the far Northwest respectively. Judging from the prominence of Cornishmen in Oxford life from the 1340s, and from their attempted colonisation of Queen's College in the 1360s, it would be wise not to under-estimate the importance of regional associations in the university as in the church.[31]

While access to most opportunities remained dependent on the vagaries of personal connection, there were more formal channels through which promising youths from ambitious families could advance themselves. Even in the thirteenth century England was served by a network of grammar schools, providing an intermediate education between acquisition of basic literacy and university entrance. Through detailed research N. Orme and J.H. Moran have revealed how the expansion of facilities continued in spite of the crises of the later middle ages, and how the really dramatic wave of school foundations in the decades around 1500 merely seems to have capped a century and a half of quiet expansion.[32] The Yorkshire-born bishops, Thomas Rotherham, Robert Stillington and John Alcock, all endowed schools in their home-towns at this time, but self-evidently educational provision was not wholly lacking in the districts in their youth. What seems beyond doubt is that the proportion of the population thinking in terms of a formal education grew markedly in the later middle ages. New school founders like Archbishop Rotherham acknowledged the widening market for basic schooling by extending the curriculum to embrace writing, account-keeping and other skills appropriate for youths destined for secular employment.[33] The size of the school population is impossible to compute, but occasional pieces of information give pause for thought. In his will of 1369 Richard Beckingham, a Yorkshire lawyer, left 2d each to sixty of the better pupils at just one of the grammar schools of York.[34] At the same time, the numbers of university students, possibly as many as 3000 at Oxford and Cambridge at the turn of the fourteenth century, must indicate immense numbers lower down the system.[35] Obviously many families and individuals found the by-no-means negligible costs of education a manageable investment, and probably found access to facilities less and less a matter of personal connection or fortuitous circumstance.

The increasing scale and institutionalisation of education inevitably served to regularise career-paths. Increasingly would-be careerists were able to make more informed decisions, economise in their commitments of time and money, minimise risks and maximise advantages by taking single purposeful steps rather than precipitate leaps. The growth of market information on education and career possibilities is observable from the early fourteenth century. Naturally it is most clearly documented in the church, as in the responses to the constitution 'cum ex eo' of 1298 which provided for beneficed clergy to be released from their cures for higher study. In the reign of Edward II at least 700 such licences were issued in the dioceses of Winchester, Worcester and Exeter alone.[36] Even more remarkable is the evidence from this same time that information on the opportunities and requirements of higher studies was available in lay circles and in areas quite remote from Oxford and Westminster. The Bruches of Bruche near Warrington, for example, were freeholders on the margins of gentility, but in the marriage contract for their eldest son in 1323 it was agreed that the father-in-law would maintain him for five years in the manner befitting a *gentilhomme*, the first year of which would be spent at school in Oxford, and the remaining four at the court of Common Pleas.[37] This programme of studies, also documented in London in the late fourteenth century, was clearly not the invention of the gentry of Tudor England.

Doubtless ambitious fathers considered the aptitudes of their sons, calculated the amount of capital available and the range of contacts that could be mobilised, and carefully weighed the advantages of the various callings. For the squirearchy a placement in the royal or an aristocratic household was the preferred form of advancement. Once their fortunes were established through law, for example, the Pastons put feet in as many doors as possible: the eldest grandson of the dour Judge Paston struggled to make his name at the court of Edward IV, while younger grandsons were in the retinues of the duke of Norfolk, the duke of Gloucester and the earl of Oxford. In the preceding generation formal education had been more important in the framing of careers: Judge Paston's eldest sons had attended inns of court, while two others studied at the University of Cambridge.[38] Lower down the social scale, but in an analogous fashion, yeomen and husbandmen placed their sons in the parson's song school, in apprenticeships in town, or in the service of their squire with the same high hopes. Though adventurism and opportunism never wholly disappeared in careerist activity, successful families tended to progress from employments where native wit and hard work were indispensable, to callings where education and capital more or less guaranteed modest affluence and respect. Ambitious tradespeople can be seen investing in the education of their sons for the church, the law, or polite society. The Cradocks of Nantwich, the Chicheles of Leicester and the Chaucers of London all operated in this fashion. In clerical dynasties like the Brantinghams of Yorkshire and the Booths of Lancashire, success in clerical administration in the older generation tended to be followed by scholarly attainment and ecclesiastical dignity in the younger generation.

As networks of careerists rose and fell, as their resources, connections and expectations expanded and contracted, their multifarious interests and activities were subject to continuous permutation. Most interesting are the veritable clans of careerists, who individually pursued their own callings but who collectively infiltrated most fields of endeavour and were active in several parts of England. The Fairfaxes and Ferribys from Yorkshire served in the retinues of northern magnates and in the royal administration, manned the church and followed the law, were involved in the wool trade, textiles and shipping. The Finchams of Fincham in Norfolk spawned a priest and a university graduate, and a fishmonger, a mercer and a silkwoman in London.[39] The Lathoms of Lancashire were distant cousins of the Stanleys, later earls of Derby, whose household the senior branch served in an honorary capacity. A younger branch of the Lathoms, established in the Cheshire towns of Congleton and Knutsford, prospered in trade, perhaps through the favour of their aristocratic kinsmen, and established sons in business in London, Denbigh and Pontefract. Their enterprises east of the Pennines were promoted by a clerical member of the family, who as secretary to Archbishop Kemp was influential as well as well-beneficed in the archdiocese of York.[40]

The manner in which ambitious families straddled a range of fields of enterprise is at first sight surprising. An unbridgeable chasm is often assumed to have lain between trade and the professions. It is true that a craftsman working with his hands or a money-grubbing stall-holder had little or nothing in common with a bishop or judge, but it is important to compare like with like. Poor clerks and minor court officials shared the world of petty artisans and retailers, while the members of merchant companies mixed freely with members of the professions. The experiences and attitudes holding them together were manifold. In all the trades and professions ability and application, education and experience, capital and connections were the ingredients of success. To a striking degree there is a shared language: commerce could be a 'studium'; there were apprentices at law as well as apprentice tailors; there were knights bachelor as well as bachelors of arts; everywhere there were masters; everywhere there was profit and advancement. In practice as well as theory there were close links between the tradespeople and professionals. Merchants, administrators and lawyers, in particular, tended to live in towns, sharing to a degree a common life-style and culture. Collective involvement in civic affairs, common association in parish gilds, and above all intermarriage, were all powerful bonds which might cut across occupational boundaries. At the same time tradesmen and professionals were not only the main suppliers, but also the greatest purveyors of goods and services, whether on their own account or as agents for their lords and corporate master. The fortunes of London merchants like Thomas Knolles and John Welles might owe something to contracts secured by their kinsmen, the celebrated soldiers-of-fortune Sir Robert Knolles and Sir John Fastolf.[41] It is small wonder that in planning their son's futures ambitious fathers, like the Londoner William Tonge, talked about securing apprenticeships, training for the priesthood and legal education in more or less the same breath.[42] It also made sense for them to opt for varied, but mutually supportive career activities. The interconnectedness of the trades and professions in so many facets of life attests the value of focusing on the larger concept of careerism.

III

The later middle ages in England was manifestly an 'age of ambition'. While the majority of the population remained rooted in a predominantly agrarian and localised economy, a growing proportion were finding themselves responding to a wide range of opportunities for enterprise and careerism. From the fourteenth century at least it is clear that neither geographical remoteness nor low birth were absolute barriers to participation in the major trades and professions. Of course, a great deal depended on a combination of connection and capital, but it would seem that informal networks of connection were widely, if rather randomly, diffused in English society, and that more formalised procedures were available to able young men with some capital to start them in life. Needless to say, the successful among the careerists were always a minority, and even for them there were major hurdles to acceptance back in landed society. The De La Poles of Hull, who rose from the warehouses of Hull to the ranks of the peerage in two generations, were never allowed to forget their origins. Still, by comparison with other European countries at the time, England was distinguished by a remarkable degree of social fluidity, and in this era the chances for advancement seemed alluring.

The significance of careerism in English life extends beyond a consideration of the rather limited record of spectacular social climbing. The fruits of careerism were often ephemeral and indirect, impossible to convert directly into solid advancement. There was a tendency for them to be dissipated, securing modest gains and losses for large numbers of kinsmen and friends. This fragmentation of the profits derived from, to use modern terms, the secondary and tertiary sectors was due in part to the casual and transitional character of the groups involved in them. There was a great deal of part-time enterprise and career activity, from the women and children involved in petty trading and commodity production to the noblemen engaged in trading ventures, soldiering and office-holding. Many young men had grounds for regarding service, clerisy and soldiering as phases in their life-cycle. Waiting on their 'livelode' or tenancy, they used the time profitably in gleaning experience, education, capital and connections, which would be put to use in landed society. The majority perforce made a life-time commitment to their calling, but few succeeded in reproducing themselves socially. Townsmen and soldiers presumably had lower than average life-expectancies, but more critical in the trades and professions generally were abysmal fecundity-rates. In theory at least clergymen were celibate; so also in practice were many young men setting out on a career. For many merchants, lawyers and soldiers, marriage came, like success, late in life, and the tendency to marry ageing widows or heiresses of declining families further limited the chances of leaving progeny.[43] Even where there were sons, trading and professional families rarely sustained themselves over a number of generations. Sometimes ability and aptitude were not inherited, sometimes they found outlets in new fields of enterprise. Moveable wealth tended to be divided among heirs, and was more vulnerable to official impost and private envy. A great deal of career activity was treading water, but the sheer volume of water churned remains impressive.

Though the traditional categories of *oratores*, *bellatores* and *laboratores* embraced most of the trades and professions, the social status of careerists in medieval England was thus problematic. For all its institutional complexity, English society was largely structured in terms of differential access to land-based power and wealth. For the most part a man's status derived from his position on a finely graded tenurial hierarchy, in which the really crucial divide lay between lords and peasants. Many careerists could be forgiven for regarding themselves as temporarily displaced members of landed society. Tradesmen and professionals, rather in the manner of servants, might in some contexts take their status from the quality of the patronage they enjoyed. Even the growth of gilds and professional identities, which gave a measure of security and dignity to the individual, seems not to have transformed them into independent social groups. Even if the trades and professions could survive adverse demographic conditions, their most promising members succumbed sooner or later to the lure of the land.[44] The acquisition of a country-seat remained the goal of all successful careerists. Throughout the middle ages and beyond land remained the soundest investment and the only heritable index of social worth. According to a contemporary adage, service was not heritage.

It is this symbiotic relationship with landed society which makes careerism of special, all-pervasive significance in English life. The relative failure of the trades and professions to develop as independent social groups, passing on esoteric skills and corporate privileges to their progeny, ironically served to diffuse commercial attitudes, professional knowledge and 'career-mindedness' far more widely. Its full impact on English landed society and its distinctive class-structure is hard to assess. The practice of primogeniture, with all its implications for agrarian development, was more readily sustained, even extended, in a world in which opportunities for alternative advancement beckoned. The economic position of the landed interest and the rural population generally was certainly strengthened by the spilling over from the town of manufacturing and business opportunities, while the calibre of the landowning classes was enhanced by the infusion of commercial and legal experience. The place of careerism in the larger transformation of English society, the transition from feudalism to capitalism, might be worthy of some consideration. According to recent neo-Marxian formulations, the focus of interest in late medieval England is the evolution of a distinctive set of class relations based on capitalist agriculture.[45] The peculiar course of English development, following the logic neither of centralised (absolutist) nor decentralised (seignorial) feudal extraction, but drawing on both tendencies in its blend of constitutionalism and economic landlordship, is hard to explain. A focus on career activity, so extensive, deeply rooted and widely diffused in late medieval England, and particularly on the manner in which it functioned in English society, forging links between communities and 'estates' and corroding regional and corportate identities, might offer some new insights. Certainly careerism helped to produce a remarkably cohesive, flexible, resilient and cohesive ruling class, which through its adroit deployment of capital and connections, and through its appeals to the rhetoric of both 'character' and credentialism, successfully maintained its hegemony and stability while proclaiming its philanthropy and openness.

The capitalist aristocracy of early modern England ruled a remarkably cohesive and homogeneous community, itself in important respects the product of the great expansion of career activity in the later middle ages. As early as the reign of Richard II it was possible to think in terms of a pool of talent, a framework of business and professional enterprise, and a community of ideas, which were demonstrably national. Customers from all corners of the realm had accounts with the London merchant, Gilbert Maghfield; wise landowners from all over eastern England paid retaining-fees to have the services of the astute barrister, Robert Tirwhit; military commanders from the South and East Anglia looked to the recruiting-grounds of the northwest for the best soldiers; haemorrhoid sufferers from distances of a hundred miles or so tottered to Newark, where John Arderne ran a successful surgery.[46] The development in the fourteenth century of an essentially national framework for commercial and profess-ional enterprise had profound implications for the integration of English society. In the political sphere the growing sense of a 'community of the realm' from the thirteenth century onwards owed something to career-mindedness as well as constitutional conflict. According to G.P. Cuttino, the forceful affirmation of national identity and interest in the reign of Edward I, and the dissemination of government propaganda and nation-alist rhetoric across the country, was largely the work of a remarkable cohort of royal clerks.[47] Through the political crises and internecine strife of the fourteenth and fifteenth centuries, professional groupings and networks, so broadly based and weighty in deliberation, provided vital ballast for the ship of state. In the economic field the close connections between land, the professions and commerce not only assisted in the growth of a national market and capital accumulation, but also in the elaboration and diffusion of business-mindedness, professional mentalities, and mercantilist concepts. Parliament was only the most public of the many forums in which noblemen, churchmen, lawyers and merchants began debating questions of 'public good' and 'common profit', inaugurating the 'discourse of the common weal' which culminated in the deafening cacophony of the 1530s.

In the world of culture, courtiers and soldiers, quite as much as princes and noblemen, led the way in the development and diffusion of new styles and tastes; lawyers, merchants and other folk followed in their wake. Advised by their confessors and consulting with craftsmen, they defined what was fashionable in piety and philanthropy as well as costume and behaviour. Their chantry endowments and educational benefactions provided the models which were followed in strings of foundations across the nation.[48] Geographically mobile clergymen, from disappointed graduates like John Wycliffe to disoriented prophets like William Langland, helped breach the walls separating scholastic thought from popular belief. In London a remarkable circle of courtiers, lawyer–administrators and merchants, including men of such diverse backgrounds as Sir John Clanvowe, John Gower, Geoffrey Chaucer and Henry Scogan, provided the context for the first great flowering of English verse.[49] This careerist milieu gave Ricardian poetry its distinctive tone: down-to-earth, practical, public-spirited, sententious, unheroic. As A. Middleton has explained, it is 'public poetry', addressing men of differing origins and occupations, and seeking 'to bring to mutual awareness, and to resolve into common understanding' their differing perspectives on the world.[50] Needless to say, the role of careerism in the promotion of lay literacy and the wide dissemination of this literature was crucial. The standardisation of the written vernacular and the homogenisation of English literary culture were well in train before the advent of the printing-press. William Caxton, entrepreneur and impresario, friend and neighbour of courtiers, scholars, bureaucrats and tradesmen, merely exploited and accelerated the trend.

In conclusion, English society in the later middle ages was bound together in innumerable strands of enterprise and careerism. Whether or not they always resulted in social mobility, they worked like leaven in English society. To the size, strength and representativeness of the groups who moved outside their 'castes' is owed in some measure the progressive integration of an increasingly informed and committed political nation, and the impressive stability of English institutions in an age of dynastic upheaval. The literary achievements of the age of Chaucer were the product of an aware and articulate community of careerists, while the spread of a standard written vernacular across the whole of the realm a full generation before the advent of printing is a tribute to the remarkable cultural unity of at least the literate elite. Meanwhile the heightened participation rate in careerism seems to have served to break down social divisions between the various trades and professions. Instead of capital, stock and skills being locked in occupational castes, they spilled over to irrigate other fields of endeavour. All in all, careerism in late medieval England played a crucial role in breaking down barriers, regional, social and occupational, to produce a much larger, but still cohesive, political and economic system. Most fundamentally it facilitated the establishment of a nation-wide infrastructure of connection, communication and commitment, without which the concerns and conceptions of the Tudor 'commonwealth' movement, and other political and economic developments of the sixteenth and seventeenth centuries, cannot be properly explained.

Notes

1   F.J. Fisher, 'London as an "engine of economic growth"' in *Britain and the Netherlands*, Vol.IV, eds. J.S. Bromley and E.H. Kossman (The Hague, 1971), pp.3–16; E.A. Wrigley, 'A simple model of London's importance in changing English society and economy 1650–1750', *Past and Present* 37 (1967), pp. 44–70.

2   For Poggio Bracciolini's comments on the ability of low-born soldiers and tradesmen to fight and buy their way into the English nobility, see G. Holmes, *The Florentine Enlightenment 1400–50* (London, 1969), p.146.

3   On social mobility see W.G. Runciman, 'Accelerating social mobility: the case of Anglo-Saxon England', *Past and Present* 104 (1984), 3–30; M.J. Bennett, 'Sources and problems in the study of social mobility: Cheshire in the later middle ages', *Transactions of the Historic Society of Lancashire and Cheshire* 128 (1979) for 1978), 59–95; F.R.H. Du Boulay, *An Age of Ambition. English Society in the Late Middle Ages* (London, 1970), esp. ch.4; L. Stone, 'Social mobility in England, 1500–1700' in P.S. Seaver (ed.), *Seventeenth-Century England. Society in Age of Revolution* (New York, 1976), pp.27–70.

4   R.W. Southern, 'From schools to university' in *The History of the University of Oxford*, Vol.I. *The Early Oxford Schools*, ed. J.I. Catto (Oxford, 1984), pp.1–36. Englishmen continued to study at Paris in some numbers well into the fourteenth century; N. Orme, *English Schools in the Middle Ages* (London, 1973), esp. ch.6.

5   J. R. Strayer, 'The laicization of French and English society in the thirteenth century' in J.R. Strayer, *Medieval Statecraft and the Perspectives of History* (Princeton, N.J., 1971), pp.251–65; M.T. Clanchy, *From Memory to Written Record. England 1066–1307* (London, 1979), passim; R.V. Turner, 'The *miles literatus* in twelfth- and thirteenth-century England: how rare a phenomenon?', *American Historical Review* 83 (1978), pp. 928–45.

6   R.A. Griffiths, 'Public and private bureaucracies in England and Wales in the fifteenth century', *Transactions of the Royal Historical Society*, 5th series 30 (1980), 109–30; R.L. Storey, 'Gentleman-bureaucrats' in C.H. Clough (ed.), *Profession, Vocation and Culture in Later Medieval England. Essays dedicated to the Memory of A.R. Myers* (Liverpool, 1982), pp.90–129.

7   A.E. Williams, 'King's clerks in England 1216–1272', Unpublished Ph.D. thesis, Emory University, 1976. Of the clerks active in the first half of the thirteenth century, roughly one quarter seem to have been foreigners and another quarter hailed from within sixty miles of London (17–18).

8   The Dominican friar Robert Holcot (d.1349) wrote: 'We commonly see that the sons of the rich and powerful will not learn, while the sons of simple poor men reach the highest ecclesiastical dignities by their character and science' (Quoted in B. Smalley, 'Robert Holcot O.P.', *Archivum Fratrum Praedicatorium* 26 (1956), 5–97, at 94).

9   K. Edwards, 'The social origins and provenance of the English bishops during the reign of Edward II', *Transactions of the Royal Historical Society*, 5th series 9 (1959), 51–79. As she feared (64), she over-stated the number of prelates from knightly backgrounds. The wordly success of

the Stapledons was a function of the bishop's achievements not vice versa: M. Buck, *Politics, Finance and the Church in the Reign of Edward II. Walter Stapledon, Treasurer of England* (Cambridge, 1983), pp.10–37.

10   G.P. Cuttino, 'King's clerks and the community of the realm', *Speculum* 29 (1954), 397.

11   J.L. Grassi, 'Royal clerks from the archdiocese of York in the fourteenth century', *Northern History* 5 (1970), pp. 12–33.

12   M.J. Bennett, *Community, Class and Careerism. Cheshire and Lancashire Society in the Age of 'Sir Gawain and the Green Knight'* (Cambridge, 1983), pp.151–5.

13   J.R. Magrath, 'Fresh light on the family of Robert de Eglesfeld, founder of Queen's College, Oxford', *Transactions of the Cumberland and Westmorland Antiquarian and Archaeological Society*, new series 16 (1916), pp. 239–72; J.R. Magrath, 'Sir Robert Parvyng kt, Knight of the Shire for Cumberland, and Chancellor of England', *Ibid.*, new series 19 (1919), pp. 30–91.

14   S.L. Thrupp, *The Merchant Class of Medieval London* (Chicago, 1948), pp.206–19, and appendix C.

15   The mayors are listed in *The Great Chronicle of London*, eds. A.H. Thomas and I.D. Thornley (London, 1938), pp.270–1, and their geographical origins can be culled from Thrupp, *Merchant Class*, appendix A.

16   R.L. Storey, 'Recruitment of English clergy in the period of the Conciliar Movement', *Annuarium Historiae Conciliorum* 7 (1975), 290–313; J.T. Rosenthal, 'The training of an elite group: English bishops in the fifteenth century', *Transactions of the American Philosophical Society*, new series 60, part 5 (1970), esp. pp.10–11. The Lancashire man Robert Hallum must be added to Rosenthal's northerners.

17   G.F. Lytle, 'Patronage patterns and Oxford colleges, c.1300–c.1500' in L. Stone (ed.), *The University in Society*, 2 vols. (Princeton, 1974), I, pp.111–49; R.N. Swanson, 'Universities, graduates and benefices in later medieval England', *Past and Present* 106 (1985), 28–61.

18   E.g. John Trillek, bishop of Hereford, Thomas Trillik, bishop of Rochester, Philip Morgan, bishop of Worcester and Reginald Pecock, bishop of Chichester.

19   M.C. Hill, *The King's Messengers 1199–1377. A Contribution to the History of the Royal Household* (London, 1961), pp.124–34. I am grateful to Dr P. Hyams for reminding me of this reference.

20   Ecclesiastical estate officials were often recruited to the royal service, as with Matthew Christian and Robert Madingly, stewards of Ely, who later became royal justices: E. Miller, *The Abbey and Bishopric of Ely. The Social History of an Ecclesiastical Estate from the Tenth to the Early Fourteenth Century* (Cambridge, 1951), pp.196–7, 267–8.

21   Grassi, 'Royal clerks from archdiocese of York', p. 17.

22   M. Jancey (ed.), *St. Thomas Cantilupe, Bishop of Hereford. Essays in his Honour* (Hereford, 1982), pp.191–201.

23   E.H. Pearce, *Walter de Wenlok, Abbot of Westminster* (London, 1920), pp.61–2.

24   Public Record Office, PROB 11/6, fos.178–9.

25   T.F.Tout, *Chapters in the Administrative History of Mediaeval England*, 6 vols. (Manchester, 1920–33), III, 215–16.

26   *Testamenta Eboracensia*, Part I, ed. J. Raine (Suretees Society 4, 1836), pp.187–8; *Testamenta Eboracensia*, Part II, ed. J. Raine (Surtees Society 30, 1855), p.233.

27   E. Rickert, *Chaucer's World*, eds. C.C. Olson and M.M. Crow (New York, 1948), p.107.

28   *A Roll of the Household Expenses of Richard de Swinfield, Bishop of Hereford, during part of the years 1289 and 1290*, ed. J. Webb, 2 vols. (Camden Society, original series 59 & 62, 1853, 1855), II, pp.xxxviii, cxiii, cxxxi.

29   Pearce, *Walter de Wenlok*, pp.60–1, 77.

30   Bennett, *Community, Class and Careerism*, pp.127–8.

31   Notable Cornishmen at Oxford at this time included the theologian William Polmorva, the doctor of medicine John Landreyn, the grammarian John of Cornwall, and the translator John Trevisa: A.B. Emden, *A Biographical Register of the University of Oxford to A.D. 1500*, 3 vols. (Oxford, 1957–9), passim; D.C. Fowler, 'New light on John Trevisa', *Traditio* 18 (1962),

289–317. For the struggle at Queen's College see *Victoria County History of Oxford*, Vol.III, eds. H.E. Salter and M.D. Lobel (London, 1954), pp.132–3.

32 N. Orme, *Education in the West of England 1066–1548* (Exeter, 1971) has added substantially to his tally for the West Country in English Schools in the Middle Ages, appendix. J.H. Moran, *The Growth of English Schooling 1340–1548. Learning, Literacy and Laicization in Pre-Reformation York Diocese* (Princeton, N.J., 1985) has likewise documented in the North (p.117) four times as many public schools as were previously acknowledged for the early sixteenth century.

33 Orme. *English Schools in the Middle Ages*, p.78.

34 J.H. Moran, *Education and Learning in the City of York 1300-1560* (Borthwick Papers no. 55, 1979), 7.

35 T.H. Aston, 'Oxford's Medieval Alumni, *Past and Present* 74 (1977), 6–7; T.H. Aston, G.D. Duncan and T.A.R. Evans, 'The medieval alumni of the University of Cambridge', *Ibid.*, 86 (1980), pp. 11–19.

36 L.E. Boyle, 'The constitution 'Cum ex eo' of Boniface VIII', *Mediaeval Studies* 24 (1962), pp. 297–8.

37 M.J. Bennett, 'Provincial gentlefolk and legal education in the reign of Edward II', *Bulletin of the Institute of Historical Research* 57 (1984), pp. 203–8.

38 H.S. Bennett, *The Pastons and their England* (Cambridge, 1922).

39 Public Record Office, PROB 11/7, fos.17–19 (Will of Lawrence Fincham, fishmonger of London); Norfolk Record Office, Hare 2019, Box 193 x 5 (Apprenticeship of Allanora Fincham in silk trade).

40 Bennett, 'Sources and problems in social mobility', 64; *Testamenta Eboracensia*, Part III, ed. J. Raine (Surtees Society 45, 1863), pp. 173–8.

41 Thrupp, *Merchant Class of Medieval London*, pp.351–2, 373; K.B. McFarlane, 'The investment of Sir John Fastolf's profits of war', *Transactions of the Royal Historical Society*, 5th series 7 (1957), pp. 95–100.

42 Rickert, *Chaucer's World*, pp.111–12.

43 Bennett, 'Sources and problems in social mobility', pp. 83–6.

44 Thrupp, *Merchant Class of Medieval London*, ch.5; J.I. Kermode, 'The merchants of three northern English towns' in Clough, *Profession, Vocation and Culture*, pp.7–49.

45 R.Brenner, 'The agrarian roots of European capitalism', *Past and Present* 97 (1982), pp. 16–113, esp.76–89.

46 E. Rickert, 'Documents and records: extracts from a fourteenth-century account book', *Modern Philology* 24 (1926–7), 111–19, 249–56; N. Ramsay, 'Retained legal counsel, c.1275–c.1475', *Transactions of the Royal Historical Society*, fifth series 35 (1985), 105; Bennett, *Community, Class and Careerism*, pp.164–5; *Treaties of 'Fistula in Ano', Haemorrhoids, and Clysters by John Arderne, from an Early Fifteenth-Century Manuscript Translation*, ed. D'Arcy Power (Early English Test Society, original series 139, 1910), pp. 1–3, 14.

47 Sir John Percival, mayor of London, and his wife adopted the same model for the schools set up in their places of birth (Macclesfield, Cheshire and Week St Mary), leaving twin endowments three hundred miles apart, and almost as far from London: Orme, *Education in West England*, pp.173–7.

48 Cuttino, 'King's clerks and community of realm', pp. 404–7.

49 D. Pearsall, *Old English and Middle English Poetry* (London, 1977), pp.194–7; J.A. Burrow, *Ricardian Poetry. Chaucer, Gower, Langland and the 'Gawain' Poet* (London, 1971), ch.3; A. Middleton, 'The idea of public poetry in the reign of Richard II', *Speculum* 53 (1978), 94–114; M.H. Hallmundson, 'Chaucer's circle: Henry Scogan and his friends', *Mediaevalia et Humanistica*, n.s. 10 (1981), 129–39. The finest works of the Northwest Midlands alliterative 'school' likewise reflect in some degree the experiences and concerns of careerists: Bennett, *Community, Class and Careerists*, pp.231–5.

50 Middleton, 'Public poetry in reign of Richard II', 98.

William Waynflete and the Educational Revolution of the Fifteenth century

VIRGINIA DAVIS

Traditionally the sixteenth century has been seen as marking a watershed in English education.[1] While, as has been said, almost every century of the late middle ages displays developments which could earn for it a name as a century of educational revolution, there were two developments in the fifteenth century which have pointed it out as the critical period when the accepted medieval system was replaced by another which was to persist until the end of the nineteenth century. Expressed in the most simplistic of terms these developments were the secularisation of education and the percolation of continental, primarily Italian, ideas on the education of the young and on the teaching of grammar in particular, through to English educational institutions at all levels. Scholars working on the educational advances of this period have stressed such developments as the expansion of higher education, the improvement in literacy rates at all levels of society and a growing lay participation in the foundation of schools all over the country. Certain key events have been seen as marking the arrival of Italian educational ideas in England, perhaps the most lauded being the refoundation of St. Paul's School in 1509 by John Colet; the appointment of the humanist William Lily as its master and the use of new printed text-books by Erasmus and by English grammarians such as John Stanbridge.

The roots of the development in the early decades of the sixteenth century lay, however, in the fifteenth century when, as remained the case until at least the Reformation, the ecclesiastical hierarchy played the leading role (Colet, for example, was Dean of St. Paul's); a spate of schools and colleges founded in the fifteenth century were episcopal foundations.[2] As a body the episcopate made a major contribution in laying a firm foundation for sixteenth century developments. Their contribution to education in the fifteenth century fully justifies speaking of an educational revolution during this period.

A clear precursor to Colet's St. Paul's was Magdalen College School, founded by the 1470s, which by 1481 at the latest had a layman as master. The teachings of Italian grammarians influenced the methods and materials used in Magdalen

College School and many of its ealiest pupils were to be influential over the next half century. The foundation of Magdalen College School was only a facet of the many-sided educational work of an important member of the English episcopate, William Waynflete, bishop of Winchester. Waynflete was involved in the mainstream of late medieval education and played an influential role in shaping the educational ideas which were to predominate in the decades after his death. As headmaster of Winchester College, provost of Eton College and as founder of Magdalen College School, Magdalen College Oxford and a grammar school in his Lincolnshire birthplace of Wainfleet, William Waynflete was the most active educationalist of his day. He was the most prolific and influential founder in the fifteenth century episcopate.

During his lengthy career (1396–1486) Waynflete was involved in a range of aspects of fifteenth century English society.[3] As bishop of Winchester, the richest see in the English church, he was a senior and influential member of the church hierarchy. Politically he was linked with Henry VI and the Lancastrian administration throughout the last years of Henry VI's disastrous first reign. Waynflete has been called a 'schoolmaster bishop', a description which emphasises the fact that he owed his promotion to the episcopate to his service to Henry VI as provost of Eton College, rather than following the more usual route for elevation to the episcopate to service in the central government and administration. Although many medieval bishops had educational interests these were often restricted to their role as founders of schools and colleges; none shared Waynflete's experience and particular interest in the practical side of teaching and schoolmastering. A recent study of schoolmasters in the late middle ages pointed out that, 'Hardly anyone who had been a schoolmaster reached a high position between 1307–1509, either in Church of State'.[4] Two other teachers did reach the forefront of public life under Henry VI – John Chedworth, bishop of Lincoln 1452–71 and John Somerset, later to be chancellor of the exchequer. Chedworth had been tutor to Robert, Lord Hungerford and Somerset had been master of Bury St. Edmunds and tutor to the king. Waynflete was the only episcopal figure of this period who had actually taught in a school; he was the sole exception to the rule that teachers were 'overlooked, forgotten and un-noticed'.[5]

This paper investigates Waynflete's involvement in English education to establish what contribution be made to the changing face of education in England during this period. The first section deals with his own education and early career, the source of his own educational experience. Subsequent sections consider his years as provost of Eton College, his foundation of Magdalen College Oxford and the two grammar schools associated with it; his promotion of the use of printed grammar texts which enabled the spread of the ideas of Italian grammarians in England and finally draws conclusions as to the importance of his contribution.

In view of the role that William Waynflete was to play in educational development in the fifteenth century it is unfortunate that almost nothing is known of his own education. He was born William Barbour in Wainfleet, on the Lincolnshire coast near Boston, and it is likely that his early education took place locally within Lincolnshire, a county which was well supplied with good schools.[6] Very little more evidence is available for the latter stages of his education. In 1416 as rector of Binbrook parish in Linconshire he obtained a *cum ex eo* licence allowing him to absent himself from his benefice for three years while studying at a university.[7] It is not known either when or where he took his degree which was in theology but the earliest reference to Waynflete as a Bachelor of Theology is found in September 1443, after he had become provost of Eton College.[8] It has usually been accepted that Waynflete was a member of New College, Oxford which drew its students from Winchester College but their records are complete and his name does not appear in them. The fact that his name does not appear in the records of any of the colleges does not mean that he did not go to Oxford; the majority of the students were attached to Halls which tended to be ephemeral and which have left few records. In the absence of any strong evidence to suggest Cambridge,[9] Oxford, which lay in the diocese of Lincoln and where he was later to found a college seems most likely. In his own lifetime the University of Oxford claimed Waynflete as an ex-student when, in 1447, the university authorities requested his help to obtain the benefaction left to them by Humphrey, Duke of Gloucester. In a letter to him they described the university of Oxford as, 'your mother who nourished you in learning'.[10]

Waynflete disappears completely from the sources during the 1420s until the very end of the decade when he reappears as *magister informator* or headmaster at Winchester College in June 1430. In September 1429 the college had sent one of their fellows to Oxford to seek a new master and Waynflete's appointment may have dated from this visit, suggesting that perhaps throughout this decade he had been in Oxford, which was still the great centre for grammar teachers.[11] It is likely that Waynflete had had some teaching experience prior to his appointment as headmaster. Wykeham had stipulated in his statutes that the master would be a man 'in gramaticam sufficienter eruditus, habens docendi peritiam, vir bone fame et conversacionis'.[12] The duties of the master were also laid down in Wykeham's statutes – they comprised the teaching or supervision of the teaching of grammar to the seventy scholars and the chastisement of the 'negligences sue alia delinquentes'. The scholars ranged in age from eight to eighteen (twenty-five in the case of Founder's Kin) and they were supposed to have grasped the rudiments of grammar and plainsong prior to their admission.[13]

Some idea of what Waynflete taught during the late 1420s and 1430s can be derived from a surviving inventory of the college library drawn up by one of the fellows in 1432, not long after Waynflete's appointment as headmaster.[14] This inventory listed the books, their value, the donor if known and the first couple of words of the second folio of each. The list was divided by subject into section; the final section *libri grammaticales* lists nineteen works. Predominant among these were the commonly used texts of Priscian and Peter Helias which formed the basis for the Arts course and had done so for several centuries. Of particular interest are the two works which were described as 'being in the hands of the master of the scholars'.[15] These were *Liber continens librum equivocorum et libri magni doctrinalis* and *Liber continens quandam compilationem de informatione puerorum cum aliis parvis tractatibus*. Neither work survives today in Winchester College Library but the *Liber continens librum equivocorum* to judge from its title, was of a type widely used by Waynflete's contemporaries.[16] Other similar works covered the four principal parts of grammar, etymology, orthography, prosody and syntax. There were almost as many different texts as there were teachers and no one set of texts or glosses was widely used. In fact prior to the 1480s when the printed works of English grammarians such as John Anwykyll came to dominate the teaching of Latin in England, masters like Waynflete had to rely heavily upon works produced on the continent which had elaborate glosses adapting them for teaching in England. By the latter half of the fourteenth century one major change had already occurred, the teaching of Latin through English rather than French had become common and it is not therefore surprising to find that this Compilation was in English – the words cited in the catalogue from the beginning of the second folio being 'ablytif case'.

Waynflete taught at Winchester College throughout the 1430s. He was, in fact, at Winchester for eleven years, a longer period than any of his predecessors and his experience was the most formative part of his early life and of great significance for his later career.

In 1441, following a visit made by Henry VI to Winchester College[17] Waynflete entered the royal service, initially in some undefined role connected with the development of Eton College which had been founded the previous year. In his foundation charter for the college the young king emphasised his desire to demonstrate his devotion to the church by copying the pious works of his ancestors and the charter shows that he saw his collegiate foundation as a symbol of his having grasped the full reins of power which he had done in November 1437.[18] The tripartite nature of Henry VI's foundation as religious college, almshouse and school was outlined in the charter; it was to consist of a provost, ten priests, four clerks, six choristers, twenty-five poor scholars and twenty-five bedesmen. In addition a master was to be appointed to teach grammar to all who wished to attend the school, freely and without exactions. The whole tone of the foundation charter clearly demonstrates that the king's intention in the autumn of 1440 was to emulate the pious works of his ancestors.

The influences which determined the form of Henry VI's foundation was to take are difficult to establish clearly. The issue is obscured further because of the major changes his foundation underwent in the first years of its existence and because, also, to modern commentators the name of Eton College is synonomous with the provision of education. This makes it particularly difficult to free oneself from the knowledge conveyed by hindsight and to view the earliest days of Eton College with detachment.

The intimate circle around the young Henry VI contained a number of men who themselves founded institutions with educational elements. Archbishop Chichele in conjunction with the king had founded All Souls College in Oxford as well as a school at Higham Ferrers. At Ewelme in Oxfordshire the Duke of Suffolk founded a triple foundation while a further triple foundation was established by Walter Lord Hungerford at Heytesbury in Wiltshire.[19] A petition addressed to the king by Walter Bingham in 1439 bemoaning the decline in the teaching of grammar in England may have helped to bring the needs of education to Henry VI's notice. Finally his secretary Thomas Beckington and his mentor Archbishop Chichele were the products of the largest educational foundation yet established in England, Wykeham's magnificent and innovative dual foundation of Winchester College and New College Oxford. This active interest among his advisors in the provision of education can hardly have failed to influence Henry VI when he came to formulate his ideas about the form his own foundation should take. The tripartite form for which he opted drew together the old and the new with a chantry, an almshouse and a school. Despite the final form that Henry's college was to take, it is clear that at the outset the school element was only conceived of as a small part of the whole, not the dominant part. Although people to fill the positions of provost, priests and choristers were named in the charter and several boys were designated scholars, the reference to the master comes almost as an afterthought and no-one was nominated to take the position. A royal chapel school and the Cambridge college of King's Hall already provided schooling for court proteges and future servants of the crown[20]; there was no actual need for the king to establish a school. Neither in 1440 was any reference made to a second university foundation to complement the school as would have been expected if Henry VI's foundation had been intended to rival Wykeham's from the outset.

In February 1441 Henry VI did establish a Cambridge college which consisted of a rector and twelve scholars[21] but no connection was set up between these two bodies. The early scholars of Eton College did not automatically proceed to Cambridge. That their options remained open can be seen from a grant made in February 1442 by John Carpenter, master of the Hospital of St. Anthony in London, to sustain five boys studying the arts in Oxford at the rate of 10*d.* per week, 'provided that they have been instructed in the rudiments of the Arts faculty at Eton College'.[22] In Henry VI's original plans the school element at Eton College was secondary; the whole tone of the foundation charter clearly demonstrates that the king's intention in the autumn was to found an ecclesiastical college imitating the foundations of his ancestors. He did not set out to emulate Wykeham's dual educational establishment despite the fact that within five years of 1440 they were closely linked in fact and in form.

William Waynflete had not been brought to Eton to act as schoolmaster. He may have done a little teaching for two scholars were named in the foundation charter but it is unlikely that much formal teaching was required until the school began to expand. When Henry VI set his foundation in motion he was not yet twenty-six years of age. In Waynflete he found what he needed, a mature and experienced man able to carry out his desires and supervise the future development of his college. Henry Sever, named as provost in the foundation charter, seems to have made little impact on the new foundation and may have proved a disappointment as provost.[23] No record of Waynflete's appointment has survived but it took place in early March 1442.[24] He was not formally sworn in as provost until after a code of statutes had been drawn up.

The great period of change for Eton College was 1443: the year when statutes closely modelled on those of Winchester College were drawn up.[25] Some small changes were made, for example, those to cover the bedesmen who were unique to Eton College or to delete Wykham's references to founder's kin privileges but in effect such alterations were minor. On 23 December 1443, at a ceremony held in the half built chapel of the college, Waynflete and the other members of the foundation swore to observe the statutes.[26] Their effect was to bring Eton closer to Wykeham's model while in the same year Eton was linked with a much altered King's College in Cambridge.[27] Three years after its initial foundation Henry VI's royal college at Eton was coming to resemble Wykeham's model. Such a development must not be seen as having been inevitable. Too often the influence of Wykeham's two colleges is accepted without question – their influence on other foundations between 1440–1480 was minimal. It was the foundation of Henry VI's college which helped to spread Wykeham's influence more widely and the transformation of this along Wykhamist lines was due primarily to the influence of William Waynflete, the first effective provost of Eton College.

The educational side of Eton College was just one aspect of the provost's responsibilities[28] although Waynflete's special interest as an ex-schoolmaster may have meant that he concerned himself more with educational sup-ervision than would otherwise have been the case. Thus, although no longer involved in the teaching of the school he was still closely involved with educational affairs. The headmaster from 1443 was William Westbury,[29] an old pupil of Waynflete's from Winchester College, and as such he must have been familiar with the curriculum which had been taught at Winchester College.

During William Waynflete's provostship the royal college at Eton, which under the king's original plan had been conceived as a fairly modest establishment, developed into a much more grandiose body on which much royal time, energy and revenue were expended. Waynflete, by virtue both of his experience at Winchester College and his appointment at Eton was in a very strong position to influence the young king's plan. The trust which Henry VI came to place in Waynflete's judgement, zeal and abilities is clearly demonstrated in the so-called King's Will of 1448 which delegated to him considerable power to continue with the king's plans for Eton College.[30] Since Waynflete's experience hitherto had been, so far as is known, solely at Winchester College, it was not surprising that he directed the king along similar lines. His own continuing approval of the idea of linking a university college with a grammar school can be seen from the form of his own later foundation at Oxford which was connected with two such schools.

The provostship of Eton College into which Henry VI thrust William Waynflete in the spring of 1442 was a challenging position. The responsibilities it carried were both numerous and onerous, being not only administrative but also diplomatic and social, requiring an ability to work successfully with a variety of people – papal envoys, magnates, bishops, bailiffs, carpenters and small boys. For Waynflete the problems were increased by the newly-founded status of the college; it would have been considerably easier to administer a well-established collegiate body which had already developed traditions and routines than it was to establish such tradition. His problems can only have been added to by the personality of the young king. During this period the college was changing, both in size and the conception of its nature, from an essentially religious foundation to one where education was of prime importance. Waynflete presided over and influenced this transformation. That he was successful in rising to the challenge is witness to his wide ranging abilities. Had he not satisfied Henry VI's requirements it is likely that Waynflete, like Sever, would have faded into relative obscurity. Instead he was promoted by the king to the bishopric of Winchester as a reward for his achievement in developing Eton within six years into a collegiate body along the same lines as the older Winchester College.

Waynflete, although highly influential at Eton College, played an exec-utive role there, acting for the royal founder. With his elevation to the bishopric of Winchester as successor to Henry Beaufort in 1447,[31] he acquired both the power and, perhaps more importantly the resources, to pursue his own educational interests further. In addition to the establishment of his own dual foundation of Magdalen College Oxford he remained concerned with the fortunes of Eton College after the deposition of Henry VI and was also intimately involved with the collegiate foundation at Tattershall College in Lincolnshire when he was acting as executor to Ralph Lord Cromwell.[32]

Through his foundation of Magdalen College and his involvement with the colleges cited above, William Waynflete continued to demonstrate his support for educational foundations in this form. The triple foundation comprising almshouse, school and college, was popular in the court circle around Henry VI – as is witnessed by the foundations of Higham Ferrers, Tattershall, Ewelme and others. Eton in its original form was the grandest exponent of the idea. Waynflete's interest, however, was in the educational side of affairs and thus he concentrated his resources closer to that of the dual foundation of Winchester and New College with educational provision as the prime aim.

Waynflete set in motion the foundation of Magdalen Hall in Oxford very shortly after having been promoted to the bishopric of Winchester. His consecration as bishop took place in July 1447; by the following June at the latest the first steps had been taken to acquire the land and site necessary as the prerequisite to the foundation.[33] On 20 August 1448 a foundation charter was issued which established a perpetual hall for a provost and forty graduate scholars.[34] From the first therefore, Waynflete envisaged his foundation on a substantial scale. In his foundation charter Waynflete described the community as a perpetual hall founded for the increase of knowledge; the emphasis was away from legal studies: philosophy and theology were the subjects to be followed, reflecting the bishop's own training as a theologian. The community was to consist of a president and forty scholars, making it a substantial body, although not as large as Wykeham's New College which provided for seventy scholars. Initially Magdalen Hall was smaller than provided for in the charter, only twenty men were named as scholars in the charter. No administrative or financial records have survived relating to this foundation but neither are there any extant statutes. Knowledge of the composition and activities of the community of Magdalen Hall depends on evidence from its foundation charter and from what is known of the careers of the early members of the Hall.

In 1458, having acquired the Oxford hospital of St. John the Baptist as a nucleus for a new foundation, Waynflete refounded his ten year old hall as a college. A comparison of the foundation charter of Magdalen College[35] with that of Magdalen Hall issued by Waynflete ten years earlier provides clues to the advantages he saw in refounding his Oxford community. Such a refoundation was not actually necessary, for Magdalen Hall did not lack any essential 'collegiate' ingredient; it could and did function adequately. Waynflete must have had his own reasons for wanting to begin again from the beginning. The wording of the two charters is very similar but the few changes which were made help to elucidate the bishop's motives. The most important of these related to Waynflete's own control over the college during the remainder of his lifetime. In this respect the new college charter of 1458 had considerable advantages over that of the hall. The latter had made no mention of what authority the bishop as founder could exercise over his foundations. That of 1458 on the other hand specifically reserved to Waynflete complete authority: '. . .reservata tamen nobis durante vita nostra plenaria potestate presidentem huiusmodi et alios scolares in collegium predictum per nos edita et edenda quociens et quando opus nobis visum fuerit mutandi, addendi, corrigendi et diminuendi'.[36] It might be expected that members of the foundation woufld show due respect to the ideas and preferences of the founder but under the original charter Waynflete would have been powerless in the face of opposition. While there is no evidence that he had met with such opposition between 1448 and 1458 he must have welcomed the greatly increased endowment provided by the acquisition of the hospital of St. John the Baptist as an opportunity to compile a more watertight foundation charter. The history of the college between this date and Waynflete's death in 1486 demonstrates that this was a very important element. The haste with which Magdalen Hall had been founded may have led him to omit such a provision in the earlier charter. Administratively and financially Waynflete was to exercise control over the college until almost the very end of his life. He concerned himself with the details of the foundation and Magdalen College was very much his own college, not merely an institution endowed from the resources of his bishopric.

Between 1458 and 1480 when adminstrative records began formally to be kept the absence of evidence makes it difficult not only to chart the growth and development of the college but also to see how closely Waynflete as founder involved himself in internal collegiate affairs. Some post 1480 evidence, however, shows him directing the fellows to elect certain men as members of the college[37] and his influence in this sphere as in others, would have been stronger prior to the promulgation of statutes in the last years of his life. To judge from his heavy financial involvement which is well documented, his other involvement is likely to have been extensive. From 1458 until his death one of bishop Waynflete's major preoccupations was the collection of lands and advowsons to ensure a lavish endowment, worth over £675 per annum, for his foundation.[38] He was, however, slow to hand them over to the college, an action that would have made the community financially independent. Throughout this period and indeed until 1481, (later if building costs are included), Waynflete retained control of the purse strings and the college was funded directly from his temporal estates.[39]

It was not until 1480, more than twenty years after the re-foundation, that Waynflete issued any statutes for Magdalen College.[40] Prior to that the internal administration of the college must have been governed by the president, William Tybard, along lines directed verbally by the bishop. The non-provision of statues which left the bishop as founder in the position of final arbiter in any matters of dispute, was in accord with Waynflete's policy towards the endowment of the college. His policy of tight control over the release of money to the president and fellows of Magdalen College gave Waynflete the opportunity to exercise authority over the development of his college. He would have to be consulted before the college could enter into any arrangements involving major expenditure. This reluctance to relinquish autonomy to the college authorities kept Waynflete in touch with and in a position to direct affairs in Oxford and ensured that it was very much his own college. The most pressing reason which led him finally to issue statutes must have been his own advanced age; by 1480 he was over eighty.

In part, the statutes were a codification of practices which were already in operation. This can be seen in the fact that payments to the lecturers who were established by the statutes were in fact recorded in the earliest surviving bursar's book of the college which begins in 1476–7.[41] The statutes were the product of a lifetime of personal experience in Winchester College, Eton College and Magdalen itself spanning more than half a century. When complete the corpus of statutes can be taken to represent the mature reflections of Waynflete on both the administration of a college and on its educational function. They were very much Waynflete's own statutes reflecting his past career and his own beliefs and interests in education.

In their basic form and in particular in their provision for the administration of the college Waynflete's statutes follow those issued by William Wykeham at the beginning of the century for the use of New College Oxford. Wykeham's administrative provisions had become the template for a number of collegiate statutes in the fifteenth century. Waynflete also restricted the eligibility of a president for Magdalen College to fellows or ex-fellows either of Magdalen itself or of Wykeham's foundations. The college was to be on a large scale; in all it was to consist of ninety-nine members – a president, forty scholars, thirty demys, four priests, eight clerks and sixteen choristers.[42] The main body of scholars thus numbered seventy, the same size as New College and Eton College.

The majority of the fellows were to study theology with only two or three being selected to study law (civil or canon) and the same small number to study medicine.[43] This selection of subjects was traditional and may reflect the idea that education was still primarily designed to serve the church. The same commitment to the idea that the college was a religious not a secular body can be seen in the statute which stated that every fellow must be ordained within a year of achieving his M.A. and that each was to preach and serve mass regularly in the college.[44] At the same time he made an effort to ensure that his college would not be excessively dominated by theologians for two of the three deans who were to be in charge of the educational side of the college were to be masters of arts not theologians.[45] A respect for education and training rather than mere longevity can be seen in his stipulation that seniority among the fellows was to be determined by their academic achievements, not by the length of time they had spent as fellows of the college.[46]

It was in his provisons for education within the college that Waynflete was particularly careful, detailed and innovatory. Waynflete's innovations came in the educational provisons of the statutes, in particular with the division of members of the foundation into demys and fellows and the arrangements for lectureships. The scholar's day was carefully divided up. Disputations were to take place twice a week during full term in the main hall of the college. One of these weekly sessions was to deal with a problem of a matter of doubt, the other with an issue relating to the solving of doubts. In the nave of the chapel was to be held a weekly discussion of theological controversies. From 7 July – 1 August, that is during the vacation period, an arts disputation was to be conducted weekly.[47] Disputations were the commonest method of teaching and practicing in the late medieval universities. Waynflete's major innovation in the sphere of teaching was to move beyond this and provide for three lecturers whose lectures were to be open to all the students, whether of Magdalen College or from elsewhere in the university. One lecturer was to teach on natural philosophy, one on moral philosophy and one on theology.[48] Their lectures were to take place (excepting feast days) from 9 October to 1 August. The educational day was to begin at 6 a.m. with the lecture on natural philosphy; at 9 a.m. came the lecture on theology and finally at 1 p.m. that on moral and metaphysical philosophy. This was an innovation which was to be repeated in early Tudor foundations in both Oxford and Cambridge.

The lectures were designed for the benefit of the forty full scholars and other members of the university who wished to attend. Separate provision was made for the junior scholars – the Demys – boys who not yet having taken their degrees would concentrate on the study of grammnar, sophistry and logic until they could demonstrate a firm grounding in these subjects.

The legislation concerning these demys was Waynflete's second important innovation. The statute relating to their position, especially the clause which prohibited boys from proceeding to further study without a proper elementary grounding in grammar, has the ring of experience about it: 'Praeterea, qui debile fundamentum fallit opus, ut experientia docet, ac etiam ut intelleximus quod quidam de nostris triginta scholaribus his diebus, priusquam in grammatica, quae omnium scientiarum mater et fundamentum esse dinoscitur, sufficienter instructi fuerint, immature divertere solent ad logicalia et sophisticalia; . . . ordinamus quod nullus eorundem de caetero admittatur ad sophistriam et logicam vel ad aliam scientiam nisi prius, judicio Presidentis et magistri informatoris in grammatica, ac alicujus Decanorum nostri collegii memorati ad id habilis et sufficiens reperiatur'.[49] In addition, the stipulation that some of the demys should devote their efforts to grammar and poetry and the other humanist arts in order to be able to instruct others, looked back to the era in which Waynflete himself had taught, the 1430s and 1440s, when there was serious concern about the absence of grammar teachers and the lack of adequate training for them; concern which had led to the foundation of Godshouse in Cambridge in 1439 as a place where teachers could be trained.[50]

Magdalen College was the most substantial of William Waynflete's foundations but it was by no means the only one. The bishop's personal concern with the teaching of grammar was reflected in his foundation of two grammar schools which would both act as 'feeder' schools for the college itself and be open to all comers. One was situated in Wainfleet, in Lincolnshire; the other was in Oxford attached to the college itself. Stipulations governing the financing and organisation of both schools were laid down in the Magdalen College statutes.[51]

The precise date when Magdalen College School came into existence as an adjunct to the college is unknown but it was functioning before the statutes were drawn up in the 1480s.[52] Within ghe founder's lifetime the school was evidently closely connected with the college and it may have been difficult to distinguish clearly between the two institutions. The master was responsible to the president of the college – it did not, unlike Winchester College, have its own warden or head, – and was to get a room and weekly commons on the same terms as the collegiate fellows.[53] While many of the pupils must have come from Oxford and the surrounding area, for the school was to be open to all who wished to attend, some of the Demys are likely to have been amongst the pupils since they were not permitted to proceed to the study of logic or sophistry until they were fully conversant with grammar.[54]

The counterpart to Magdalen College School at Wainfleet in Lincolnshire was not an identical body. While also a grammar school open to all, it was much more traditional in conception, incorporating a chantry element; its master had to be in religious orders.[55] This must reflect both its rural location which one would expect to be more conservative in its expectations and also Waynfleet's own age; the foundation at Wainfleet is closer to what one might expect a man of his generation would found. Magdalen College School was the larger of the two, with both a master and an usher;[56] the master was not required to be a priest and in fact the first recorded master, John Anwykyll was a married man.[57] The difference between these two foundations was to be reflected in their subsequent development – while the school in Wainfleet was never to become more than a rural school, serving a fairly limited area in Lincolnshire, within a decade of its foundation Magdalen College School had become one of the leading grammar schools in England and was foremost in the introduction of the new grammar teaching being pioneered on the continent.

The manifestation of humanism in England during the second half of the fifteenth century took a very different form from that seen in contemporary Italy where classical values and the cult of the antique predominated. In England the approach was more practical – humanist ideas were not seen as ends in themselves but were applied, especially within the universities to further scholasticism. Humanism was initially a medium for improving and enriching other studies, not the sole object of study.[58] A major landmark in the spread of this practical humanism was the introduction of Greek as a subject in Oxford and Cambridge in the early sixteenth century.[59] This step was preceded by a revolution in the teaching of Latin which took place in the last quarter of the fifteenth century. Although the middle years of the fifteenth century had seen a renewed interest in and concern about the teaching of grammar and ecclesiastics and laymen alike founded schools to provide education at a popular level,[60] teaching methods had changed little. Texts such as Donatus and the Doctrinale of Alexander which had been the staple grammar works since the late twelfth century were still in use and boys being taught in the 1470s would have used books and done exercises similar to those being used by Waynflete when teaching in Winchester College half a century earlier. In the early 1480s a revolution in grammar teaching began. It was stimulated and inspired by works written by contemporary Italian grammarians but it manifested itself in text books for the first time being produced by native grammarians and teachers specifically for use in English schools. It was a revolution which would have been impossible without the aid of the printing press which was becoming established first in London and then in the 1470s in Oxford and Cambridge. This revolution was led by Magdalen College School and actively encouraged by William Waynflete.

Printing was crucial for the dissemination of the early works of the Magdalen grammarians. A press existed in Oxford from 1478;[61] by 1479 Theodoric Rood, the town's first printer was living in a tenement rented from

Magdalen College.[62] Thus Rood had from the first a connection with Waynflete's college and it is not therefore surprising to find that his press played an important role in publishing works emanating from Magdalen College School which helped to spread continental ideas about the teaching of grammar in England.

The first of three grammar books printed in Waynflete's lifetime, the *Longe Parvula*, has survived only as an anonymous fragment although it is possible that it may have been the work of John Anwykyll, headmaster of Magdalen College School.[63] Anwykyll was certainly responsible for the second and most important of fifteenth century English grammar books, the *Compendium totius grammatica*. Two editions of this, neither of which survives in full, were printed in Oxford in 1483.[64] One of these editions included the *Vulgaria Terentii* which Rood also printed separately in these years.[65] The *Vulgaria Terentii* was a short work, of only thirty-two leaves, which contained sentences derived from the plays of Terence together with their English translations. It was in effect a phrase book of classical Latin which would be useful for general conversations such as those of schoolboys or young students.

Of Anwykyll's own career, prior to his appointment as master of Magdalen College School, little is known beyond the fact that he had graduated as a master of grammar from Cambridge.[66] The full title of his work, however, is significant – *Compendium totius grammaticae ex variis autoribus, Laurentio, Servio, Perotto, diligeanter collectum et versibus cum eorum interpretatione conscriptum, totius barbariei destructorum et latine langue oranamentum non minus preceptoribus quam pueris necessarium.* Anwykyll could have become familiar with the works of the Latin authors mentioned in Oxford. Perotti's own grammar, only published in 1473, was in the library of John Nele, William Waynflete's chaplain and household treasurer.[67] Valla's treatise *Elegantiae* was in the libraries of both Lincoln College and Balliol College.[68] In view of Waynflete's close involvement in the affairs of his college throughout his life and of his interest in the proper teaching of grammar reiterated in the collegiate statutes, it is difficult to believe that he was not involved with the original decision to appoint Anwykyll as grammar master. The appointment of a man familiar with contemporary continential grammatical developments indicates clearly that Magdalen College and Bishop Waynflete were open and welcoming to ideas and influences from contemporary Italy.

William Waynflete's personal connection with this revolution in the teaching of grammar was not just as the founder of the body which played a leading role in these changes, but as direct patron of the *Compendium Totius Greammaticae*. The earliest surviving complete edition of Anwykyll's work, printed at Deventer in 1489, contains a dedicatory preface which praised Waynflete as patron of the work:

Te Gulielme pater multum celebrissimus qui nunc
Ecclesie presul vintoniensis ades
Fama canet tantos et te celebrabit ad annos
Dum fuerit stabili firmis in ace polus
Hoc opus auctor enim te persuadente joannes [Anwykyll]
Edidit unde tibi fama perennis erit.[69]

The tradition of grammatical innovation established by Waynflete at Magdalen College continued after his death. In June 1487 an agreement was drawn up between Anwykyll and the college under which Magdalen was to pay to him an annual pension of £10 '. . . et ob exccellentiam scientie et aliorum meritorum dicti Johannes et ad dicte schole et scholarium communem utilitatem, continuationem et profectum, consideratis multimodis vigiliis et laboribus quos idem magister Johannes perpessus est circa novam et perutilem formam docendi pro eadem schola conceptam et perscriptum per eundem. . .'[70]

The foremost grammarians of the early sixteenth century, Stanbridge and Lily, were both products of the Magdalen tradition.[71] In addition, the first teacher of Greek at the University of Oxford, William Groceyn, was intimately connected with Magdalen College as reader in divinity there in the last years of the founder's lifetime, between 1483–1488.[72] When Richard III visited the College in 1483, Groceyn featured prominently in the disputation arranged by Waynflete and the college for the entertainment of the king.[73] There is no evidence that Richard Mayew, president of Magdalen College 1480–1508, had any special interest in grammar.[74] This reinforces the importance of the founder in establishing a strong grammatical tradition. Waynflete's involvement in the introduction of the new learning is reflected in the sixteenth century tradition that he introduced the study of Greek into the College.[75] Although unfounded and erroneous, the very existence of such a tradition reflects the bishop's prominent position in the new developments as seen by his immediate successors.

His contemporaries recognised Waynflete as a person of importance in English humanistic circles of the period. He was highly complemented as a patron of learning when Lorenzo da Savona, an Italian franciscan, dedicated a work to him in the 1480s. Lorenzo had studied in Padua and Bologna before coming to England. There he completed his *Rhetorica*(1478) which has been described as 'constructed on modern lines and obviously inspired by classical models'.[76] Lorenzo was not only familiar with continental educational developments but was the leading Italian rhetorician in England in the 1470s and 1480s. His choice of Waynflete as the dedicatee of the second of his works written in England, indicates that, despite his advanced age, the bishop was considered an important patron of learning. This work was a poem entitled *Triumphus Amoris Jesus Christi*.[77] As a preface it has a lengthy dedicatory epistle addressed to Waynflete. In distinctly neo-classical language it praises Magdalen College as Waynflete's major contribution to humanistic study in England.

Waynflete was ready to accept and promote new ideas and developments as can be seen by his attitude to the new developments in the teaching of grammar. Further striking evidence of this is the indulgence which he issued in the early 1480s which is of note because it is the earliest known printed indulgence to be issued by a member of the English episcopate.[78] It was issued in conjunction with three fellow prelates – the bishops of Ely, Norwich and Chichester. Of these four men Waynflete was the oldest; Goldwell and Morton were relatively young men and both had explicit interests in continental humanist development. Waynflete's name appears as the first of the four named in the indulgence. That a man in his eighties should take advantage of the opportunities offered by the new mechanical developments suggests that he was forward looking and open-minded to the end of his life.

The fifteenth century was one during which England was open to extensive continental influences in the field of scholarship. Some members of the episcopate travelled to Italy and forged close connections with Italian scholars. Waynflete did not have these personal connections. In him, however, can be seen a mingling of the old and the new. He promoted the teaching of grammar in Oxford, reflecting his own training as a schoolmaster but using new continental-style texts. He can be seen also to have appreciated the value of the new printing presses. Above all he was open to new developments.

Waynflete's training as a schoolmaster dominated his life. His success as provost of Eton College made possible his promotion to the episcopate. The resources – financial, political and administrative – at his disposal as bishop of Winchester were ploughed back into education and forward looking education at that, rather than that of his own youth. Magdalen College and Magdalen College School with their particular emphasis on the teaching of grammar and the provision of a solid educational grounding were fitting memorials to the lasting interests of a man who throughout his lengthy career played an outstanding role in the promotion of the educational revolution in England. The changes in methods and types of schools being founded between the 1420s, when he began his career teaching Donatus to schoolboys at Winchester College and his death in 1486, were much shaped by William Waynflete's efforts and interests.

NOTES

1 I am grateful for the suggestions made at the delivery of this paper at Keele in July 1985. I would also like to thank Dr. Michael Hicks for his comments.

2 For educational foundations in the later middle ages see N. Orme, *English schools in the middle ages* (London 1973) and on the episcopate in particular see H. Jewell, 'English bishops as educational benefactors in the later fifteenth century', in *The church, politics and patronage in the*

fifteenth century, ed. B. Dobson (Gloucester 1984) and J.T. Rosenthal, 'Lancastrian bishops and educational benefaction', in *The Church in pre-Reformation society: essays in honour of F.R.H. Du Boulay*, ed. C.M. Barron and C. Harper-Bill (London 1985).

3   See V.G. Davis, 'The life and career of William Waynflete, bishop of Winchester 1447–1486', (unpublished Ph.D. thesis Trinity College Dublin 1985). The only published work on Waynflete is R. Chandler, *The life of William Waynflete* (London 1911).

4   N. Orme, 'Schoolmasters' in C.H. Clough, ed. *Profession, vocation and culture in later medieval England* (Liverpool 1982), p. 226.

5   *Ibid.*, p. 227.

6   It has often been stated that Waynflete was educated in Winchester at William Wykeham's recently founded Winchester College, (e.g. *D.N.B.* article on Waynflete and more recently, Joan Simon, *Education in Tudor and Stuart England* (Cambridge 1966), p. 13. Its records of scholars are complete and do not include Waynflete's name and while some day boys attended as oppidans, it is unlikely that Waynflete, from Lincolnshire and with no local connections, could have done so. The misunderstanding may have arisen from a reference by Waynflete's chaplain Thomas Chandler, a reference of whose to William Say, one of Henry VI's chaplains, has been misunderstood as referring to Waynflete, see Emden, *B.R.U.O.*, p. 2001.

7   Lincoln Record Office, Register XV, Philip Repington, fo. 154r. Waynflete was rector of Binbrook from January 1416, the month in which he exchanged his earlier benefice of Salomby which he had only held for three weeks, with his brother who held Binbrook, *ibid.*, fo. 77v.

8   Eton College Records (henceforth E.C.R.) 39/30.

9   He cannot be identified with the William Waynflete who was a clerk at the Exchequer in the early 1420s and who then went on to become a fellow at King's Hall Cambridge. This other Waynflete was a B.C.L. not a B.Th. PRO E28/49; PRO E404/37/174; Trinity College Cambridge Library, account books of King's Hall, vols 7,8.

10 'Credimus enim semper tibi ante oculos esse quanto tenearis amore in matrem que te spirituali conceptum utere in lucem cognicionis eduxit', *Epistolae academicae Oxon.*, ed. H. Anstey (2 vols O.H.S. 35,36, 1898), I, p. 258.

11 Bonaventure, 'The teaching of Latin in later medieval England', *Mediaeval Studies* 23 (1961), p. 15.

12 Winchester College Muniments 22106, bursars' accounts 1429–30.

13 T.F. Kirby, *Annals of Winchester* (London 1892), p. 484.

14 'Catalogue of books belonging to the college of St. Mary of Winchester in the reign of Henry VI', ed. W.H. Gunner, *Archaeological Journal* 15 (1858), pp. 59–74.

15 *Ibid.*, p. 74.

16 'The teaching of Latin in later medieval England', pp. 13–18.

17 Henry VI may have gone to Winchester to seek the advice of his great-uncle Cardinal Beaufort or he may have gone to Winchester for the express purpose of visiting Winchester College as has been suggested, (Kirby, *Annals of Winchester*, p. 192) but it must not be assumed that because the visit resulted in the employment of William Waynflete its purpose was to seek a master for Eton College.

18 The charter is printed in A.F. Leach, ed. *Educational charters and documents* (Cambridge 1911), p. 404.

19 Orme, *English schools in the middle ages*, pp. 195–202; on Heytesbury see M. Hicks, 'St Katherine's Hospital, Heytesbury: prehistory, foundation and refoundation 1408–1472', *Wiltshire Archaeological and Natural History Magazine* 78 (1984), pp. 62–9.

20 For King's Hall see A. Cobban, *The King's Hall within the University of Cambridge in the later middle ages* (Cambridge 1969).

21 *V.C.H. Cambridgeshire* III, pp. 376–7.

22 *V.C.H. Buckinghamshire* II, p. 153; Carpenter became bishop of Worcester and established a grammar school at Westbury-on-Trym.

23   Sever became chancellor of Oxford after leaving Eton College, *B.R.U.O.*, pp. 1672–3; in 1443 some members of the university wrote to the pope requesting that he use his influence with the king in Sever's favour, *Epistolae academicae Oxon.* I, pp. 223–5. This was a surprising request since not only had Sever served the king at Eton but had been his confessor in the 1430s. Had Sever won royal favour in these activities such a letter would hardly have been necessary.

24   The last reference to Sever as provost occurs in a deed of 5 March 1442, *Calendar of Patent Rolls 1441–46*, p. 50 while a manor court roll for the manor of Cottisford (Oxon.), dated 13 March 1442 describes the court as being the first one held under Waynflete's provostship, E.C.R. 26/120. The appointment must have been made between these dates, a time when the king was in residence at Sheen, not far from Eton.

25   E.C.R. 54/10; H.C.M. Lyte, *Eton College*, (London 1898), p. 18.

26   These statutes no longer exist. They predate those published by Heywood and Wright in *The ancient laws of the fifteenth century. . . for the public school of Eton College* (London 1850) which date from *c.* 1447–55. The notorial instrument of 21 December 1443 which records a ceremony in which Waynflete and other fellows swore to uphold the statutes refers to a still earlier corpus of statutes of which nothing is known, E.C.R. 54/10. The Eton statutes are not quite as Leach described them in *V.C.H. Buckinghamshire* II, P. 157, '. . .a mere transcript of those of Winchester. . .'. A careful comparison reveals some changes – as mentioned above, these are primarily of phrasing to fit the royal status of the founder.

27   In July 1443 William Millington, rector of the College of St. Nicholas in Cambridge founded in February 1441 was appointed provost of a reconstituted body, the royal college of St. Mary and St. Nicholas at Cambridge (King's College). A public instrument made in Eton College chapel on 13 September 1443 shows a link between the two royal foundations being forged for the first time, three years after their initial establishment, 'Et qualiter pauperes indigentes que scolartes dici Collegii Regalis Beate Marie de Etona postquam fuerint prius gramatice rudimentis sufficenter imbuti ad dictam Collegium Regale Beate Marie et Sancti Nicholi. . . affirmientur liberalibus ibidem studiis ac ceteris scientiis et facultibus perfectuis imbuendi iuxta ordinacione et statuta serenissiimi principis et domini nostri regis. . .in hac parte edita,' E.C.R. 39/30.

28   Waynflete's responsibilities were far more wide-ranging than they had been as *magister informator* at Winchester College; he was in regular communication with the young king and with leading royal advisors. Matters as diverse as the purchase of cloth for liveries, the provision of books for the scholars and fellows, the organisation of temporary and permanent buildings and the administration of the estates and manors which comprised part of the college's endowment all fell within the range of his responsibilities.

29   *B.R.U.O.*, p. 2000–1.

30   The King's Will was a document setting out Henry VI's intentions concerning the future development of his two foundations. It was a detailed and specific document dealing in particular with the arrangements made to finance the building works. It was drawn up in 1448, after Waynflete had ceased to be provost of Eton, but the overall supervision of the scheme was entrusted to him. In it Henry VI praises Waynflete's '. . . high trought and fervent zele . . .' and speaks of the '. . . grete and hool confidence whiche I have unto hym. . .', E.C.R. 39/78, m. 2. 26.

31   Cardinal Beaufort died in early April 1447 and the king immediately instructed the cathedral chapter to elect Waynflete as his successor, *The register of the common seal*, ed. J. Greatrex (Hampshire 1978), pp. 99–101.

32   Tattershall was essentially a chantry for the souls of Henry VI, Lord Cromwell and his wife Maud but one section of statutes (which Waynflete was involved in drawing up) reflects Waynflete's own personal interests; 'The master shall hire a clerk or priest to teach grammar to the choristers and to all the sons of the tenants of the lordship of Tattershall and of the college without charge.' *De L'Isle manuscripts* (H.M.C.) I, p. 182.

33 *The cartulary of the hospital of St. John the Baptist*, ed. H. Salter (3 vols O.H.S. 1914–20), (henceforth *Cart. St. John*) p. 248.

34 Magdalen College Deeds, *Chartae Regis*, 50; it is printed in Chandler, *Life of William Waynflete*, appendix 9, pp. 323–30.

35 The 1458 charter is printed in *Cart. St. John*, pp, 425–9.

36 '. . . reservata tamen nobis durante vita nostra pelnaria poteste presidentem huiusmodi et alios scholares in collegium predictum per nos edita et edenda quociens et quando opus nobis visum fuerit mutandi, addendi, corrigendi et diminuendi,' *ibid.*, p. 429.

37 In a letter sent to the college in March (1485) Waynflete ordered that, '. . . at oure next election among other and before all other, the seid Master William [Hewster, a college chaplain] be elected unto the more and greater number contrary statutes by us made notwithstanding', Chandler, *Life of William Waynflete*, appendix 29, p. 289.

38 Details of his acquisitions, the sources of the property and the bishop's main agents in these transactions are traced in J. Mills, 'The foundations, endowment and early administration of Magdalen College Oxford', (Unpublished Oxford B.Litt. thesis 1973).

39 Four manors in Oxfordshire and Berkshire – Adderbury, Brightwell, Harewell and Witney – between them contributed an average of £123 annually to the college: money was also paid directly to the college from the central episcopal treasury at Wolvesey, Mills, 'The foundations, endowment and early administration', pp. 21–4.

40 There are two contemporary manuscripts of the statutes. Bodleian Ms Rawl. Q.c. 14 was copied *c.* 1485 and includes the complete code of statutes including Waynflete's later emendations. The second manuscript is Magdalen College Ms. 277 which is a copy of the code of statutes containing alterations made by Waynflete in July and November 1443. This may be the volume of statutes for which 16d was paid for binding in the accounts for 1483–4; it may have been bound because it was now felt to be complete. Writing on the final folio of the manuscript is thought to be in Waynflete's own hand. The printed copy of the statutes is taken from the Bodleian manuscript with corrupt passages corrected by collation with B.L. Harl. Ms. 1235 and B.L. Hargrave Ms. 148, *Statutes of the colleges of Oxford* (3 vols London 1853–4) II, pp. 5–91. (Henceforth *Magdalen Statutes*).

41 Magdalen College Bursars' Book, fo. 5.

42 *De numero scholarium, Magdalen Statutes*, pp. 5–6.

43 *Ibid.*

44 *De tempore assumendi sacros ordines, ibid.*, p. 34.

45 *De decanorum officio et eorum electione, ibid.*, pp. 24–5.

46 *De senioritate sociorum, ibid.*, pp. 27–8.

47 *De disputatione sociorum et scholarium faciendim, ibid.*, pp. 34–5.

48 *De officiis lectorum, ibid.*, pp. 47–8

49 *De electione scholarium vocatorum Demys, ibid.*, p. 16.

50 In a petition to the king, William Byngham, the founder of Godshouse had emphasised the '. . .grete scarstee of maistres of Gramer, whereof as now ben almost none . . . be hade in your Universitees. . .' and claimed that '. . .the clergie of this youre Reaume . . . is like to be empeired and febled, by the defaute and lak of Scolemaistres of Gramer.', Leach, *Educational charters and documents*, p. 402.

51 *Magdalen Statutes*, p. 77.

52 An entry in the college register for 1480 implies that the school had been taking place in the lower hall of the college since at least the previous year, Magdalen College Register A, fo. 3r. It is likely to have established some time earlier than this – the companion school in Lincolnshire had been in existence since the mid 1460s, Magdalen College estate papers 165/6, B. Parry-Jones, *Five hundred years of the Magdalen College School at Wainfleet* (Wainfleet 1984).

53 *De magistro seu informatore grammaticorum, Magdalen Statutes*, p. 76.

54 *De electione scholarium vocatorum Demys, ibid.*, p. 1.

55 *Ibid.*, p. 1.

56 *De magistro seu informatore grammaticorum, Magdalen Statutes*, p. 76.

57 *B.R.U.O.*, p. 39.

58 On the spread of humanist ideas in England and their impact see R. Weiss, *Humanism in England during the fifteenth century*, (3rd ed. Oxford 1967); N. Hurnard, 'Studies in intellectual life in England from the middle of the fifteenth century to the time of Colet', (Oxford D.Phil. thesis, 1935, unpublished).

59 Simon, *Education in Tudor and Stuart England*, p. 83.

60 Orme, *English schools in the middle ages*, chapter 6.

61 H. Carter, *Oxford University Press: a history* (Oxford 1973), p. 6.

62 *Cart. St. John III*, pp. 272, 276; Rood was from Cologne and is described as 'Dyryke Doucheman' or 'Dyryke Rood' in the rentals. For details of his career see *Oxford University Press*, pp. 6–7.

63 F. Madden, *The early Oxford press 1468–1640* (Oxford 1895), pp. 3, 257. It has been attributed to John Stanbridge, successively usher and then master at Magdalen College School, who was later to write a number of grammatical textbooks, *B.R.U.O.*, pp. 1754–5. In 1479, however, Stanbridge was aged only twelve and was still a pupil at Winchester College.

64 G. Duff, *Fifteenth century English books* (Oxford 1917), nos. 28, 29.

65 *Ibid.*, nos 29, 30, 31;*Oxford University Press*, p. 8.

66 *B.R.U.C.*, p. 39; Anwykyll is not referred to as headmaster until 1483 but in 1474–5 he was granted permission at Cambridge to incept in grammar in two years time and in 1475–6 he was fined 13s 4d for not incepting, *Grace Book A 1454–88*, ed. S.M. Leathes, (Cambridge 1897), pp. 106, 111. He may have come to Oxford shortly after this date.

67 J. Fletcher, 'A fifteenth century benefaction to Magdalen College library', *Bodleian Library Record* 9 (1974), p. 271.

68 Weiss, *Humanism in England in the fifteenth century*, pp. 94, 168.

69 Anwykyll, *Compendium totius grammaticae* (Deventer 1489), p. 1; the dedication was composed by Pietro Carmeliano, an Italian who assisted first Rood and later Caxton with editorial work, Carmeliano later became Latin secretary to Henry VII, see W. Nelson, *John Skelton: laureate* (Columbia 1939), pp. 20–21.*B.R.U.O.*, p. 358.

70 Magdalen College Register A, fo. 54v; printed in *Register of the presidents . . . and other members of Magdalen College Oxford*, ed. J.R. Bloxam (7 vols Oxford 1853–85), III, p. 718.

71 *B.R.U.O.*, pp. 1147, 1754–5.

72 *Ibid.*, p. 821.

73 Magdalen College Register A, fo. 27v; '. . .facta est alia solempnis disputatio theologica, etiam in praesentia regis, per . . . magistrum Willelmum Groceyn responsalem. . .'; printed in *Register of the presidents . . . and other members of Magdalen College*, new series, ed. W.D. Macray, (8 vols London 1894–1915), I, pp. 11–12.

74 *B.R.U.O.*, pp. 1247–8.

75 L. Humphridus, *Epistola de Graecis literis et homeri lectione* (Basle 1558), cited in H.L. Gray, 'Greek visitors to England 1455–1456' in *Anniversary essays in medieval history by students of C.H. Haskins*, ed. C.H. Taylor and J.L. LaMonte, (Boston 1929), p. 111.

76 Weiss, *Humanism in England in the fifteenth century*, pp. 162–3, 199; A.G. Little, *The grey friars in Oxford* (O.H.S. 20 1892), pp. 265–6.

77 Lambeth Palace Library, Ms. 450.

78 Lambeth Palace Library, Maitland fragment 5.

Fluid Prejudice: Scottish Origin Myths in the Later Middle Ages

MARJORIE DREXLER

The title of this paper has been borrowed from the writings of Mark Twain; his complete quotation runs, 'The very ink with which all history is written is merely fluid prejudice.'[1] This is a criticism which can be levelled against the historical works of any age. Try as we might, none of us can rid our work of the effects of our upbringing and training; it would indeed be an unusual individual who did not have any favourites. The best we can hope for is to keep these biases under control. On the other hand, this weakness is a lucky break for historiographers, for these preferences, or prejudices, are what allow them to become acquainted with the historians they study.

More to the point, it was a rare Scottish historian from the later Middle Ages who did not prefer his own nation and the prouder moments in its history to all others. These authors were also men with a purpose – several purposes actually – the first and foremost of which was to prove beyond any shadow of a doubt that the Scots had always been, were then, and would always be independent of any and all other nations, but most especially of the English. The very early history of their nation, in other words their origin myths, provided these historians with a convenient place to put forward their arguments on this issue; after all, information on that period was sketchy at best, so there were few cumbersome facts to get in the way of their proving a point. In these origin myths we find highlighted most of the characteristics these men deemed essential to being truly a Scot, characteristics which, by the end of the fifteenth century, had become an integral part of most Scots' image of themselves. These stories and the way they are told can also help us understand the Scots' attitude towards their southern neighbours. To most of these men, to be a Scot required hating the English as naturally as to be alive required breathing. This important prejudice is, perforce, not stated outright in the myths themselves, for even the most rabidly anti-English writer could not legitimately heap abuse on that nation until he reached that point in his narrative when the Scots and English actually came into contact with one another, and by that time we have left behind the ages covered by the myths.

Nonetheless, this hatred had a great effect on their construction and development.

During the century and a half after these myths were put down in their most enduring form, they became ingrained in the popular imagination of the Scots; by the early sixteenth centry, to belittle these myths was to belittle their nation, so secure were these stories in most Scots' sense of national identity. This paper will begin with the fourteenth century works which established the tradition and end with a dispute that erupted in the early sixteenth century. Thus the subject of this paper is not only not the English history advertised in the title of this conference, it also extends itself beyond the stated time limits.

By the time the historians we will be studying began to work, the Scots had been editing and adapting their origin myth for centuries.[2] We will begin with the crisis which forced the Scots to take yet another look at their far distant past: Edward I's claim to Scotland and the resultant Wars of Independence. Edward I was a very thorough man who wanted to win on all fronts, including the diplomatic, so 1301 found the Scots and English lawyers presenting their nations' ancient histories to Boniface VIII and his curia. The English myth as presented there is, more or less, that which the Scots would spend two or more centuries refuting. Very briefly, Brutus, the grandson of the Trojan hero Aeneas, led a number of his compatriots to Albion, that is, to the mainland of Britain. Later he divided his new kingdom among his three sons: Locrine, the eldest, received England; the youngest, Camber, got Wales; and to the middle son, Albanacht, he gave Scotland. As it turned out, Albanacht was later killed in battle against invading Huns, and on his death, his kingdom reverted to his elder brother, Locrine, thereby setting the precedent for southern rule of Scotland.[3]

Edward tried to make a personal claim to Scotland through Brutus, but the Scottish lawyer, Baldred Bisset, made quick work of that claim; after all, during Brutus' reign, 'All the natives of the kingdom of the Angles were Britons, who were afterwards cast down by the Saxons, the Saxons by the Danes, and again the Danes by the Saxons, and the same Saxons by the Normans, that is by William the Bastard and his accomplices, from whom this same king is recognised to have descended, not from the Britons.'[4] What's more, while the Britons had indeed lived in Scotland, they had since been conquered by the Picts who were in turn overrun by the Scots, so their history is irrelevant to the matter at hand. What was relevant, from Bisset's point of view, was the skeletal Scottish myth he had chosen from those available to him. In it Scota, the daughter of Pharaoh, landed in Ireland before sailing to Scotland with the stone seat of the kings and a large armed band with which she conquered the Picts and their kingdom.[5]

This myth turned up again in a document used to negotiate with the English in 1321, only this time the Scots added the claim that Scota had been followed by 113 Scottish kings who had kept the kingdom free in spite of the wars which had surrounded them.[6] Lastly, the Declaration of Arbroath, addressed in 1320 to John XXII, referred vaguely to the Scots' early wanderings from Scythia to Scotland via Spain. Once again, the emphasis is on the 113 kings who had made up the Scots' native, and invincible, dynasty.[7]

From these early myths would be drawn the themes which would be central to the later historical works: the Scots' long wanderings and illustrious ancestry; their independence; and their long line of kings.

Next to nothing is known about John of Fordun, compiler of the first historical narrative completed after the Wars of Independence, the *Chronica Gentis Scotorum*, except his name and what has been passed on to us by Abbot Walter Bower who continued Fordun's work in the middle of the fifteenth century. Bower considered his predecessor something of a hero, for, according to the abbot, 'that ferocious torturer, Edward…king of England, called Langshanks and tyrant' had destroyed or stolen all the Scottish historical material he could get his hands on, lest it be used against him. Nevertheless, some documents survived, and Fordun, inspired by patriotic zeal, had 'travelled throughout Britain like a proof-laden bee, conversing and arguing with historians while examining their books, eventually producing a history of the Scots'.[8] Whether this biography is a product of Bower's fertile imagination or his nearly inexhaustible supply of popular lore will never be certain. It is certainly not an impossible tale; given the first Edward's policies and the destruction wrought by years of war, an earnest student of history may well have taken advantage of Edward III's safe-conducts allowing Scots to study in England.[9] From other sources it has been established that Fordun was a priest[10] possibly in Aberdeen.[11] Using the *Chronica* itself as evidence, it is likely that Fordun was a Lowlander, though perhaps not from the town of the same name, who first wrote in 1363, completed the final version of his history between 1384 and 1385,[12] and probably died soon after. If Bower's stories are true, then John of Fordun came closer than anyone else in this study to being a professional historian. He certainly knew his audience, for his stories caught the Scots' imagination and influenced every general history of Scotland for the next century and a half at least.

The *Chronica Gentis Scotorum* was addressed to the Scottish kings who were, Fordun proclaimed, the legitimate heirs of the throne of England through their ancestress, St. Margaret, wife of Malcolm III, whose family had been displaced by William the Conqueror.[13] In other words, the *Chronica* was designed to prove that not only did the English have no legitimate claim to Scotland, it was the Scots who should be ruling England.

Fordun spliced together his origin myth from those published during the Wars of Independence and from still earlier traditions, filling out his tale with contemporary folklore or his own inventions as he tried to reconcile all the contradictory stories he had come across. In this he was quite successful.

He introduced a useful character at the start of his myth, one Gaythelos, son of Neolus, a Greek prince who had gotten into so much trouble at home that he had been forced into exile. Gaythelos made his fortune in Egypt where his victories earned him Pharoah's daughter, Scota, for his wife. Confident his children would inherit their grandfather's throne, Gaythelos was prepared to stay in Egypt, but instead found it necessary to set sail again. Fordun set forth several reasons for his departure, allowing the reader to decide for himself whether, for instance, Gaythelos was heeding the warnings sent by God through Moses or whether he was simply trying to save himself.[14]

Whatever his motives, Gaythelos and his company of Greeks and Egyptians set sail for parts unkown about the time Scota's father was drowned in the Red Sea. This mixed band wandered for forty years before Gaythelos, their king, led them to Spain where they settled down and built Brigancia. It was there that Gaythelos gave his people a set of laws which Fordun claimed was still in use.[15]

But all was not well. Gaythelos had already noticed that while the Scots, as they had come to be called, were always victorious over their hostile neighbours, continual war was costing lives, and the king blamed himself for this, figuring that he should have brought them to an uninhabited land. Therefore, he sent scouts to the island, Ireland, he had seen from a high mountain in Spain. Their reports were favourable, so Gaythelos, who would not live long enough to go to this promised land prepared for the Scots by their gods, sent his sons north to secure for themselves that most precious of blessings, a succession of kings of their own nation, free from all foreign domination.[16]

Not all the Scots followed Gaythelos' sons, Hiber and Hymec, north to Ireland, which those two had renamed 'Scotia' in honor of their mother. Indeed, in his attempt to reconcile the earlier traditions, Fordun noted three separate migrations. The second was led by the sons of the Scottish king, Micelius Espayn; they took control of Ireland with or without the co-operation of their kindred who were already there. Last of all came Simon Brec and his party. This Simon, the favourite son of the Scottish king still ruling in Spain, was sent north with the Stone of Destiny, the marble throne of the Scottish kings which at last secured the Scots' hold on Ireland, for they believed that wherever the Stone was, their nation would some day rule.[17]

Meanwhile, some Scots, led by Ethacius Rothay, moved on to the Hebrides, but when the Picts arrived in Ireland looking for a home of their own, the mainland of northern Britain was still empty, and the Scots advised them to go there. The Scots also gave them wives on the condition that the Picts practice matrilinear succession. The families of some of these women followed them to their new home and, struck by the fertility of the land, decided to stay in Albion. Their growing numbers alarmed the Picts who tried to oust them by force, but to no avail.

With a greedy eye for the richness of the land, an ambitious prince, Fergus, son of Ferechad, decided to leave Ireland in order to protect those Scottish pioneers, and, as symbols of his authority, he brought with him the Stone of Destiny and the Scottish royal banner complete with lion rampant. The Scots and Picts allied and spent most of the next five hundred years or so fighting with the Romans or Britons. Caesar's peace initiatives, for instance, were rebuffed; the allies doubted that he had any understanding of the true meaning of peace, and besides, their freedom was their most precious inheritance and they intended to preserve it.[18] Luckily for them, Caesar was distracted by trouble in Gaul.

Much to the delight of their enemies, a dispute over a hunting dog caused the Picto-Scottish alliance to fall apart.[19] This allowed the Roman leader, Maximus, to convince the Picts and Britons to join his campaign against the Scots which ended in a decisive Roman victory. The Scottish king, Eugenius, and his son were both killed and the remainder of the nation faced slavery or exile; as it was unthinkable that a Scot would ever consent to be a slave, all sought temporary shelter in Norway, the Hebrides or with their late king's brother, Echach and his son, Erth, who still lived in Ireland.

The Picts discovered fairly quickly that Roman domination was not to their liking and, as soon as Maximus was dead, they helped the Scots return to Albion, this time led by Fergus, son of Erth, their forty-fifth king since Fergus, son of Ferechad. This second Fergus, with his brothers Loarn and Fenegus, re-established the Scottish kingdom with apparent ease, then went on to rule in Pictland as well. Furthermore, contemporary seers foretold that the Scots would eventually rule the entire island of Albion.[20]

The Scots, meanwhile, did not really trust their Pictish allies, and, true to form, when Aurelius Ambrosius, the British leader, asked for help against the Saxons, the Scots went to his aid while the Picts joined the pagans. Relations between the northern neighbours went from bad to worse, and when the Scottish king Alpin invaded Pictland trying to make good his claim to the throne, he was captured and executed. Naturally, his son Kenneth wanted vengeance, but his council was too thoroughly shaken to act and Kenneth was forced to resort to a trick. Dressed in a cloak covered with shimmering fish scales, he entered the chiefs' quarters in the middle of the night and convinced its sleepy occupants that they were having a vision sent from Heaven commanding them to obey their king by destroying their neighbours.[21] With the chiefs' moral fibre thus restored, a war was declared, the upshot of which was the complete destruction of the Pictish kingdom, a just retribution for their sins.

Fordun's introduction of this new character, the Greek Gaythelos, served several purposes in the Chronica. First, the Scots could now claim to have been ruled by a king, and not a queen, right from the very beginning. That long line of kings was a source of very great pride to them and, no doubt, contributed to their sense of superiority over their oft-conquered neighbours. [22] Gaythelos provided a figure analogous to Moses; the Book of Exodus was, after all, the outline around which Fordun had fashioned his myth, thereby bolstering his tacit claim that the Scots were one of God's chosen people. The presence of Gaythelos and his Greeks explained the division of the Scots into Highlanders and Lowlanders, for elsewhere in the *Chronica* Fordun claimed that from the Greeks were descended the wild, savage, and by and large, unsavoury Gaels who had taken their name from Gaythelos, while from the Egyptians came the peace loving and civilized Teutonic, Lowland Scots. [23] Finally, Gaythelos and his men allowed the Scots one more bit of one-up-manship which further weakened English claims through their myth; after all, if the English were proud of their Trojan descent, what better nation could the Scots choose for their ancestors than that which had defeated the Trojans? The joining of the Greeks with the glorious and mysterious Egyptians gave the Scots an ancestry second to none in Europe.

John of Fordun was not a subtle teacher. Given the continual wars with England, it is not surprising that he stressed the independent nature of his nation. His tone is one of complete self-confidence; he practically swaggers as he makes the claim that England should be ruled by the Scots. The Stone of Destiny had been hauled to London by Edward I had it not? Fordun repeated the tradition that wherever the Stone was, the Scots would eventually rule; it was now only a matter of time.

John of Fodun's myth has been given here in such detail because, one way or another, it found its way into the work of every medieval Scottish historian who followed him. Those who wrote in Latin were more or less completely dependent on the *Chronica*. Jumping ahead to the 1440's, we come to the first of these, Abbot Walter Bower, who, despite being the busy custodian of his house and servant of his king and pope, found time to comply with the request of a local landowner, Sir David Stewart, for a transcription and continuation in Latin of Fordun's work. The result was the *Scotichronicon*, a wide-ranging compilation of sixteen books which, as Bower promises in his preface, has something for everybody: theology, political thought, natural science and even history. Bower continued to revise this manuscript until the time of his death in 1449 while bowing, only ever so slightly, to popular demand for an abridgement. He did produce a second volume but as he added almost as much as he omitted, it is an abridgement only in name.

Bower's method was simple; he would copy a portion of Fordun's *Chronica*, sometimes as little as a phrase, then he would add his own opinion or extra information. He was most interested in events nearest his own time, and as Fordun's myth suited his purposes nicely, he copied it almost verbatim into both of his volumes, a rare compliment to Fordun's work. To this Bower added a verse history of the coronation stone; this verse, which he claimed was ancient, followed the Scots' progress from Egypt to Argyll and even included a kinglist.[24] Bower loved everything Scottish and shared all his predecessor's attitudes towards his nation and its neighbours. He was so pleased with his own compilation that he ended his *Scotichronicon* with a short prayer adapted from the words of St. Brigitte, 'Christ, he to whom this book is not pleasing is not a Scot.'[25]

Abbot Bower seems to have been right about that. The *Scotichronicon* was so popular that no new general histories of Scotland were compiled in Latin for over 80 years; all extant manuscripts are either copies or abridgements of Fordun's *Chronica* or one of Bower's adaptations. Furthermore, even that most selective and independent of editors, the compiler of the *Book of Pluscarden*, included the origin myth, either because he suspected that Bower had not tampered with this part of Fordun's work and respect for Fordun kept him from doing so himself, or because the myth made all the points he wanted.

There is only one extant general history of Scotland written in Scots during our period, Andrew of Wyntoun's *Treatise*, begun sometime before 1406 and revised until sometime soon after 1420. This work, given the number of extant manuscripts, was more popular than any other work of its kind except Bower's *Scotichronicon* and its redactions, and is proof that, as long as they did not expect their words to reach beyond the borders of their kingdom, the Scots of the early fifteenth century were not all willing to accept Fordun's carefully constructed myth lock, stock and barrel.

Andrew of Wyntoun wanted to instruct and entertain the household of Sir John of Wemyss, a gentleman with property in Fife near the house of St. Serf where Wyntoun was prior. Considering the scandalous stories he tells about the Scottish royal family and the way he pokes fun at the foibles of his compatriots, it seems highly unlikely that Wyntoun, unlike Fordun and the others who chose to work in Latin, ever expected his work to reach the ears of his king, let alone the English or any other foreigners.

Wyntoun included no less than three different, and brief, origin myths in his *Treatise*, summing up with a disclaimer of responsibility for the accuracy of any of them. In the shortest of these, a wise, but nameless, Scythian was banished from Egypt at the time of the drowning of Pharaoh. This man led an equally anonymous party of refugees around Africa to Spain where they settled; 1200 years later, in 352 BCE, their descendants migrated to Ireland.[26]

The account most like Fordun's begins again with a Scythian, this time one Sir Neville, who somehow came to power in Greece. His son, Gedeyelle-Glays, married Scota, daughter of Pharaoh and confidently looked forward to exploiting the riches of Egypt once his children had inherited the throne there. However, following the drowning of their

Pharaoh, the Egyptians banished all foreigners, so Gadeyelle-Glays led his family and a band of exiles to Spain where they built the city now known as Santiago de Compostella. It was from there that he spied Ireland. Gedeyelle-Glays was dead by the time his explorers returned with their favourable reports, so it was one of his younger sons who led the Scots to their easy conquest of the island. Sometime later, a number of Scots moved still further on, this time to settle next to the Picts and Britons in the north of Britain.[27]

Wyntoun said he drew his third myth from the *Brut*, a work by his compatriot, John Barbour, best known for his biography of Robert Bruce. This tale is very similar to that John of Fordun had credited, accurately, to Geoffrey of Monmouth. In it, Gurgunt-Badruk, king of the Britons, was sailing near Orkney when he was met by thirty ships from Spain. The leader of the wanderers, whose name was Partoloym, asked for permission to settle in Britain; this was refused. Gurgunt-Badruk sent them instead to Ireland, which was then empty, and it was from these people that the 'Irishery', as Wyntoun called them, were descended.[28]

Wyntoun admitted that he found his sources for this period both confused and confusing but his common sense made him discount some of the more outrageous claims he had come across which loyalty to a party line might otherwise have forced him to accept. He had his doubts about the reliability of all these tales, and was willing to vouch only for the fact that the Scots had, at some time, come from Spain to Ireland and that they still held that island and Scotland.[29] Such a conclusion utterly destroyed Fordun's carefully laid foundation for the Scots' claim to special status in the eyes of the Lord. Wyntoun tried much harder to believe that the Scots had settled in the north of Britain before the Picts, but here, too, he ran into difficulty. There were simply not enough Scottish kings to fill the expanse of time. The way Wyntoun figured it, there were ten kings separating Fergus, son of Eric, and Kenneth mac Alpin; but, if Fergus and his people had arrived in Scotland before the Picts, then those ten reigns had to span more than 1200 years. Wyntoun feared he might bore hs audience if he tried to reconcile all the kinglists, so, declaring himself open to suggestions, he concluded that the period between the reigns of Fergus, son of Eric and Kenneth mac Alpin could have been no more than 300 years,[30] which was fairly close to the mark. This drove him to the inevitable conclusion that the Picts had been well established in Scotland long before the Scottish migration. That earlier Fergus, the son of Feredach, whom Fordun had sent to Scotland hundreds of years before Fergus, son of Eric, in order to solve this very problem never enters Wyntoun's *Treatise*.

As for the Picts themselves, their history in the *Treatise* is just an outline of that given in the *Chronica*, to which Wyntoun added an annotated kinglist which is clearly related to Fordun's and an oblique reference to a Pictish conquest of the Scots. Wyntoun did not give much space to his description of the Scottish conquest of Scotland. Kenneth mac Alpin did not have to resort to tricks before his chieftains attacked the Picts; indeed, so thorough was he in his work that some sceptics questioned whether the Picts had ever existed though others wondered if the Highlanders might be descendants of the Picts because of their great physical stature and strength.[31]

All of Wyntoun's origin myths are so sketchy that many of the points on which Fordun rested his arguments in favour of innate Scottish independence and their long line of kings have been completely destroyed. While the *Treatise* as a whole makes the Scots' love of freedom amply clear, Wyntoun seldom used this to explain their migration from one place to another, and he also failed to repeat or invent those speeches in which the ancients declared their love of independence. Wyntoun's brevity removes the Scots from their privileged position as a chosen people and fails to explain adequately the division of the Scots into Highlanders and Lowlanders. To add insult to injury, Wyntoun repeated that foreign story which left the Scots dependent on the Britons in a manner that would have suited Edward I and his lawyers to a tee.

Writing just over two decades after Fordun had completed his carefully constructed myth, Wyntoun drew on many traditions and did not favour any, perhaps out of respect, or perhaps because he did not care. After all, he and his intended audience did not need to have the legitimacy of the Scots' independent possession of Scotland proved to them with either historical precedents or legal proofs. Furthermore, none of them expected these stories to reach hostile ears; none of them were going to twist or misinterpret his narrative on purpose. It was safe for Wyntoun to let down his guard, thereby providing us with evidence that, left to themselves, the Scots did not always take these myths and the attendant legal wranglings all that seriously.

The next surviving work is another written in the vernacular, though it is, in all likelihood, a translation from Latin; therefore, this work is far more closely related to the *Chronica* than to Wyntoun's *Treatise*. This tract, entitled 'Heir is assignyt ye Cause quhy oure natioun vas callyt fyrst ye Scottis' deals with the origin myth in great detail. The dates of the extant manuscripts range from 1460 to the reign of James V; the one we will be studying was revised until 1482, but all of them are based on the same source.

Nothing is known for certain about who wrote 'ye Cause'. Whoever he was, he was very familiar with Fordun's myth, but his attitude about his nation's future could not have been more different from the earlier author's. Fordun was completely confident in the strenth and security of his nation and the brightness of its future; for all he provided the Scots with a history useful to lawyers and diplomats, he did not feel any need to whitewash that history. The Scots may have God on their side in the *Chronica*, but they are not perfect. Something had happened by the mid-fifteenth century, though, which made 'ye Cause's' author and those who chose to translate his work feel the need to clean up the origin myth making it not just more presentable but unassailable by anyone who might try to use it to malign the Scots. This was an author on the defensive; he systematically rewrote the myth, smoothing over or omitting many episodes which might have been used to raise uncomfortable questions about the Scots' integrity.

There is never any mention in 'ye Cause' of the division into Highlanders and Lowlanders, and without this Fordun's portrayal of Gaythelos' misspent youth suddenly becomes an embarrassment. As Gaythelos and his Greeks could no longer be the eponymous ancestors of the despicable Gaels, their waywardness reflected badly on the whole nation, so the story had to be changed. In 'ye Cause' the story starts with an alliance between Greece and Egypt; when the Ethiopians invaded Egypt, the king of Athens sent his son, Gayel glas to aid his allies. He was, of course, victorious, and the grateful Pharaoh gave him Scota as his wife. In case any reader should wonder why a nation would take its name from a woman, the author was careful to explain that it was because 'the custome was than to call natioun eftir women and not eftir men as in asia affrica and europa the thre pryncipale partis of the world'.[32]

Nor was Gayel glas exiled by the Egyptians; he and his company, made up mostly of lords and gentlemen, chose to heed the warnings of the plagues and left. This raises the question, 'Why didn't he go home?' It seems that the customs of the times prevented this, and besides, Gayel glas had been told by his pagan gods to go to a new land. And what about those who dislike the Scots on the suspicion that they were descended from the Egyptians, the oppressors of the Israelites, on both sides? They should remember that it was Egypt which had once sheltered the Holy Family.

The author of 'ye Cause' greatly simplified the story of the migration to Ireland. The Scots' first stop on the Iberian peninsula was Portugal which was named for Gayel glas,[33] then they settled in Spain. Once his son, Iber Scot, came of age Gayel glas sent him to explore Ireland. No explanation is ever given for how Gayel glas knew the island was there; perhaps the author feared that the claim that Gayel glas had seen Ireland would inspire so much derision that he felt it was worth sacrificing the details which had helped Fordun establish Gaythelos as a second Moses.

Iber Scot found it easy to conquer the giants who were Ireland's only inhabitants, and he named it *Scotia* for his mother. Sometime later, Rathus Rothia led the first Scottish settlers to Rothesay, followed by another company under Simon Brek. As these migrations had begun 300 years before the fall of Troy, and Brutus could not even have been born for another century,[34] then the Scottish nation was a good 400 years older than the British and in no way dependent on them.[35]

Many years later, the Picts were exiled from their Scythian homeland and journeyed to Ireland looking for wives and homes; the wives they were given, but they were sent over to Britain for the land. There the Pictish population grew until their numbers brought them into conflct with ths Scots already there. At this point the author adopts Fordun's first Fergus, this time called fergus Ferchar, the saviour prince of the Scottish settlers who brought the Scottish royal standard to Scotland with him. It is the second Fergus, the son of Eric, who is omitted here along with much of the rest of Fordun's myth because this author would never admit that the Scots had been forced to choose between slavery and exile. The wars against the Romans are set up as examples of the Scots' prowess in defending their freedom, but no wars with the Picts are ever mentioned until the brief report of the complete destruction of the Pictish kingdom and nation.

Like Fordun, the author of 'ye Cause' claimed a long line of kings for the Scots, 120 direct descendants of Fergus ferchar;[36] also like Fordun, he did not name them. He had little interest in such details. What he wanted to do was produce an origin myth which was as presentable as possible and which proved beyond a shadow of a doubt that the Scots had always been independent. In case the reader had not gotten this message from the narrative itself, he explained, 'Saw yat we may say yis day in verite yat yar is na land no na nacioun so fre fra ye begynnynge of ye warld na has standyn sa lang tyme in fredome as has ye scottis for yae hafe beyne xviii hunder zeris and mare unconquest and neuir was subieckit to na natioun or king to yis day bot euir undir our awin king of oure awin blude be rycht line discendand fra oure first king ferguse befor said to him yat now rignis quhome god kepe'.[37] Thus, even with so many embarrassments trimmed away, the essentials remain: the Scots' independence, their ancient dynasty, and their glorious ancestors. Having established these to his own satisfaction, the author then heaped abuse on the English in what seems to have become the traditional manner.

By the end of the fifteenth century, these elements were part and parcel of the origin myth with which most Scots defined who they were and from where they had come. It is easy, therefore, to understand their astonishment and outrage when, in 1521, John Major announced to the world that much of it was bunk.

This announcement might not have mattered so much to the Scots if Major, one of the last of the scholastic theologians, had not been a scholar and teacher with an international reputation at the University of Paris and if he had not had his *Historia Maioris Britanniae tam Angliae…* published in

Paris, making it readily available to a European audience. In addition, the *Historia* was addressed to Major's young sovereign, James V, who was expected to learn from the examples set out in it and arrange his foreign policy accordingly. Major's theological training and standing at the University left him feeling more than equal to turning almost every entry into a lesson of some sort. His theme, whose importance overwhelmed all others in the *Historia,* was the need for a union of the Scottish and English crowns, for as long as the two kingdoms were independent, the Scots could not be conquered and the English could not stop trying to conquer them, resulting in their mutual destruction. The recent slaughter at Flodden in September 1513 could not have been far from Major's thoughts when he put forward such an argument. He set up the whole of his work to prove the need for unity, beginning with the title *Historia Maiioris Britanniae;* no less an authority than Fordun himself had rejected the use of the term 'Great Britain' when speaking of the island occupied by Scotland and England. Major not only ignored this prohibition, but then went so far as to state that the present inhabitants of the island were all Britons[38] whether they cared to admit it or not. He even tried to divide the *Historia* equally between the two nations, but that he could not quite manage.

Major applied to the study of history the same principle he said he had used in his study of theology: that a man of sense should think for himself without inordinate love of his own nation or hatred of his enemy[39] No other stance he could have taken could have separated him more radically from his predecessors; the very things he was trying to avoid had been their reasons for writing.

After repeating much of Fordun's myth through the arrival of the Scots in Spain, Major summarily dismissed it as 'a figment'.[40] Unlike Wyntoun who was suspicious of the myths because their gaps and contradictions confused him, Major saw these tales for exactly what they were: inventions devised to counter English claims to sovereignty over Scotland. As Major put it, the English had claimed Trojan descent, so the Scots had chosen the Greeks, conquerors of Troy, as their progenitors, then improved on the tale by adding the Egyptian royal line. since all histories and linguistic studies proved that the Irish had come from Spain, then the inventors of the tales had had to pretend that the Greeks and Egyptians had stopped in that country. Reminiscent of Wyntoun, Major declared that only two statements drawn from these stories could be substantiated: the Irish had come from Spain and the Scots from Ireland. The rest was a mixture of truth and falsehood, and was, in Major's estimation, doubtful and unprofitable.[41]

Major had equally little use for the English tales and their claims through Brutus and his sons. One of Major's main sources of English history and opinions of the Scots was Ranulph Higden's *Polychronicon* whose authorship he incorrectly ascribed to its publisher, William Caxton. Major despised that work. In it he found examples of everything he disliked in a historian; Major's attitude was epitomized by his aside that Caxton was, after all, an unlettered man, and so he had reproduced whatever the English commonly said about their Scottish enemies.

Moving on to the latter part of the myth, Major set aside the Scots' claims to having settled in Scotland before the Picts, but even he could not rid himself completely of Fordun's influence, and, from the start of his discussion of the migration to Scotland, Major seems much more willing to accept the traditions as they had been handed down. He accepted the existence of the first Fergus, the son of Ferechad, and the eventual choice of exile over slavery made when the Scots were defeated by the Romans and Picts. His story of their return and subsequent conquest of the Picts is substantially that found in the *Chronica,* but some of the lessons Major drew from the account were not. For instance, Major wondered whether the Scots' conquest of Pictland had been just and he denounced the inhuman slaughter of the Pictish priests, women and children;[42] Fordun had admitted to no such qualms.

Yet despite Major's radical break with the narrative tradition established by Fordun, the theme which emerges from both the pared down myth and the *Historia* as a whole, is surprisingly similar to that which, at first glance, he seems to repudiate. In the *Historia* the Scots are just as independent as they had always been and were still fully capable of defending their kingdom since, Major declared, his contemporaries were just as warlike as the first settlers had been 1850 years before;[43] try as he might, Major could not disguise his pride in that. It is the conclusion Major draws from his evidence that separates him most from the pleasure Fordun took in the maintenance of the status quo and the hope of eventual conquest of England. Major was no pacifist in the strict sense of the word, but he wanted peace, and the only way he could see for the Scots to find any was through the intermarriage of the Scottish and English royal families until an heir to both kingdoms was born.[44] As his treatment of both the Scottish and English origin myths attests, Major was far more concerned with the welfare of the inhabitants of the two kingdoms than with pandering to their national pride.

Judging the *Historia* by the goals Major had set for it, his work was a failure. Even Major's friend Gavin Douglas did not like the *Historia* and urged Polydore Vergil not to use it,[45] though Vergil ignored him. Most important, it did not receive a warm welcome in the court of its addressee, James V; no translations of it were commissioned and James rejected Major's advice utterly, for when the time came, he chose a French bride.

The historical work which did receive royal approval is the last to be studied here, Hector Boece's *Scotorum Historiae a Prima Gentis,* published in Paris in 1527. In it, Boece embraced Fordun's origin myth and all its attendant prejudices whole-heartedly, and it was his story that the Scots and their king, to whom it was addressed, wanted to hear. There were two royal commissions for its translation into Scots and a third Scots translation is extant. When James V went courting in France in 1537 he took a copy of the *Scotorum Historiae*, perhaps in translation, along with him; selections from it were translated into French to acquaint Queen Magdalene with her new realm.

The author of this popular work had been a lecturer at Paris, but by the time he started the *Scotorum Historiae* he was principal of the new University of Aberdeen which he had helped organize. Boece was a humanist; even so, he spoke of John Major's theological writings as 'brightest torches'.[46] It is amply clear from the *Scotorum Historiae* that he did not think the same of the *Historia;* indeed, Boece set to work specifically to counteract the effects of Major's publication.

The origin myth presented in the *Scotorum Historiae* is an inflated version of Fordun's with many details invented to fill the gaps. Gaythelos and his obstreperous cronies are forced to flee Greece once again and seek refuge in Egypt where their victory against the Ethiopians at Memphis brought Gaythelos Scota for his wife.[47] Fear of the plagues sent by Moses' God led Gaythelos and his mixed band to set off on their journey to Spain via Numidia and Portugal. According to Boece, it was the growth of his people, whom he had already named Scots in an effort to unite them, which turned Gaythelos' attention to finding them a new home. About the only claim about Gaythelos from the *Chronica* that Boece did not repeat was that he had seen Ireland from Spain; instead, the king is said to have heard rumours about the island and consequently sent explorers to it.[48] Once more there were three migrations to Ireland, the last led by Simon Brech in 695 BCE.[49] The first Scots had settled in the Hebrides well before the Picts; in 330 BCE, Fergus, now the son of Ferquhard, came to Scotland to be their king and protect them from the attacks of their Pictish and British neighbours.[50]

Over the next six centuries the Scots, usually with their Pictish allies, made many courageous stands, especially against Roman aggression from the south. This gave Boece plenty of time to write speeches proclaiming the need to defend the independence of the kingdom at any and all costs. Then, in 379 AD, the Scots were forced into exile, not, as Fordun had said, to Ireland, but to Denmark where Eirth, nephew of the late Scottish king, married a princess, Rocha.[51] Their son, Fergus, took part in a Danish raid on Rome before turning his attention to the restoration of the Scottish kingdom when the Picts sent out their call for help. By 422 AD he had made it to Argyll where he was seated on the Stone of Destiny; by the time he died fighting the Romans, the Scots were again in possession of their kingdom.[52]

The Picts received short shrift from Boece. His account of their arrival is confused. The one point about which he was adamant was that they had arrived in what is now Scotland about 250 years after the Scots.[53] Most of his account deals with their relations with the Scots, during which they were often treacherous. Once Kenneth mac Alpin convinced the nobles to co-operate with him, the Picts were doomed. Those who survived his attacks hoped to restore their kingdom once the Scots had allowed themselves to be weakened by the luxuries introduced by the tyrant, Donald; as it turned out, the Picts were too divided amongst themselves to take advantage of the situation.

John of Fordun had claimed that the reigns of forty-five kings separated those of the two Ferguses, but he had named only two. Boece reduced the number somewhat to thirty-nine and found names for them all. Even in this he was dependent on the *Chronica* since he had drawn most of the names from Fordun's genealogy of David I via Simon Brech to Japhet. Thus, the cherished kinglist was firmly re-established as the cornerstone of Scottish history. Even so, Boece's kinglist is not one to inspire great confidence in the innate worth of kings. Of the 101 Scottish kings in the *Scotorum Historiae*, 28 were tyrants, all of whom died in some appropriately unpleasant manner; another fourteen were capable of doing only a mediocre job due either to circumstances or personal weakness. This left only fifty-nine, less than two-thirds, who actually did their job well, and very few of these were endowed with any exceptional virtue. Boece left young James V with little doubt about exactly what a good king should and should not do.

One of the most important tasks for the king was to lead his subjects back from the ways of luxury and ease which they were following. Paradoxically, while Major, the proponent of union, was completely confident about the Scots' ability to defend themselves, Boece had his doubts. He traced the degeneration of his nation from their prime in a golden age in a manner very popular at the time, but in his case it was not simply a device. Perhaps it was the Scottish troops' refusal to follow the Duke of Albany across the Tweed in 1523 compounded with the horror of the defeat at Flodden which undermined Boece's confidence in his nation's prowess. He harped continually on the Scots need to reform, and in an interesting break with another tradition, he held up the Highlanders' simpler and tougher way of life as an example of a step in the right direction. By constantly demanding that the Scots free themselves from enervating foreign influences, Boece worked himself into a cleft stick, for, if the Scots had been weakened by foreign, and especially English, luxuries, then why need they fear their despised southern neighbours who should, by this time, be thoroughly degenerate themselves? Boece never addressed this question; he just kept nagging.

Boece and Major, and the themes presented in their narratives, represent two sides of a debate about foreign policy which raged during the early years of the reign of James V: should the Scots maintain their Auld Alliance with France and accept the continuation of hostilities along the Border, or, should they bury the hatchet and ally with England. Support of Fordun's myth was a natural rallying cry for those who favoured the maintenance of the French alliance and, at the very least, wished to guarantee continued Scottish independence. As a nationalist of the staunch, old-fashioned sort, Boece's pride in his nation's history, its illustrious ancestors, and ancient royal dynasty was complimented by his hatred of the English, all feelings most of his compatriots took for granted. They liked the glorious past presented in Fordun's pioneering work; in the course of the fifteenth century it had become part and parcel of most Scots' image of their nation. The narrative and policy put forward by Major were rejected. Ironically, although the man at the centre of this uproar, James V, ignored Major's advice and chose French brides, his father's marriage to Margaret Tudor, daughter of Henry VII, would one day result in the birth of an heir to both kingdoms, James VI. So, while Major lost his battle to the nationalists, in the end it was he who won the war.

NOTES

1 Mark Twain, *The Portable Mark Twain* (New York: 1962) 567.
2 See Edward J. Cohen, 'Myth and Identity in Early Medieval Scotland' *Scottish Historical Review*, XIII (Oct. 1985) 111–135.
3 E.L.G. Stones, ed., and trans., *Anglo-Scottish Relations* (Oxford: 1970) 195–197.
4 Walter Goodall, ed., *Joannis de Fordun Scotichronicon cum Supplimentis ac Continuatione Walteri Boweri* (Edinburgh: 1759) II, 215.
5 *Ibid.*, II, 216.
6 P.A. Lineham, 'A Fourteenth Century History of Anglo-Scottish Relations in a Spanish Manuscript', *Bull. Inst. Hist. Res.* XLVIII (1975) 113–114.
7 James Ferguson, *The Declaration of Arbroath* (Edinburgh) 7.
8 Walter Bower, *Codex Hayanus...*, National Library of Scotland, ADV. MS. 35.1.7, fo. 1.
9 *Rotuli Scotiae in Turri Londinensi et in Domo Capitulari Westmonasteriensi Asservati* (London: 1814) I, 877.
10 National Library of Scotland ADV. MS. 35.6.7, fo. 1.
11 British Library Royal MS. 13. E. x, fo. 28.
12 Ranald Nicholson, *Scotland: The Later Middle Ages* (Edinburgh: 1974) 277.
13 William F. Skene, ed., *Johannis de Fordun Chronica Gentis Scotorum* (Edinburg: 1871) I, 387.
14 *Ibid.*, I, 11–12.
15 *Ibid.*, I, 18.
16 *Ibid.*, I, 15.
17 *Ibid.*, I, 23–24.
18 *Ibid.*, I, 47–48.
19 *Ibid.*, I, 67.
20 *Ibid.*, I, 90.
21 *Ibid.*, I, 146–147.

22 This claim to a long line of kings was based on fact. The death of Margaret, Maid of Norway, brought to an end a dynasty which could, through the female line, trace its ancestry back to the rulers of Scottish Dalriada. 'In 1290 no other kingdom of Europe could claim with equal conviction to be governed by a royal house enjoying an unbroken existence of seven centuries.' Geoffrey W.S. Barrow, 'Robert Bruce and the Scottish Identity' (Edinburgh: 1984) 1.

23 Skene, *Fordun*, I, 42.

24 Bower, *Codex Hayanus*, 13,81.

25 Goodall, *Scotichronicon*, II, 517.

26 Francis J. Amours, ed., *The Original Chronicle of Andrew Wyntoun* (Edinburgh: 1914) II, 205.

27 David Laing, ed., *The Orygynale Cronykil of Scotland* (Edinburgh: 1872) I, 100.

28 Amours, *Original Chronicle*, II, 199–201.

29 Laing, *Orygynale Cronykil*, I, 99.

30 Amours, *Original Chronicle*, III, 141.

31 *Ibid.*, II, 111–113; III, 136.

32 British Library, Royal MS. 17. d. xx, fo. 299^r.

33 *Ibid.*, fo. 300^r.

34 *Ibid.*, fo. 299^v, 300^r.

35 *The Bannatyne Miscellany* (Edinburgh: 1855) III, 36.

36 Royal MS. 17. d. xx, fo. 301^r.

37 *Ibid.*, fo. 302^v–303^r.

38 John Major, *Historia Maioris Britanniae tam Angliae quam Scotiae* ... (Paris: 1521) 6.

39 *Ibid.*, 13. Ricardo Garcia-Villoslada, *La Universidad de Paris Durante Los Estudios de Vitoria O.P.*, Analecta Gregoriana XIV Series, Facultatis Historiae Ecclesiastica Sectio B (2) (Rome: 1938) 143–144. P. Hume Brown, ed., *Collected Essays and Reviews of Thomas Graves Law* (Edinburgh: 1904) 118, 121.

40 Major, *Historia*, 17.

41 *Ibid.*, 17.

42 *Ibid.*, 37.

43 *Ibid.*, 13.

44 *Ibid.*, 13.

45 John MacQueen, 'National Spirit and Native Culture', in *The Scottish Nation*, ed., Gordon Menzies (London: 1972) 70

46 James Moir, *Hectoris Boetii Murthlacensium et Aberdonensium Episcoporum Vitae* (Aberdeen: 1894) 89.

47 Hector Boece, *Scotorum Historiae e Prima Gentis Origine* ... (Paris: 1527) 1.

48 *Ibid.*, 2.

49 *Ibid.*, 3–4.

50 *Ibid.*, 6.

51 *Ibid.*, 117–118.

52 *Ibid.*, 121–126.

53 *Ibid.*, 'Scotorum Regni Descriptio', 4.

Cheshiremen at Blore Heath:
A Swan Dive

JAMES L. GILLESPIE

'There Dutton, Dutton kills, a Done doth kill a Done,
A Booth, a Booth, and Leigh by Leigh is overthrown;
A Venables against a Venables doth stand,
A Troutbeck fighteth with a Troutbeck, hand to hand;
There Molineux doth make a Molineux to die,
And Egerton the strength of Egerton doth try.
O! Cheshire, wer't thou mad? of thine own native gore
So much until this day thou never shed'st before!
Above two thousand men upon the earth were thrown,
Of which the greatest part were naturally thine own.
The stout Lord Audley slain, with many a captain there,
To Salisbury it sorts the Palm away to bear.'

These lines of the Elizabethan poet Michael Drayton have become the almost de rigueur introduction to the discussion of the Battle of Blore Heath by Cheshire historians.[1] In his description of the slaughter, Drayton was following a tradition popularized by Edward Hall's Chronicle: 'In this battail, wer slain, xxiiij C. persons, but the greatest plague lighted on the Chesshire men, because one halfe of the shire, was one the one part, and the other on the other part. . .' Contemporaries also remarked upon the casualties sustained by the men of the palatinate: 'And there was the lorde Audeley slyne, and many of the notable knyghtes and squyers of Chesshyre that had resceued the lyuery of the swannes. . .'[2] The battlefield itself gained the name of Deadman's Den among the local inhabitants.[3] Blore Heath's reputation as a slaughtering ground for the Cheshire gentry has remained intact to the present day. Writing in 1981, a troika of leading British scholars reasserted the validity of the tradition. Michael Bennett, a master of the palatinate's history, speaks of 'The Battle of Blore Heath, in which large numbers of local gentlemen fought and were slaughtered on both sides. . .'; Ralph Griffiths, the leading biographer of Henry VI, wrote: 'In all, about 2000 men were feared slain,. . .. The Cheshire contingents fared particularly badly. . ..'; and Anthony Goodman asserted in his *The Wars of the*

Roses: 'Cheshire gentlefolk rallying to the young prince of Wales suffered high casualties at Blore Heath in 1459.' A great deal of ink has been spilled on the Cheshiremen at Blore Heath; it remains to be seen how much blood these gallants actually shed on St. Thecla's day in the thirty-eighth year of Henry VI.

The battle resulted from the efforts of Margaret of Anjou to prevent the earl of Salisbury who had set out from Middleham with his retinue from effecting a rendezvous with the earl of Warwick and the duke of York. Henry VI had moved from Coventry to Nottingham in an effort to intercept Salisbury, but the earl avoided the main Lancastrian army by shifting his line of march westward. The task of blocking Salisbury, therefore, fell to a force of retainers of the young prince of Wales under the command of James Tuchet, lord Audley. Audley, with a numerically superior force, encountered Salisbury as he approached Market Drayton along the road from Newcastle-under-Lyme. The two armies fought at Blore Heath, and Salisbury won a decisive, albeit precarious, victory. The details of the battle have engendered a scholarly war. A monograph was even produced on Blore Heath in 1912, but it is unlikely that a definitive account of the battle is possible on the basis of the surviving sources.[5] The point at issue, in any case, is how many Cheshiremen survived the affray.

The fratricidal nature of the conflict seems to have been over dramatized. The bulk of Salisbury's force was composed of Yorkshiremen; a surviving partial account of the Earl's retainers lists ten men from Richmondshire, three from the North and West Ridings and three men each from Durham and Northumberland.[6] There were, however, some Cheshiremen in the Earl's ranks. The 'Parliament of Devils' that assembled at Coventry on 20 November 1459 to avenge the Lancastrian cause in the aftermath of the flight of the Yorkist lords from Ludlow urged Henry VI to attaint Thomas, lord Stanley. Stanley was accused of failing to heed a summons to the royal host and of impeding the tenants of the prince of Wales in the Cheshire hundreds of Wirral and Macclesfield from joining forces with Lord Audley. In addition, 'William Stanley his Brother went, with many of the said Lordes Servauntz and Tenauntz, grete nombre of people, to the Erle of Salesbury, which were with the same Erle at the distressying of youre true Liege people at Bloreheth,'[7] William Stanley, however, was the only substantial Cheshireman who has been identified in Salisbury's army, and the vast majority of the Stanley retinue itself hailed from Lancashire.[8] The Coventry parliament made no accusations against any other Cheshiremen for their support of Salisbury, nor is there any evidence for such support in the records of the palatinate. Perhaps most telling on this point is the lack of a single surviving inquisition post mortem for a member of the Chester gentry who was slain in the Earl's ranks.

It is possible that William Stanley may have lost two brothers-in-law in Audley's army. His sister Margaret had married Sir William Troutbeck, who was certainly a casualty of the battle, and his sister, Elizabeth married Sir Richard Molineux, a Lancashire knight who may also have perished at Blore Heath. If Molineux was killed in the battle, it is doubtful that the Stanleys mourned their departed brother-in-law. Molineux's father had had a severe quarrel with the Stanleys 'which threatened to become a private war'.[9] Thus, it was not surprising to find the sons of the two old Lancashire protagonists on opposite sides at Blore Heath. As for Troutbeck, there is no evidence that Stanley ever crossed swords with him – or with Molineux for that matter. Francis Twemlow summarized the issue of the fratricidal nature of the battle: 'On the whole it seems that Blore Heath was no worse in this respect than most battles in our Civil Wars; and that the behaviour of the Cheshire gentry compares favourably with that of the aristocracy in other counties, such for instance as that of the Neville family in Yorkshire.'[10] Few Cheshiremen shared in Salisbury's triumph.

A great many Cheshiremen shared in Audley's defeat. Assertions that Audley's army was a 'Cheshire army' are clearly overdrawn.[11] Tuchet drew retainers from his estates in Shropshire, Staffordshire and Derbyshire as well as Cheshire, and a number of Lancashire men were reported captured by the Yorkists after the battle.[12] The only member of Lord Dudley's contingent who can be identified, Nicholas Leverson, who received a £20 grant for his service at Blore Heath 'where he was wounded and maimed and left on the field for dead, and spoiled of horses, goods and harness,' seems to have been a Staffordshire man.[13] Clearly, however, the Cheshiremen comprised the core of Audley's army. Margaret of Anjou had visited Chester in 1455 to recruit followers as part of her policy of creating an inner citadel centered on Coventry for the Lancastrian monarchy. As Richard II had enlisted the support of his personal earldom through the distribution of the livery of the white hart, Margaret distributed white swans on behalf of her son.[14] The white swan had been used by Edward III as well as the countess of Hereford, wife of Henry Bolingbroke; it thus had special associations with the Plantagenet as well as the Lancastrian lines.[15] The Queen had relied heavily upon the elder Thomas, lord Stanley to control Cheshire until his death in February, 1459. The younger lord Stanley was the earl of Salisbury's son-in-law, and he was, therefore, viewed as a less reliable instrument than his father had been, even before Blore Heath. Royal power does seem to have suffered as a result in Wirral, but Wirral was never, in spite of the protests of the Coventry parliament, a major source of soldiers. A muster roll of 1417 lists the provenance of 405 archers from Cheshire; a mere 18 of these hailed from Wirral. Other documents tell a similar tale.[16] Macclesfield was another matter; it was a good recruiting ground. Audley with the aid of his second in command John Sutton, lord Dudley, also a prominent Cheshire landowner, seems to have successfully filled the void in royal power in this hundred. The southern portion of Macclesfield which marched upon the field of battle contributed handsomely to Audley's army.

That army was, according to *Gregory's Chronicle,* composed of the 'Quenys galentys', or as *Benet's Chronicle* put it: 'octo millia hominum bellatorum de Galantibus regine'.[17] Surely such a gallant collection of Lancastrian martyrs must have left behind a noble memorial. In addition to Audley, who perished at Blore Heath, and John Sutton, baron of Malpas, lord Dudley, who was captured by the Yorkists, the names of fourteen Cheshire gentlemen and one gentleman from Lancashire, whose family had long been connected with Cheshire, have been listed as Lancastrian casualties of the battle of Blore Heath. Two of these alleged casualties can be dismissed immediately. George Ormerod identified Sir John Troutbeck as a casualty, but, as Richard Brooke pointed out over a century ago, Ormerod had simply confused John Troutbeck with William Troutbeck.[18] John Troutbeck's inquisition post mortem makes it clear that he was already dead prior to the battle.[19] Sir Robert del Bothe has also been placed upon the field by Ormerod on the basis of sepulchral evidence. Ormerod has reconstructed the damaged inscription on Bothe's memorial brass to read that Sir Robert del Bothe died on the feast of St. Thecla in 1460, and his wife, Douce, on the morrow of the Blessed Virgin, 1453. In a note Ormerod remarked that the inscription 'possesses considerable interest, and is the only inscription now remaining in the county relating to any of the warriors who fell at Blore Heath'.[20] Sadly, Ormerod botched the reading of this 'only inscription now remaining'. J.P. Earwaker working from a sketch of the memorial made by Randle Holmes during the reign of the Virgin Queen has demonstrated that the correct reading places Bothe's death on the feast of St. Edith the Virgin (16 September), 1460; it was Douce who died on the morrow of the feast of St. Thecla, 1453. Earwaker curtly added that Bothe had in any case died a year late for Blore Heath and that there is no feast of the Blessed Virgin in the Catholic calendar![21] Thus, only a baker's dozen of potential recorded casualties remain among the Queen's Cheshire gallants, and the ease with which these first two gentlemen and the 'only inscription now remaining' have been dismissed may give pause concerning the reliability of the remaining list.

These thirteen gallants seem plausible candidates for Lancastrian martyrdom at Blore Heath, and they, therefore, deserve closer examination than their two obviously bogus colleagues. The men of this group are: Adam Bostok of Bostok, Esq., Sir Hugh Calveley, Sir John Done of Utkinton, Richard Done of Crowton, Esq., Sir Robert Downes of

Shrigley, John Dutton of Hatton, Esq., Peter Dutton of Dutton, Sir Thomas Dutton of Dutton, Sir John Egerton of Egerton, Sir John Legh of Booths, Sir William Troutbeck of Dunham-on-the-Hill, Sir Hugh Venables of Kinderton and Sir Richard Molineux who was from Sefton, Lancashire, but a man with long-standing Cheshire connections.[22] Indeed this entire group of prominent Cheshire gentry was interconnected. The Bostoks and the Duttons had supported Sir John Egerton in his dispute with the Breretons over the division of the barony of Malpas which Ormerod characterized as 'a little, but determined war, extending over some forty years'.[23] Adam Bostok and Hugh Venables had each served as parties to recognizances that members of the other's family should keep the peace, and John Donne held lands from each of them.[24] Donne was William Troutbeck's brother-in-law, and Hugh Venables had also married a Troutbeck. William Troutbeck's father and grandfather had long been associated in Cheshire affairs with Lord Audley.[25] Donne had married Troutbeck's sister, Cecilia. Sir Hugh Calveley received a licence in 1454 to alienate some lands and tenements held of the earl of Chester to William Troutbeck during the lifetime of Cecilia with remainder in tail-male on Cecilia's death to the Donnes of Utkinton.[26] Richard Donne of Crowton was distantly related to the Donnes of Utkinton, and he held lands from them.[27] Sir Thomas Dutton was related to Sir Richard Molineux and Sir Thomas Stanley by marriage; and John Dutton of Hatton had served as a surety for Sir John de Legh.[28] Clearly these representatives of the leading families of Cheshire who had acted in concert prior to 1459 would seem to be likely companions-in-arms at Blore Heath.

These gentlemen had had considerable experience of the world prior to 1459. Only Troutbeck, John and Peter Dutton, and Richard Donne were under thirty. Sir Hugh Venables was thirty-two, and Thomas Dutton, Hugh Calveley and John Donne were in their late thirties. Bostok, Egerton and Legh were all in their mid to late forties. Molineux was over fifty and Sir Robert Downes was pushing sixty.[29] Most of the group had had some experience in local service to the government, and nearly all had been involved in local disorders which required that they become parties to peace recognizances. In addition to the Egerton–Brereton feud, the Bostoks had waged a long-standing battle with the Abbots of Vale Royal that had become a local cause célèbre.[30] All of these gallants were descended from families with a long tradition of military service to the crown. Adam Bostok, John Donne and John Legh were the direct descendants of three of the seven watch commanders of Richard II's Cheshire bodyguard upon which Margaret of Anjou's distribution of the livery of the white swan seems to have been patterned.[31] Yet, for all their local experience and hereditary proclivities, none of these men seems to have ever been engaged in a full-scale military operation prior to Blore Heath. Indeed, their commander, Lord Audley, had not been in the field since 1431.[32] This may explain how a numerically superior force managed to be routed on St. Thecla's day.

That these gallants of the Queen stood shoulder to shoulder at Blore Heath is probable; that they fell side by side in the rout is more problematical. In four cases, Sir John Donne, Richard Donne, Sir Thomas Dutton and Sir Hugh Venables, the survival of inquisitions post mortem confirm that the gallant gentlemen did indeed perish on the Sunday next before the feast of St. Michael the Archangel in the thirty-eighth year of Henry VI. Sir William Troutbeck's writ diem clausit extremum provides similar confirmation for his demise at Blore Heath, and this is confirmed by Troutbeck's inquisition post mortem held in the next reign.[33] The name of Sir John Egerton may also be added to the casualty list with some assurance. His inquisition post mortem states that 'the said John died on Tuesday next before the Feast of St. Michael the Archangel'; Egerton, therefore, very likely succumbed to wounds he received on the field at Blore Heath.[34] No other Chester inquisitions post mortem provide 23 September 1459 as the date of death.[35] To this half dozen definite victims, may be added another two probable casualties. Sir Thomas Dutton's son, Peter Dutton, is numbered among the dead, and although there is no documentary confirmation of his death, there is no reason to question it either. Peter does not appear in the records after 1459, and since he died at the same time as his father, there would be no reason for the palatinate's bureaucracy to take notice of his demise. The lack of any official notice of the death of Sir John Legh is more troubling, but once again the lack of any reference to him after the battle provides circumstantial proof of his death. Finally, there is an additional gentleman who may have breathed his last on St. Thecla's day. John Dutton of Hatton clearly survived the battle. On 18 June 1462, John Dutton of Hatton was granted the issues of the frithmote of Delamere forest until he had satisfied himself of £100 expended by him in going to Chester with certain armed men at the king's command.[36] Sir Thomas Dutton of Dutton did, however, have a brother John who may have perished at Blore Heath. Once again there is no incontrovertible proof that any John Dutton died in the battle, but if a John Dutton did, later historians got the wrong man.

Indeed, historians have gotten several wrong men! Adam Bostok continues to show up on the Cheshire recognizance rolls after 1459; he even served as a subsidy collector in the Nantwich hundred under Edward IV. Bostok's inquisition post mortem was held in 1475.[37] Sir Hugh Calveley survived Bostok by twenty years on the evidence of his inquisition post mortem, and once again the entries in the Cheshire recognizance rolls continue after Blore Heath. Hugh does seem to have been a Lancastrian partizan since a 500 mark recognizance was required of him on 23 December 1461 as a pledge of his allegiance to Edward IV.[38] It is doubtful if Edward would have been overly concerned with the allegiance of this gallant of Queen Margaret had he perished with his companions of the white swan in 1459. If Sir Robert Downes perished as a result of Blore Heath, he must have suffered a lingering death. His inquisition post mortem, which refers to him as Robert Downes, Esq., states that he died on 25 April 1460. The memorial erected by his son in Prestbury Church in 1495 makes no mention of Blore Heath.[39] The writ diem clausit extremum for that Lancashire liveryman of the swan, Sir Richard Molineux was dated 12 August 1462, and the *Victoria County History of Lancashire* concedes that the claim that Molineux died at Blore Heath 'is perhaps merely a family tradition'.[40] Thus, the baker's dozen of Cheshire gallants has been culled to eight or perhaps nine men who joined their commander, lord Audley, in death on the field at Blore Heath. When this result is compared with the assertions that over two thousand men lost their lives in Audley's army, the words of a popular song come to mind: 'Is that all there is?'

Well, that's not quite all. In addition to Audley's second-in-command, John Sutton, lord Dudley, Jean Waurin records that 'messire Thomas Fiderne' was captured by the Yorkists.[41] This was Sir Thomas Fitton of Gawsworth, Macclesfield, and Waurin's rather confused account of Blore Heath is confirmed on this point by the Chester recognizance rolls. On 29 April 1460, Fitton and sixty-seven of his followers received a general pardon in consideration of the good service they had performed at the battle of Blore Heath.[42] Sir Thomas received knighthood as a result of his distinguished service on the field on St. Thecla's day, and the men of his company were the only group to be singled out for a pardon.[43] The pardon which was granted by the prince of Wales in his capacity as earl of Chester was issued with the special assent of Edward's very dear mother, Margaret of Anjou.[44] Dorothy Clayton has argued that the men named in the pardon were not the same men described in the pardon's account of Sir Thomas' service at Blore Heath '*cum quampluribus sibi adherentibus*', but were rather men who 'had been involved with Sir Thomas in crimes committed before Blore Heath which were totally unconnected with the battle'. Clayton has marshalled evidence of such earlier criminal activity in support of her position, but it is hardly surprising to find Fitton and his followers associated in this way. Such evidence would seem to strengthen rather than deny the ties that would cause these Cheshiremen to assemble together in Fitton's company for the march to Blore Heath. Soldiering and criminal activity have never been mutually exclusive professions, and to deny those pardoned with Fitton their place at Blore Heath seems needlessly disingenuous.[45] It seems, therefore, that Fitton and his company were among the most devoted of the Queen's gallants.

These gallants of the swan, however, were hardly among the flower of Cheshire society. The Fittons of Gawsworth were a solid gentry family that was to achieve great prominence in the following centuries until the last male member of the family died, appropriately enough, fighting for King Charles I in 1643.[46] In 1459, Thomas Fitton was a young squire who had just entered upon the estates of his grandfather without licence. Fitton was a tenant of lord Audley for part of that estate, and it is, therefore, no surprise to find him in Audley's army at Blore Heath.[47] The men who followed Fitton were drawn largely from Macclesfield from among his own relations and tenants. These men have long been known from the calendar of Cheshire recognizance rolls compiled by Mr Peter Turner and from Earwaker's version of the same entry on the recognizance rolls.[48] Unfortunately, both of these printed versions of the pardon are not only incomplete but misleading as well. The original document lists the social status as well as the provenance of all but one recipient. The printed versions ignore the first point which has only been noted by J.T. Driver in passing and not with complete accuracy.[49] The matter of provenance is included in the printed document only when the place of origin is spelled out; the frequent references to 'de eadem in eodem comitatu' in the entries which follow those that include specific place names have been ignored.

Sir Thomas was the only man of armigerous status included in the company, but an additional twenty men warranted the title of gentleman. Eight of these gentlemen were members of the Fitton family. Three of Sir Thomas' uncles and two of his brothers followed him to Blore Heath. All these men, save Thomas' brother Edward who had established himself at Peover, were from Gawsworth. In addition, three members of the Fittons of Pownall joined the company. The Fittons of Pownall were a junior branch of the family whose ties to the Fittons of Gawsworth had been reaffirmed by the marriage of John, son of John Fitton to Sir Thomas' aunt. This John was joined by his father and by his own brother in the host. Roger Davenport of Bramhall, another of the gentlemen in the Fitton contingent, had married another of Sir Thomas' aunts. Davenport was the eldest son of the family, but his father was still alive and in control of the family lands that included land held from the Stanley family.[50] The tie that brought four gentlemen of the Mainwaring family from Mobberly in Bucklow hundred into the fold is more obscure. Hugh Mainwaring, the father of two members of the army had been tied to Sir Thomas' father a decade earlier when the elder Fitton was a party to a recognizance for Hugh's appearance before the auditors of the duchy of Lancaster. One of Hugh's sons, Ralph, who with his brother served with Fitton, had also been involved in a 1446 recognizance to keep the peace with Adam Bostok as one of his sureties. Another Mainwaring gentleman also named Ralph who served with Sir Thomas had served on a 1449 commission of arrest with Thomas' grandfather, and there are other commissions yoking members of the two families.[51] The final Mainwaring gentleman, whose Christian name was unknown to Turner and Earwaker, was Robert. A close examination of the manuscript also yields the Christian name of Henry Stafford of Bothoms, Derbyshire, the only man not from Cheshire to serve with Fitton. The tie between Stafford and Fitton has not been discovered.

The remaining half dozen gentlemen were small fry indeed; they seem to have been tenants or dependants of the Fittons in Gawsworth, Sutton, Puddington and Capesthorne. Thomas Rode of Rode had earlier been associated with Thomas Fitton's grandfather and Ralph Mainwaring in a commission of arrest, and he may well have organized and commanded the ten-man contingent of yeomen from Rode that served under Fitton.[52] Edward Ward was a younger son of the Wards of Capesthorne who has no other claim to distinction.[53] The other gentlemen included two John Suttons from Sutton, Richard Mascy of Gawsworth and a Richard from Puddington whose last name has been lost due to a tear in the manuscript. These are hardly the stuff which one would expect to find among the Queen's gallants. Having been duly chastized for my own overly generous categorization of Cheshire gentry in the past, it is only the courtesy of the compiler of the pardon that supports these liverymen of the swan's claim to gentility.[54]

The bulk of Fitton's force was composed of yeomen who probably served as archers, yeomen bowmen. Twenty-six such yeomen were drawn from the Fittons' seat at Gawsworth, ten came from Rode and one each from Siddington, Sutton, Pownall and Eaton. The provenance of John, son of Richard de Kingsley, otherwise called John Nicson is not given; the compiler of the document seems to have tired of the man after such a long name. Nicson's status is also ignored by the compiler. Traditionalists interested in names will no doubt be reassured to learn that three members of the Stubbs family fought for Lancastrian constitutionalism with Thomas Fitton at Blore Heath; those of a more contemporary bent will be pleased to know that John Stede was also there to combat the foes of the crown. In terms of numbers, however, the Bosdons and the Passes with four men each lead the yeomen families. In fact one of the Bosdons, Thomas, was listed as a knave rather than a yeoman. Laurence Westbroke was listed as a cook, William Aynesworth as a miller, John Henshaw as a husbandman, Edmund Hordon of Bosley as a laborer and John Stede as a shepherd of some sort (qy? 'Falspie').[55] Such are the men who marched to Blore Heath.

Once again, however, the question is who marched home and who was carried home from the battlefield. Earwaker, basing his claim on the use of the term 'late' in Mr Turner's calendar argued that of 'those who accompanied Sir Thomas Fitton, of Gawsworth, to the field, no less than thirty-one were slain, a fact which bears witness to the severity of the fighting'.[56]

Turner, however, who had long misled historians about Richard II's Cheshire archers through his inconsistent citations of marginalia, was again capricious in his inclusion of 'late' (*nuper*) in his calendar entry.[57] In fact, including John Nicson, only seven men are not referred to as being 'late' of someplace. Two of these entries are consecutive as are three later ones. Thus, either the compiler was simply negligent in these few cases, or Fitton's contingent was wiped out. It is hard to believe that a group of dead yeomen carried such clout with the prince of Wales as to lead him to provide them with a posthumous pardon. When it is noted that an entry on the recognizance roll prior to the battle refers to Thomas Fitton 'late of Gawsworth', confidence in the demise of the parties so designated in the pardon is somewhat shaken.[58] Closer inspection of the pardon reveals that Fitton himself was referred to as one of the 'late of Gawsworth'. Among the yeomen so designated was Thomas Stubbs who later received a new pardon on 8 November 1478 as Thomas Stubbs, 'late of Gawsworth'.[59] '*Nuper*' would seem to mean no more than 'last known address' in these cases. Earwaker's casualty count, therefore, is even shakier than the evidence upon which it is based. Clearly, several members of the Fitton contingent did die; Blore Heath seems to have provided the Fitton family with a means of pruning unneeded younger males from the family tree. The extent of the carnage, however, cannot be stated with any precision.

Chroniclers and modern historians must be credited when they aver that Cheshire suffered losses at Blore Heath. The testimony of Margaret Troutbeck, the widow of Sir William Troutbeck who died with Audley and the sister of William Stanley who triumphed with Salisbury, confirms this. A patent of 26 April 1460 reads:

> On the complaint of Margaret, late wife of William Troutbeck, Kt., shewing that he held certain lands in Salop of the king by knight service, and was killed at Blore Heath, Co. Stafford, in the king's service, with James, lord of Audley, and because William was promoted of late to the order of knighthood at his no small costs and was afterwards killed with 100 persons and more and spoiled of horses, harness and other goods to the value of 400 *l.* and more, the king, considering the premises and that William has four children by her and that she cannot support them and has paid 100 *l.* to the treasurer of England for the wardship and marriage of William, son and heir of her husband, has granted to her the said wardship and marriage, and so from heir to heir.[60]

A sad tale, but also a unique tale on the record.

Troutbeck is one of only nine Cheshire gallants whose death at Blore Heath can be confirmed with any certainty. The vast majority of the yeomen who fought with Sir Thomas Fitton were of such low status that neither their lives nor their deaths have left any impression on the surviving records of the palatinate apart from their criminal adventures and the pardons they earned on St. Thecla's day. Thus, two conclusions are possible concerning the Queen's Cheshire gallants of the swan, conclusions that are by no means mutually exclusive. The impact of the battle upon the morbidity of the gallants of Cheshire society has been greatly exaggerated; many of the gallants of the swan simply took a dive! This is the first conclusion, and the second is like unto it. Contrary to much historical wisdom, the brunt of the casualties in this battle of the Wars of the Roses must have fallen more heavily on lesser men than on their leaders.[61] Audley died, but few other gentlefolk seem to have accompanied their commander on his last journey. If Cheshiremen died in great numbers at Deadman's Den, it was not the gallants of the swan, who seem to have flown from the field, who were to be found hallowing the Staffordshire earth.

ACKNOWLEDGEMENTS

I wish to thank the staffs of the Cleveland Public Library, the Widener Library, Harvard University, the Firestone Library, Princeton University and the Sydney Jones Library, The University of Liverpool for their cooperation. The photographic departments of the Newberry Library, The University of Wales and The Public Record Office also provided valuable assistance. Special thanks go to Miss Desiree Tango, for whom this paper is a swan song, for technical assistance with its production. That such fine support has not produced greater results lies with me. '*Parturiunt montes, Nascetur riduculus mus.*' Horace, *Ars Poetica*, 9.

NOTES

1   Michael Drayton, *Polyolbion*, 22; J.H. Hanshall, *The History of the County Palatine of Chester* (Chester, 1817) p.35; R. Brooke, *Visits to Fields of Battle in England* (London, 1857) p.21; M. A. Hookham, *The Life and Times of Margaret of Anjou*, 2 vols. (London, 1872), 2:51–52; J.P. Earwaker, *East Cheshire*, 2 vols. (London, 1877–1880), 2:2; J.T. Driver, *Cheshire in the Later Middle Ages* (Chester, 1971), p.18; cf. D.J. Clayton, 'The Involvement of the Gentry in Political, Administrative and Judicial Affairs of the County Palatine of Chester, 1442–1485,' (University of Liverpool Ph.D. thesis, 1980), pp. 111–112, a reference kindly provided me by Professor Ralph Griffiths at the 20th International Congress on Medieval Studies during the presentation of an earlier version of this paper.

2   H. Ellis, (ed.), *Hall's Chronicle* (London, 1809), p. 240; J.S. Davies, ed., *An English Chronicle of the Reigns of Richard II, Henry V and Henry VI*, Camden Society, old series, 64 (London, 1856), p. 80.

3   E.A. Thomas, 'The Lords Audley, 1391–1459,' (University of Wales M. A. dissertation, 1976), p. 19.

4   M.J. Bennett, "'Good Lords" and "Kingmakers": the Stanleys of Lathom', *History Today* Vol.
    31 (1981):14; R.A. Griffiths, *The Reign of King Henry VI* (Berkeley, 1981), pp. 820–21; A.
    Goodman, *The Wars of the Roses* (London, 1981), p. 201. My thanks to Dr. Bennett for
    sending me a copy of his article.

5   Cf. W. Snape, 'The Battle of Blore Heath in 1459,' *Gentleman's Magazine* 82 (1812): 602–605;
    W. Beamont, 'The Battle of Blore Heath,' *Journal of the Archaeological and Historic Society of
    Chester* 1 (1850): 81–100; Brooke, pp. 21-37; J.H. Ramsay, *Lancaster and York*, 2 vols.
    (London, 1892), 2:214–15; F.R. Twemlow, *The Battle of Blore Heath* (Wolverhampton,
    1912); A.H. Burne, *More Battlefields of England* (London, 1952), pp. 140–49; Thomas, pp.
    14–20; Clayton, pp. 107–108. Burne's account is the most convincing for the battle itself.

6   A.J. Pollard, 'The Northern retainers of Richard Neville, Earl of Salisbury,' *Northern History* 9
    (1976):57, 66–68.

7   *Rotuli Parliamentorum* 16 vols., (London, 1832), 5:369–70; Clayton, pp. 118–119; B. Coward,
    The Stanleys, Lords Stanley and Earls of Derby, 1385–1672, Chetham Society, 3rd. ser., 30
    (Manchester, 1983), pp. 9–10; Bennett, 'Good Lords,' p.14.

8   Goodman, p. 27.

9   Earwaker 2:603; E. Baines, *The History of the County Palatine and Duchy of Lancaster*, 2nd edn.,
    4 vols., (Manchester, 1836) 4:204; Twemlow, p. 36; *Victoria History of the Counties of England:
    Lancaster*, 8 vols. (London, 1906–1914), 3:69.

10 Twemlow, p. 37.

11 Goodman, p. 28.

12 Griffiths, p. 820; Thomas, pp. 46–66.

13 C(alendar) (of) P(atent) R(olls), 1452–1461, p. 595.

14 D. & S. Lysons, *Magna Britannia* (London, 1806–22), 2:308; Griffiths, pp. 777–790; B.P.
    Wolfe, *Henry VI* (London, 1981), pp. 316–17; cf. Clayton, p. 108 which raises doubts about
    the visit.

15 Beamont, p. 87; A. Strickland, *Lives of the Queens of England*, 3rd. edn., (London, 1864–65),
    3:293.

16 R. Stewart-Brown, *The Wapentake of Wirral* (Liverpool, 1907), pp. 60–63, 178; J.T. Driver p.
    14. If the example of my great-grandfather, William Davison of Birkenhead, who sought refuge
    in tzhe United States as a deserter from the thirteenth hussars is any indication, Wirral men
    were not the most reliable Cheshire soldiers.

17 J. Gairdner, ed., *Three Fifteenth-Century Chronicles*, Camden Society, 3rd. ser., 17 (London,
    1880), p. 204; G.L. Harriss, ed., 'John Benet's Chronicle,' *Camden Miscellany*, 24, Camden
    Society, 4th ser. 9 (London, 1972), p. 224; cf. Ralph Flenley, ed., *Six Town Chronicles of
    England* (Oxford, 1911), p. 147 n. 6.

18 G. Ormerod, *The History of the County Palatine and City of Chester*, T. Helsby, (ed.), 2nd edn.,
    3 vols, (London, 1882), 2:41; Brooke, p.26 n 2.

19 P(ublic) R(ecord) O(ffice) Chest. 3/45/9; :'Index to Inquisitions, etc. – Counties of Chester and
    Flint,' Twenty-Fifth Report of the Deputy Keeper of the Public Records (London, 1864), p.
    57.

20 Ormerod, 1st. edn. (London, 1819), 3:311; Beamont, p. 96; Hookham, 2:51 n. The error is
    corrected by Helsby, Ormerod, 3:598.

21 Earwaker, 2:75–76; British Library, Harleian Ms. 2151; Clayton, p. 115.

22 Beamont, pp. 96–97; Ormerod, 1:499, 649; 2:41, 133, 245, 623–24, 796; 3:192; Barnes,
    4:204; D. King, *The Vale Royal of England* (London, 1656), p. 99. for the Molineux tie to
    Cheshire see J.L. Gillespie, 'Thomas Mortimer and Thomas Molineux: Radcot Bridge and the
    Appeal of 1397,' *Albion* 7 (1975): 161–173.

23 C(alendar) (of) R(ecogizance) R(olls) (CRR) (of the Palatinate of Chester), Thirty-Seventh
    Report of the Deputy Keeper of Public Records (London, 1876), p. 231; Ormerod, 2:623.

24 CRR, pp. 65–66, 212.

25 Ormerod, 2:245; Thomas, pp. 91, 95.

26 CRR 117.

27 Ormerod, 2:133, 136; CRR p. 212.

28 Baines 4:204, 216; CRR p. 452.

29 PRO Chest 3/39/16, Hen.VI/5; Chest 3/43/31H.VI/6; Chest 3/45/38 H.VI/3; CRR pp. 65, 116, 212, 214, 235–37, 246–57, 721; 'Duchy of Lancaster: Calendar of Rolls of the Chancery of the County Palatine,' Thirty-Seventh Report of the Deputy Keeper of the Public records (London, 1876), p. 176.

30 CRR, p. 178.

31 J.L. Gillespie, 'Richard II's Cheshire Archers,' *Transactions of the Historic Society of Lancashire and Cheshire*, 125 (1975): 1–39; Driver, p. 17.

32 Griffiths, p. 820.

33 PRO Chest 38 Hen. VI. 15, 3/45/38 H. VI/1, 2, 4, 9; CRR pp. 213, 721. PRO Chest. 3/46/4 E. IV/4. This information is summarized in tabular form by Clayton, p. 115. Clayton does not, however, note the discrepancy in the date of Sir John Egerton's death.

34 PRO Chest 3/45/5.

35 'Index to Inquisitions, etc.,' pp. 32–60.

36 CRR, p. 238; cf. Clayton, p. 115.

37 CRR, p. 67; PRO Chest 3/48/1.

38 PRO Chest 3/53/2; CRR, p. 117; Clayton, p. 116.

39 PRO Chest 3/45/38 H. VI/3; Earwaker, 2:193.

40 'Duchy of Lancaster: Calendar of Rolls of the Chancery,' p. 176; *Victoria History*, 3:69 n.11.

41 '. . .et y furent prins le baron de Duclay et messire Thomas Fiderne. . ..' J. Waurin, *Recueil des Chroniques et Anchiennes Istories de la Grant Bretaigne*, ed. W. & E. Hardy, 5 vols. (London, 1864–91), 5:269.

42 CRR, p. 279.

43 Earwaker, 2:551.

44 PRO Chest 2/153 mm. 10–10d.

45 Clayton, pp. 116–117. For the details of the criminal activities of Fitton and his followers, see p. 117 nl. and the references cited therein.

46 Earwaker, 1:22; Cheshire society has received admirable treatment from M.J. Bennett, *Community, Class and Careerism* (Cambridge, 1983); Coward; and J.S. Morrill, *Cheshire 1630–1660* (Oxford, 1974).

47 CRR, pp. 279–80.

48 Earwaker, 2:2.

49 Driver, p. 18.

50 Ormerod, 3:824; Earwaker, 2:564.

51 CRR, pp. 497–98, 523.

52 CRR, p. 523.

53 Ormerod, 3:723; Earwaker, 2:408.

54 Cf. Bennett, *Community*, p. 210 n.65.

55 Cf. H. Kurath & S.A. Kuhn, *Middle English Dictionary* (Ann Arbor, 1956 –), 3:379.

56 Earwaker, 2:3.

57 Cf. Clayton, pp. 117–118; Gillespie, 'Richard II's Chester Archers,' p. 7.

58 CRR, pp. 278–279.

59 CRR, p. 693.

60 C.P.R., 1452–1461, p. 582.

61 I.e. C. Ross, *The Wars of the Roses* (London, 1976), p. 119; Goodman, pp. 200–201.

The Pre-episcopal Career of William Alnwick, Bishop of Norwich and Lincoln

ROSEMARY C.E. HAYES

William Alnwick was bishop of Norwich from 1426 to 1436 and bishop of Lincoln from 1436 until his death in 1449. His Norwich episcopate is probably best known for the heresy trials he conducted between 1428 and 1431[1] and for the disputes he had with the abbots of Bury St. Edmunds (William Curteys)[2] and St. Albans (John Whethamstede).[3] His Lincoln episcopate is remembered for his tireless visitations of religious houses[4] and for the long running dispute he had with John Macworth, the difficult dean of Lincoln Cathedral.[5] Visual reminders of his episcopates include parts of the West front of Norwich cathedral and the ruins of his episcopal palace at Lincoln.[6] Sadly, his tomb, by the West door of Lincoln cathedral, was destroyed during the Civil War and the wooden spires he had built on Lincoln cathedral's towers were brought down at the beginning of the nineteenth century.[7]

A number of general studies of the pre-episcopal careers of the English and Welsh bishops of the fifteenth century have appeared in the last twenty years, making it possible to judge, to some extent at least, how typical Alnwick was of the episcopate of the period. Lita-Rose Betcherman began the series with an article which laid great stress on the need to have been in royal service, and rather too much emphasis on the involvement of factions in the making of bishops.[8] This was followed by Joel T. Rosenthal's statistical examination which correlated the bishops' social backgrounds and education with their subsequent careers and promotions.[9] The most important contribution has come from Richard G. Davies who has studied both the pre and post episcopal careers of all the English and Welsh bishops of the period 1375–1443.[10] Of particular interest was his unravelling of the actual process of promotion. He illustrated the fact that, although the government's choice of bishop usually succeeded, the pope, whose position was never simply that of a rubber stamp, was sometimes able to impose his own will. One theme, for the period 1375–1443, brought out by Davies is the replacement, on the episcopal bench, of the old career civil servant (the last example seems to have been Thomas Langley) by the law graduate who had spent at least part of his career in ecclesiastical administration, particularly in the Canterbury province. He considers Alnwick something of a throwback to the old career civil servant[11] but, in fact, there is some indication that Alnwick had claims to be one of those who started their career working for the archbishop of Canterbury.[12] Finally, J.M. George Jr.[13] has shown how, during the personal rule of Henry VI, these law graduates gave way, to some extent, to men trained in theology, many of whom had served the king in a personal capacity as confessor.

William Alnwick's date of birth is unknown. It has been stated that he was thirty-eight (relatively young for a man of unknown origins) at the time of his promotion in 1426, thus suggesting 1388.[14] A birth date of around 1390 would seem to fit in with the fact that he became a bachelor of civil law, a degree that took ten years to achieve, in 1415. It is known that he came from Alnwick in Northumberland but neither the names nor social origins of his parents are known. Piero da Monte, papal collector in the 1430s, described him thus: '*rusticanus homo . . . . . . ex vili genere natus*'.[15] Some doubt may be thrown on this statement by the fact that Da Monte was a hostile witness as he was an associate of John Whethamstede, abbot of St. Albans, who carried out a lengthy dispute with Alnwick in the 1430's. Also, the letter in which he thus describes Alnwick is addressed to Pietro Barbo, for whom he was attempting, with difficulty, to secure collation to a Lincoln prebend from the bishop. Nevertheless, the very fact that nothing is known of Alnwick's family points to there being some truth in the allegation. It was not unusual for bishops of the period to be of lowly or unknown birth (other examples being Brouns, Lyndwood and Bubwith) but Alnwick did better than most in the wealth of the dioceses he attained. In contrast to the general agreement on the lowliness of Alnwick's birth, A.F. Leach[16] claims that Alnwick was a Percy, brother of the earl of Northumberland. However, this statement seems to have arisen from a misreading of the foundation records of a chantry founded at Alnwick in 1448 by Bishop Alnwick and members of the Percy family.

Alnwick has been identified with several people:[17] a Premonstratensian canon of Alnwick who was involved in the 1407 rebellion; a Benedictine monk of St. Albans, 1428 to c.1434, and prior of Belvoir, 1435; and the recluse of Westminster who became first confessor general of the Bridgettines of Twickenham, c.1416 to c.1418. However, it is quite wrong to identify any of these men with the secular clerk who was to become the bishop and, indeed, simultaneous appearances make it impossible.

Possible relatives include, apart from the men of the same name with whom he has been misidentified, a John Alnwick to whom he acted as patron after he became bishop.[18] His only identifiable relative was a niece, Agnes,[19] who married a Richard Hayton, had a daughter and predeceased Alnwick. Perhaps her husband was the Richard Hayton, coroner of York, who died in 1421.[20] Another possible connection is William Hayton, a clerk of the signet while Alnwick was king's secretary and later secretary himself. (It may be more than coincidence that he left office as secretary at about the same time as Alnwick resigned the privy seal.)[21]

Nothing is known of Alnwick's very early life and education. He made bequests in his will to the parish church of Alnwick, the abbot and convent of Premonstratensian canons of Alnwick and the Carmelite friars of Hulne (three miles away). Perhaps one of these provided his earliest education. He was one of several clerics who seem to have owed early advances to more senior churchmen (other examples are John Kemp, Spofford and Brouns who were patronised, respectively, by Chichele, Beaufort and Repingdon). It is evident that he considered he owed much to Stephen Scrope, archdeacon of Richmond and nephew of the executed archbishop of York. In his will, he established a five year chantry 'for my soul and the soul of Master Stephen le Scrope, sometime archdeacon of Richmond, and the souls of the faithful departed'. When Scrope died, in 1418, Alnwick was an executor of his will and was bequeathed 'i flatt *pecia de auro cooperto*', one silver-covered salt-cellar bearing Scrope's arms, two books outright and four books for his lifetime which were to go to York Minster library after his death.[22]

The first certain notice we have of Alnwick reflects Scrope's patronage. On 7 July 1411, William Alnewyk, unmarried clerk of the diocese of Durham, was appointed papal notary under faculty of the archdeacon of Richmond.[23] Three weeks later, on 28 July, we find him exercising this office in drawing up the instrument of resignation of a church in the Durham diocese.[24] This establishes an early connection with Thomas Langley, bishop of Durham, with whom Alnwick was to serve for many years on the minority council of Henry VI. Langley may well have played a part in advancing the careet of his fellow Northerner. Later, in 1428, the two were to join with a John Hore of Childerley, Cambridgeshire, in founding a hostel at Cambridge for Benedictine students from Croyland. This was later called Buckingham College and developed into Magdalene College.[25] When Langley died, in 1437, Alnwick was an executor, and beneficiary, of his will.[26]

By 1411, Alnwick had probably commenced his studies at Cambridge, and it seems likely that it was Scrope, who was chancellor of the university in 1414, who enabled him to pursue his education there. The first benefice Alnwick is known to have received was Goldsborough which was situated in Scrope's archdeaconry. There is no record of his institution there but, on 3 April 1415, he was granted leave of absence from the church, for five years, to pursue his studies at an English university.[27] Alnwick was not even ordained as an acolyte until 21 December 1415[28] so his institution at Goldsborough was uncononical to say the least. This indicated a less refined ecclesiastical conscience than he was later to display and, more importantly perhaps, that he was a clerical high flier.

While it would be wrong to state that any cleric (except perhaps for those from the noblest families) had his eye on the episcopate from the start of his career, the majority of those who achieved this position started with a training in law, and Alnwick was no exception. He was a bachelor of civil law by 1415, a licenciate by 1417 and a doctor by 1419.[29] At the same time, he advanced through holy orders, being ordained subdeacon, on 14 March 1416,[30] and deacon on 21 May 1418.[31]

Alnwick's Cambridge career does not seem to have been entirely peaceful. On 20 June 1415, the chancellor of the university, and the mayor and sheriff, were ordered to arrest him, together with William Buckworth, Robert Berkford, John Nowell and Roger Strangwys, and bring them before the king in chancery with all speed.[32] No reason is given for this commission of arrest and Emden is unable to give any information about Alnwick's fellow students. However, in May, a writ had been issued requiring the university's chancellor to provide the royal chancery with the names of scholars in canon and civil law failing to attend the law schools and pay the proper fees.[33] Perhaps Alnwick and his companions had been among the names submitted. Whatever the reason for his arrest, Alnwick cannot have been under a cloud for long for, in about 1418, Cambridge town chose him as one of two arbitrators to settle a vehement dispute between it and the university.[34]

Before this date, William Alnwick had come, by some means, to the attention of Henry Chichele, archbishop of Canterbury. On 23 February 1416, the archbishop commissioned Alnwick, together with William Bukkeworth (surely the same as the Buckworth arrested with him), bachelor of canon law, and John Cok, rector of the parish church of Lavenham, to prove the will of Richard, earl of Oxford, which they did sitting in the Cambridge parish church of St. John and sealing the instrument with '*sigillum officialitatis Eliensis, quod ego Willelmus Alnewyk predictus ad manus habeo*'.[35] A few months later, the archbishop again commissioned Alnwick, this time with John Judde, doctor of canon law, to hear and determine a dispute over a will in the Ely diocese.[36] There is no more direct evidence of Chichele using Alnwick in diocesan or provincial administration before he entered royal service, but, on 20 December 1419, Alnwick was instituted, by the archbishop's collation, to the rectory of Hollingbourne, Kent.[37] This rectory, which had a perpetual vicar, was, according to E.F. Jacob, one of the parishes, exempt from the archdeacon, which the archbishop used to maintain and reward his legal friends and assistants.[38] This collation is perhaps evidence that Alnwick was more closely connected with the archbishop and his administration than has hitherto been supposed and that he belongs to the group of bishops (notably John Kemp, Stafford, Lyndwood and Bekynton) who benefited from early patronage by the archiepiscopal see. There is no record of Alnwick's ordination to the priesthood, but perhaps Chichele saw that he had been properly ordained before collating him.[39] A further sign of the archbishop's patronage *may* be the institution, in 1418, of a William Alnwick to the rectory of Goodnestone next to Faversham, at the presentation of Thomas Chicche esquire.[40] However, as this William Alnwick is only described as chaplain, not licenciate of civil law, and the next rector was instituted in succession to John Alnwick,[41] it would perhaps be dangerous to identify the rector of Goodnestone with the future bishop.

However important service to the archbishop of Canterbury was for the early promotion of rising clerks, most fifteenth century bishops owed their eventual promotion to work for the crown. Like many others, Alnwick's pre-episcopal career is most noted for his royal service. It is not known how he came to the attention of Henry V, perhaps through the Cambridge disputes, perhaps through Chichele. There may even have been some connection through Richard Caudray, his near-contemporary at Cambridge, who was scribe of the archbishop's court of audience in 1414–15, engaged in the French negotiations in 1419 and king's secretary in 1420.[42] However he came to the king's notice, Alnwick was in France and one of those appointed, on 7 July 1420, to treat with the ambassadors of the duke of Brittany for correction of the abuses of the truce.[43] This was the first of several diplomatic commissions for Alnwick. It may be that it was his training in civil law, a common qualification for diplomatic service, which attracted him to the king's attention. On 5 December 1420, he was appointed to array several retinues.[44] Two days later, he was collated to the archdeaconry of Salisbury by Bishop Chaundler of Salisbury.[45] This archdeaconry was the first major benefice to fall to him and, as no connection with Chaundler has been established, Alnwick probably owed it to his royal service (or possibly to Chichele who had great connections with Salisbury). There is little evidence that Alnwick treated his archdeaconry as much more than a sinecure and, indeed, his absence in France over the next two years would have precluded any official activity even if he had felt so inclined.[46] On 5 January 1421, Alnwick's diplomatic experience was extended by his appointment, with John Saint John, mayor of Bordeaux, to negotiate with the ambassadors of Charles lord de la Bret and Francis lord of S. Basile. These negotiations resulted in the latter two renouncing the appeal made to the French court by Amanen lord de la Bret and doing homage to Henry V.[47]

Henry V was in England between 1 February and 11 June 1421 and William Alnwick accompanied him.[48] He may have been the king's secretary as early as 15 April when he assisted, in Henry's presence, at

Lincoln, in the arbitration by Fleming, bishop of Lincoln, between the dean and chapter of the cathedral.[49] He was certainly secretary by 1 May when he was commissioned with Philip Morgan, bishop of Worcester, and John Stafford, the keeper of the privy seal, to treat with Genoese ambassadors.[50] Because of the personal nature of the appointment, acheived merely by the handing over of the signet, it is very difficult to date kings' secretaries accurately. The latest mention for Richard Caudray, his predecessor, is dated 2 June 1420,[51] and Alnwick may have been appointed at any time after that. Whenever it came, the appointment was a sure sign of royal favour.[52]

The signet, which was very much the king's personal instrument, was still viewed with suspicion as an instrument of warranty, only fully acceptable in the privy seal office. However, Henry's absence in France, especially after June 1421 when he left the privy seal behind, increased the importance of the signet. It then became, in the absence of the privy seal, the natural instrument for communicating with the administration in England. It was used for issuing warrants not only to the privy seal office but also to the chancery for letters of minor importance. On at least one occasion, even the exchequer was ordered to accept warrants sealed under it.[53] The secretary was also responsible for the issue of the king's private letters and some minor diplomatic correspondence.

There is no evidence that Alnwick, as secretary, received a fixed salary or livery from the great wardrobe although he did receive five measures of scarlet cloth for Queen Katherine's coronation.[54] Otherwise, he probably had to make do with the fees of the office[55] and with the benefices that came to him as a royal clerk. While he was acting as secretary, Alnwick was collated[56] to the York prebend of Knaresborough-cum-Bickhill which Stephen Scrope had held at the time of his death[57] and which Alnwick continued to hold until his promotion to the episcopate.[58] He also received from the king the prebend of Gauray in the cathedral of Bayeux.[59]

While in England with the king, Alnwick attended the council meeting at Lambeth, on 6 May 1421, in which a statement was made to Henry of the revenues and expenditure of the kingdom. This marks his first appearance in the records of the king's council.[60] He also seems to have taken part in the assembly which met at Westminster, on the next day, to discuss the reform of the Benedictine order.[61] On 22 May 1421, he was appointed, with Bishop Edmund Lacy of Exeter, Sir John Colville and Master John Stokes, doctor of laws, to redress infractions of the truce with Brittany.[62] Alnwick returned to France with the king and was perhaps responsible for drawing up Henry's will, at Dover, before they embarked.[63]

An entry in the patent rolls for 1424 describes William Alnwick as having been both secretary and confessor to Henry V.[64] It may have been to assist him in carrying out the latter responsibilities that he received a papal indult for a portable altar, on 15 March 1422.[65] On the same date, John Stopyndon was addressed as king's secretary in a papal letter.[66] This is the only evidence that Alnwick was replaced and is possibly a mistake of the papal chancery. Stopyndon may have been a clerk of the signet. It is likely that Alnwick continued as secretary until the king's death. He was in attendance when Henry died, on 31 August 1422,[67] and returned to England by 5 November in time for the burial and formal reading of the will on the 7th.[68]

The first Parliament of the new reign lasted from 9 November to 18 December 1422.[69] Alnwick attended its sessions and handed over draft letters patent, approved by the king before his death, on behalf of the priory of Ivychurch in the Salisbury diocese.[70] Although he was not one of those appointed to the minority council on 9 December,[71] a place was soon found for him in the royal administration. William Kinwolmersh, who had been reappointed treasurer, died before the Parliament closed[72] and, at the council meeting of 16 December, it was decided that John Stafford should replace him as treasurer and that Alnwick would replace Stafford as keeper of the privy seal.[73] As a former king's secretary, a post which worked closely with the privy seal office, Alnwick was the natural choice, and was, in fact, only one of a number of men (including Nicholas Bubwith and Thomas Bekynton) who progressed from one office to the other in the period. He was to retain his new office until 1432 when he was replaced by his secondary, William Lyndwood.[74]

The keeper of the privy seal was one of the three major administrative offices.[75] While its position was obviously inferior to that of the chancellor or treasurer, the office was of particular importance during the minority of Henry VI. The privy seal was the principal instrument of the minority council, being used to communicate with the chancery, exchequer and numerous lesser offices. It was also used for sealing correspondence not requiring the use of the great seal, diplomatic correspondence being of particular importance. The close connection between the council and the privy seal office is reflected in the fact that the clerk of the council wa usually a privy seal clerk. In the early years of the minority this was Richard Caudray, Alnwick's Cambridge contemporary and predecessor as Henry V's secretary. The keeper's own executive authority was strictly limited to certain routine matters. However, as an ex-officio member of the council, he was in a position of some influence.

The regularity of Alnwick's attendance at the council can, to a certain extent, be traced through its records.[76] There are records for 294 dates on which the council met in the first four years of Henry VI's reign (i.e. between September 1422 and August 1426). For 87 of these dates (30%) there is no complete indication of attendance. There is a record of attendance for 210 dates.[77] On 127 of these days, when meetings were held at one location, Alnwick's presence was recorded. On 8 days he attended meetings at more than one location and on 6 days he was present at one location and absent at another. Thus his presence was recorded on 141 out of the 210 days, or 67% of the time. However, of the 69 days on which his presence was not recorded, there was only one date, 2 June 1426, when his absence was actually noted.[78] 35 days (mainly in 4 Henry VI) are occasions when the only evidence of attendance is signatures on the front of a council document. These signatures cannot be taken as a complete record of attendance. In fact, on six occasions when his signature does not appear (3, 4 and 6 July and 18 November 1424, and 25 and 26 July 1426)[79] other evidence confirms his presence. Indeed, a council document of 3 July, 1424, does not contain his signature on the front although on the dorse he is said to have been present.[80] On 4 July 1424, it had been decided that in passing their bills 'the names of thassenters be writen of their own hand'[81] and this is, presumably, what these signatures represent. However, there are remarkably few documents that Alnwick has signed. If his absence from the signatures does not denote his absence from council meetings, it seems unlikely that he dissented from almost all decisions made during this period. Was the keeper of the privy seal's assent perhaps assumed – an assumption that would have been strengthened by the fact that the instruments used to further the council's decision were usually sealed with the privy seal? Perhaps the keeper was regarded merely as an executive rather than advisory member of the council. Despite these difficulties, it is clear that Alnwick regularly attended council and may well have exercised a steady if not outstanding influence over its actions.[82]

Alnwick's service to the minority government was not confined to his work in the privy seal office and attendance on the council. The diplomatic work he had begun for Henry V was continued. On 3 December 1423, he was commissioned with Philip Morgan, bishop of Worcester, John Stafford, treasurer, Ralph Lord Cromwell, Sir John Pelham, knight, Robert Waterton, esq., and John Stokes, D.C.L., to treat with Scottish ambassadors regarding the liberation of James, king of Scotland.[83] On 14 February 1424, he was appointed one of the embassy, led by John Kemp, bishop of London, which met the Scottish king and ambassadors in Durham, concluding a truce on 28 March.[84] On 14 July 1425, he was appointed, with the bishop of Durham, Lord Cromwell, John le Scrope, Robert Umfreville and William Haryngton, to meet Scottish commissioners at Berwick, on 15 August, to redress infractions of this truce.[85]

In addition, on three occasions, between December 1423 and June 1426, he served on commissions to hear appeals from the court of

Admiralty, thus utilising his legal training.[86] He attended Parliament where he acted as proctor for Archbishop Bowet of York, in September 1423, and Bishop Spofford of Hereford, in April 1425.[87] He was one of the lords of the council who made loans to the king, on 3 March 1425.[88] His loan of 100 marks was the smallest made, compared with the greatest, 1,000 marks from Chichele, and the second smallest, 200 from Stafford. This is perhaps a reflection of the fact that he was the only member of council who did not receive payment for attendance, receiving no more than his 20s a day salary as keeper of the privy seal.[89]

It has been stated that Alnwick was the young king's confessor by May 1424.[90] Davies considers it odd that a civil lawyer in the service of the royal administration should have held this post, and, in fact, it is not certain that he did, at least at this early date. The evidence most commonly cited is the patent roll entry, for 16 May 1424, which in fact states that Alnwick *had been* Henry V's confessor.[91] A George Arthurton seems to have been Henry VI's confessor at this date.[92] The only source which describes Alnwick as the king's confessor before his promotion to Norwich is a chronology of the bishops of Ely.[93] This cannot have been composed before Bishop Morgan's death in 1435, by which time Alnwick did hold the post,[94] so it is possible that the chronicler was mistaken as to date. There is not much evidence that Henry VI had any particular affection for Alnwick, such as he showed to some of his other confessors, although, later, the bishop was to cooperate enthusiastically with Henry's educational foundations.

Alnwick's duties as a royal official and member of the council cannot have left him with much time to devote to the ecclesiastical administration with which he had started his career. On the same day that he was appointed keeper of the privy seal he was granted, for life, the wardenship of the hospital of St. James by Westminster.[95] There is no evidence that he treated this office as anything more than a sinecure, a fate that seems to have been suffered by several of the London hospitals at this time. As bishop of Norwich he used the hospital quite often as his London base, and it may have been at his instance, and would, surely, have been with his consent, that its lands were granted to the newly founded college of Eton in 1449.[96] The one instance we have of his using the hospital before his promotion was on 4 February 1426, when, acting on Chichele's behalf, he oversaw the probate of the will of John Fordham, bishop of Ely.[97] Another notable will, that of Richard Whittington, was proved before him and William Lynwood, acting as the archbishop's commissaries, on 21 April 1423.[98]

It was perhaps Alnwick's respect for Chichele which prompted his presence in the Salisbury diocese during the archbishop's metropolitical visitation in the autumn of 1423. On 30 September, again on 7 October,

Alnwick personally inducted rectors into their parishes.[99] It is not known whether this was all he did as archdeacon but it is at least indicative that he was slightly more conscientious than he has previously been given credit for. In November of the same year, he was again involved in the dispute between Dean Macworth and the chapter of Lincoln cathedral when he was mandated by the pope to confirm part of the agreement made between the dean and chapter.[100] This involvement was probably of assistance when, after his promotion to Lincoln, he came himself to tackle the dean.

From the time of his collation to the archdeaconry of Salisbury, in December 1420, Alnwick would have been required to attend the convocation of the southern province of the English church. However, it is perhaps significant of the fact that his main attention was given to royal rather than ecclesiastical service that the only mention of him in the records of convocation, before he became bishop of Norwich, is of his coming, with other members of the king's council, to the convocation of 12 October 1424 – 17 February 1425, to appeal, unsuccessfully, for a 'notable subsidy'.[101]

Indeed, although it seems that his service to the church was not as neglibible as has hitherto been presumed, it would be wrong to suppose that his promotion to the episcopate resulted directly from anything other than his royal service.[102] As keeper of the privy seal, he was an obvious candidate for promotion. Only one keeper, during the period, John Prophete, failed to attain the episcopate and so, after Alnwick's appointment to the privy seal, it was not unlikely that he would be a candidate in the event of a suitable vacancy.[103]

The events leading up to Alnwick's promotion are complicated.[104] On 20 October 1423, Archbishop Bowet of York died. The council's choice to succeed him was Bishop Philip Morgan of Worcester,[105] and they chose John Stafford (the treasurer, and therefore one ahead of Alnwick in the queue for the episcopacy) to succeed Morgan. However, the pope, Martin V, provided Bishop Fleming of Lincoln to York. Fleming was 'persuaded' to stand down by the council.[106] During the ensuing deadlock, on 24 October 1424, Bishop Bubwith of Bath and Wells died. The council wrote to the pope officially nominating Stafford for this see, at the same time suggesting Alnwick for the Worcester diocese.[107] Stafford was duly provided to Bath and Wells.[108] On promotion he would have vacated his position as dean of St Martin's le Grand, a very valuable benefice in the king's gift and Alnwick succeeded him to this dignity.[109]

Meanwhile, there was continued difficulty over the archbishopric of York, which was only resolved after negotiations between the duke of Bedford and Martin V. These negotiations eventually resulted in the translation of Bishop Kemp of London to York[110] and the provision of

William Gray to London. The death of John Wakering, bishop of Norwich, on 9 April 1425,[111] was followed, on 19 November, by that of Bishop Fordham of Ely. The council urged the monks of Ely to elect Alnwick but they chose their prior instead.[112] This was unacceptable to the council which met, on 14 January 1426, with Bedford who had returned from France.[113] It was resolved to confirm Kemp at York and to ask the pope to provide Morgan to Ely, unless he had already been provided to Norwich, and Alnwick to Norwich unless he had already been provided to Ely in response to the council's earlier letters. Martin produced the required letters of provision on 27 February. Alnwick received the temporalities on 4 May and was consecrated by Archbishop Chichele at Canterbury on 18 August.[114]

Betcherman sees the disputed succession to York as an expression of factions on the council. She suggests that Chichele and the duke of Gloucester were supporting Morgan against Bishop Beaufort and the pope for Fleming, with the duke of Bedford successfully intervening on behalf of his own candidate, Bishop Kemp. She continues: 'Ely and Norwich, both 'fat' sees, were reserved for the Gloucester–Chichele forces. They went to Philip Morgan the disappointed candidate for York and William Alnwick, a partisan of theirs whose reward as keeper of the privy seal was overdue'.[115]

Was Alnwick's promotion due to his connection with a faction? He certainly seems to have been attached to Chichele but it is at least doubtful that Chichele was part of a Gloucester faction and it is even more difficult to establish a link between Gloucester and Alnwick. Certainly, in later years, any connection there may have been between Gloucester and Alnwick seems to hav disappeared. Gloucester supported the abbots of St. Albans and Bury St Edmunds in their attempts to preserve their exemption from the jurisdiction of Alnwick as bishop,[116] and Alnwick was one of those who tried Gloucester's wife for witchcraft.[117] In fact, there are more indications to link him with the Beauforts. Alnwick was a supervisor of the will of Thomas, duke of Exeter in 1427,[118] and the processional cross that he gave to Lincoln cathedral was engraved 'orate pro animabus domini Thome Bewford, etc.'[119] It is possible that he was friendly with Marmaduke Lumley, a fellow Cambridge graduate of the Durham diocese, who was related to the Beauforts and at whose consecration he assisted.[120] As bishop of Norwich, he was to patronise William Ayscough, later bishop of Salisbury, who has been identified with a Beaufort–Suffolk party.[121] Other close associates seem to have been Thomas Langley, bishop of Durham,[122] and Ralph Lord Cromwell.[123] In fact, there is not much to prove that Alnwick was particularly attached to either a Beaufort or a Gloucester faction. He was present at the council meeting, of 26 February 1425, which decided to hand over the Tower of London to

Richard Woodville, the act that seems to have done most to provoke Gloucester's fury against Beaufort.[124] However, he was also one of the arbitrators between Beaufort and Gloucester, in March 1426,[125] and he did not lose his position as keeper of the privy seal when Beaufort and Stafford lost theirs as chancellor and treasurer.[126] Indeed, it is far more likely that, rather than being a member of any particular faction, Alnwick was, as Griffiths states, one of 'a solid core of devoted servants of Henry V who continued to protect the fortunes of his son'[127] and that his connection with the duke of Exeter arose out of this rather than any attachment to the bishop of Winchester.

In fact, William Alnwick, with his legal training, early experience in ecclesiastical administration and history of royal service, was a natural candidate for promotion. He had had little time since his entry into the royal administration to devote his abilities to ecclesiastical service, but there are interesting pointers to his career as bishop: notably his involvement in Henry V's campaign to reform the Benedictines and the attempts to reconcile Dean Macworth with the Lincoln chapter. Perhaps the best indication for the future was the conscientious reliability that he seems to have displayed as king's secretary, keeper of the privy seal and member of the minority council. Henceforth this was to be directed mainly to the administration of his bishoprics and the service of the Church.

ABBREVIATIONS

BRUC	A.B. Emden, *A Biographical Register of the University of Cambridge to 1500*, Cambridge (1963).
BRUO	A.B. Emden, *A Biographical Register of the University of Oxford to 1500*, 3 vols, Oxford (1957–9)
CCR	*Calendar of Close Rolls*
CPL	Ed. W.H. Bliss and J.A. Twemlow, *Calendar of Entries In the Papal Registers Relating to Great Britain and Ireland: Papal Letters (1198–1492)*, 14 vols, H.M.S.O. (1893–1960).
CPR	*Calendar of Patent Rolls*
Foedera	Ed. T. Rymer, *Foedera, Conventiones, Litterae, Et Cujuscunque Generis Acta Publica Inter Reges Angliae Et Alios Quosvis Imperatores, Reges, Pontifices, Principes Vel Communitates (1101–1654)* 3rd edition, 10 vols, The Hague (1739–45).
HBC	Ed. F.M. Powicke, *Handbook of British Chronology*, 2nd edition (1961).
POPC	Ed. N.H. Nicolas, *Proceedings and Ordinances of the Privy Council of England (1386–1542)*, 7 vols (1834–7).

Reg.   Ed. E.F. Jacob, *Register of Henry Chichele, Archbishop of*
Chichele   *Canterbury 1414–43*, 4 vols, Canterbury and York Society,
              Oxford, XLII, XLV, XLVI, XLVII (1937, 1943, 1945
              1947).

RP   Record Commissioners (ed. J. Strachey), *Rotuli Parlia-*
              mentorum: ut et petitiones et placita in parliamento, 7 vols
              (1832).

NOTES

1   The records of these were edited by N.P. Tanner as *Heresy Trials In the Diocese of Norwich,*
    1428–31, Camden Society, Fourth Series, XX (1977). The trials were, incorrectly,
    attributed to Alnwick's predecessor, John Wakering, by F. Blomefield, *An Essay Towards A*
    Topographical History of the County Of Norfolk, III (1806, second edition), 140–1, 530.

2   Discussed by J.W. Elston, 'William Curteys, Abbot of Bury St. Edmunds 1429–1446',
    unpublished Ph.D. thesis, University of California, Berkeley (1979), 340–59.

3   J. Amundesham, *Annales Monasterii Sancti Albani*, ed. H.T. Riley, Rolls Series, 2 Parts
    (1870–1), Part II, I, 300–69.

4   Ed. A. Hamilton Thompson, *Visitations of Religious Houses in the Diocese of Lincoln 1436 to*
    1449, Canterbury and York Society, XXIV, XXXIII (1919 and 1927).

5   A. Hamilton Thompson, *The English Clergy and Their Organisation in the Later Middle Ages*,
    Oxford (1947), 90–7; ed. H. Bradshaw and C. Wordsworth, *Statutes of Lincoln Cathedral*, 2
    parts in 3 volumes, Cambridge, Part I (1892), 401–8, Part II (1897), *passim*.

6   Blomefield, *op.cit.*, III, 531–2; A. Hamilton Thompson, *Visitations, ut supra.*, XXIV, xxiii.

7   T. Allen, *The History of the County of Lincoln, From the Earliest Period to the Present Time*
    (1834), 160.

8   'The Making of Bishops in the Lancastrian Period', *Speculum*, XLI (1966), 397–419.

9   'The Training of an Elite Group: English Bishops in the Fifteenth Century', *Transactions Of*
    The American Philosophical Society, New Series, LX, Part 5, Philadelphia (1970).

10 'The Episcopate in England and Wales, 1375–1443', unpublished Ph.D. thesis, University of
    Manchester (1974); 'The Episcopate' in *Profession, Vocation and Culture in Later Medieval*
    England. Essays Dedicated to the Memory of A.R. Myers, ed. C.H. Clough, Liverpool (1982),
    51–89.

11 *Ibid*, 64.

12 See below, 5–6.

13 'The Episcopate and the Crown, 1437–50', unpublished Ph.D.thesis, Columbia University
    (1976).

14 *Ibid*, 44. George cites no authority for this statement.

15 J. Haller, *Piero Da Monte: Ein Gelehrter Und Papstlicher Beamter Des 15 Jahr I Iunderts*, Rome
    (1941), 74.

16 A.F. Leach, *The Schools of Medieval England* (1915), 269.

17 These misidentifications are discussed by A. Hamilton Thompson in *Visitations, ut supra*,
    XXIV, xv–xviii, and by D. Knowles in *The Religious Orders in England*, 3 volumes, Cambridge
    (1948–59), II, 367–8.

18 *BRUO*, I, 27.

19 She is mentioned in his will, Lambeth Palace Library: Register John Stafford (Canterbury),
    fos. 178d–179d, translated in Hamilton Thompson, *Visitations, ut supra*, XXIV, xxiv–xxx.

20 *CCR, 1419–22*, 177.

21 J. Otway-Ruthven, *The King's Secretary and the Signet office in the Fifteenth Century*, Cambridge (1939), 13–4 and *passim*.

22 *Testamenta Eboracensia*, I, Surtees Society (1936), 385–9.

23 *CPL*, VI, 333.

24 Ed. R.L. Storey, *The Register of Thomas Langley, Bishop Of Durham, 1406–37*, Surtees Society, CLXIV (1949), 160–1.

25 *CPR, 1422–9*, 475; C.H. Cooper, *Annals of Cambridge* I, Cambridge (1842), 178–9.

26 *Historiae Dunelmensis Scriptores Tres*, Surtees Society, IX (1839), ccxli–cclvii.

27 Borthwick Institute: Reg. 18: Register Henry Bowet (York), I, fo. 267. His estate as rector of Goldsborough was ratified on 25 March 1419 (*CPR, 1416–22*, 214) and he had resigned the benefice by 30 July 1421 (Ed. A. Hamilton Thompson, 'The Registers of the Archdeaconry of Richmond, 1361–1442, From the Abstract Made by Matthew Hutton (BM Ms Harl 6978)', *The Yorkshire Archaeological Journal*, XXV (1920), 205).

28 Cambridge University Library: Ely Diocesan Records: G/I/3: Register John Fordham (Ely), fo. 265.

29 *BRUC*, 11.

30 Guildhall Library: Ms 9531/4: Register Richard Clifford (London), fo. 76.

31 Register Fordham (Ely), *ut supra*, fo 269v.

32 *CPR, 1413–16*, 347. There are a number of similar commissions in the patent rolls at the time.

33 C.H. Cooper, *op. cit.*, I, 157.

34 *Ibid*, I, 162.

35 *Reg. Chichele*, II, 116–8. Was it by chance that this seal was at hand or was Alnwick involved in the administration of the diocese of Ely?

36 21 November 1416 (*Ibid*, IV, 41). – Judde was the bishop of Ely's official (Register Fordham (Ely) *ut supra*, fos. 149, 165, 201).

37 *Ibid*, I, 176.

38 *Ibid*, I, lxxvii. Alnwick had resigned the rectory by 24 May 1421. (*Ibid*, I, 199).

39 Bishop Fordham's Ely register (*ut supra*) contains no record of ordinations between September 1419 (fo. 272v) and December 1420 (fo. 107v), and it is possible that Alnwick was ordained priest in the Ely diocese during this period.

40 5 February 1418. (*Ibid*, I, 166).

41 16 December 1420. (*Ibid*, I, 196).

42 *BRUC*, 127.

43 *Reports of the Deputy keeper of the Public Records*, XLII (1881), 375. Among other clerical diplomats were bishops John Kemp, Morgan, Stafford, Lyndwood, Brouns, Bekynton and Moleyns.

44 *Ibid*, 393.

45 Wiltshire County Record Office: D1/2/8: Register John Chaundler (Salisbury), part I, fo. 40v. Richard Gourley was instituted as his proxy. Alnwick received papal dispensation to hold an incompatible benefice with the archdeaconry, on 4 May 1421 (*CPL*, VII, 205). The archdeaconry was valued at not more than 100 marks. He succeeded John Stafford to this dignity as, indeed, he was to succeed him to both the keepership of the Privy Seal and the deanery of St. Martin le Grand. See below.

46 Almost all the mandates for induction addressed to the archdeacon of Salisbury are also addressed to his official, a post already in existence when John Stafford was archdeacon. This seems to indicate that an absentee archdeacon was not unusual. (Register Chaundler (Salisbury), *ut supra*, *passim*.)

47 *Foedera*, IV, III, 197–9.

48 A.L. Brown, 'The Privy Seal In The Early Fifteenth Century', unpublished D.Phil. thesis, University of Oxford (1955), 106.

49 *CPR, 1416–22*, 404–6.

50 *Foedera*, IV, IV, 28–30.

51 Ed. J.L. Kirby, *Calendar of Signet Letters of Henry IV and Henry V (1399)–1422)* (1978), xii.

52 Bubwith and Bekynton were among other royal secretaries who went on to become bishops. For general discussion on the office of king's secretary which follows, see Otway-Ruthven, *op. cit.*, *passim*; A.L. Brown, *op. cit.*, *passim*.

53 On 27 November 1421, Henry sent a letter under the privy seal to the treasurer and barons of the exchequer ordering them to allow signet letters and chamberlain's bills in the account of the keeper of the great wardrobe. (PRO: Memoranda Rolls, E159: 2 Henry VI, Hilary rot. 29.)

54 PRO: Great Wardrobe Accounts, E101/407/4: 9 Henry V, fo. 36d.

55 The fee was 6s 8d per signet letter. (Otway-Ruthven, *op. cit.*, 84.)

56 3 May 1421. (Register Henry Bowet (York), *ut supra*, I, fo. 72.)

57 *Ibid*, fo. 61v.

58 *CPL*, VII, 17.

59 *Foedera*, IV, IV, 49. Not Bayonne as Otway-Ruthven (*op. cit.*, 170) states.

60 *POPC*, II, 315.

61 PRO: Exchequer K.R. Ecclesiastical Documents, E135/1/2. This meeting may have influenced him when he later came to inspect the religious houses in his diocese.

62 *Reports of the Deputy Keeper of the Public Records*, XLIV, 626; or 21 May (*Foedera*, IV, IV, 27).

63 10 June 1421 (B.P. Wolffe, *Henry VI* (1981), 29). The will was supplemented by codicils, also probably drawn up by Alnwick, late in August 1422.

64 *CPR, 1422–9*, 226. (Original: PRO Patent Rolls: C66/415, m. 10.)

65 *CPL*, VII, 323.

66 *Ibid.*, VII, 222.

67 *POPC*, III, 247–8.

68 R.A. Griffiths, *The Reign of King Henry VI. The Exercise of Royal Authority, 1422–1461* (1981), 19, 21.

69 *HBC*, 530.

70 *RP*, IV, 179. This may be an indication of some feeling of duty to the Salisbury diocese.

71 *Ibid.*, IV, 171.

72 He was dead by 15 December when Alnwick was collated to the St. Paul's prebend of Wildland in succession to him. (Ed. G. Hennessey, *Novum Repertorium Ecclesiaticum Parochiale Londinense* (1898), 55.)

73 *POPC*, III, 8. He was paid from 19 December (PRO: Exchequer Warrants for Issues: E404/39/121).

74 *HBC*, 192.

75 For the position of the KPS in the early fifteenth century see A.L. Brown, *op. cit.*, *passim*. The close connection between the privy seal office and the minority council is indicated by the council records, notably the PRO series C81 (Warrants for the Great Seal) and E28 (Exchequer, Treasury of Receipt, Council and Privy Seal) and the records published in *POPC*.

76 These figures are based on the recording of attendance in the council records in *POPC*, III, and in the PRO series C81/1544 and E28/38–47. See table.

77 On 3 dates, 20 and 21 December 1422, and 20 July 1426, there is a record of the attendance at one location but not at another.

78 *POPC*, III, 198.

79 *Ibid.*, III, 148–54; E28/45–8; C81/1544. – In all cases where there is a document endorsed with the names of those present he is included, but his name is not among the signatures.

80 E28/45.

81 *POPC*, III, 150.

82 That his position was considered one of some influence is indicated by the petitions

addressed to the KPS and those considered at his request among the council records (E28/38–47, *passim*).

83 Ed. J. Bain, *Calendar of Documents Relating to Scotland Preserved in H.M. P.R.O. London*, IV, Edinburgh (1888), 189–90; C81/1544/53; *Foedera*, IV, IV, 99.

84 *Foedera*, IV, IV, 108–12. The other ambassadors were Thomas Langley, bishop of Durham, the earls of Northumberland and Westmoreland, Lord Dacre, Baron Graystoke and Sir Robert Umfreville. While he was in the north the privy seal was handed over to the care of his secretary, Robert Foxe (E28/44, 28 February, 1424).

85 *Foedera*, IV, IV, 117.

86 5 December 1423 (CPR, 1422–9, 160–1); 15 May 1425 (*Ibid.*, 280); 1 June 1426 (*Ibid.*, 343).

87 PRO: *Parliamentary Proxies*: SC10/47/2348; Ed. A.T. Bannister, *Registrum Thome Spofford, 1422–48*, Canterbury and York Society (1919), 86.

88 POPC, III, 167–8.

89 POPC, III, 154–8. Out of this he was obliged to maintain a household for the clerks and servants of the office. (A.L. Brown, *op.cit.*, 327.)

90 E.g. BRUC, 11; Griffiths, *op.cit.*, 72; Davies' thesis *ut supra*, 363, 465, Appendix I, v–vi.

91 See note 64.

92 Griffiths, *op.cit.*, 53, 56.

93 BL: Cottonian Ms. Titus AI, fo. 144v. One version is printed in Henry Wharton, *Anglia Sacra* (1661), I, 667.

94 CPR, 1429–36, 506.

95 16 December 1422 (CPR, 1422–9, 14, 17).

96 N. Blakiston, 'The Archives of Eton College', *Archives*, V (1961–2), 124.

97 *Reg. Chichele* , II, 328–9.

98 *Ibid.*, II, 243–4.

99 *Ibid.*, 212–3.

100 CPL, VII, 272–3.

101 *Reg. Chichele*, III, 88–89.

102 Piero da Monte described him as 'verum regiis precibus exaltatus' (J. Haller, *op.cit.*, 74).

103 In the years 1399–1450 the Keepers of the Privy Seal were: Richard Clifford (bishop of Worcester, London); Thomas Langley (bishop of Durham); Nicholas Bubwith (bishop of London, Salisbury, Bath and Wells); John Prophete ; John Wakering (bishop of Norwich); Henry Ware (bishop of Chichester); John Kemp (bishop of Rochester, London, Canterbury); John Stafford (bishop of Bath and Wells, Canterbury); William Alnwick; William Lyndwood (bishop of St. Davids); Thomas Bekynton (bishop of Bath and Wells); Adam Moleyns (bishop of Chichester).

104 The best description of events is contained in Davies' thesis, *ut supra*, 340–63. Unless noted otherwise, the source for dates of bishops' deaths and promotions is HBC, 206, 240, 265.

105 CPR, 1422–9, 169.

106 POPC, III, 210–2.

107 2 November 1424 (BL: Cottonian Ms. Cleopatra, CIV, fo. 175).

108 CPL, VII, 408.

109 CPR, 1422–9, 348. (It was valued at up to 300 marks (CPL, VII, 274).) On 4 February 1426, Alnwick used the seal of the commissary of St. Martin's on the letters of probate of John Fordham's will (*Reg. Chichele*, II, 329).

110 20 July 1425.

111 Norfolk and Norwich Record Office: Reg. 5/8: Register John Wakering (Norwich), fo. 125.

112 BL: Cottonian Ms. Titus AI, fo. 144v; Henry Wharton, *Anglia Sacra*, I, 667.

113 POPC, III, 180–1. Alnwick is not among those recorded as present.

114 CPL, VII, 476; CPR, 1422–9, 333; *Reg. Chichele*, I, 93–4.

115 Betcherman, *op.cit.*, 408–9.

116 See above, 1.
117 Ed. F.W.D. Brie, *The Brut, or Chronicles of England*, Early English Text Society, CXXXVI (1908), 480.
118 *Reg. Chichele*, II, 355–64.
119 Ed. W. Dugdale, *Monasticon Anglicanum*, VI (1846), 1280. (The 'etc.' is Dugdale's.)
120 Borthwick Institute: Register 19: John Kempe (York), fos. 17r-v.
121 Norfolk and Norwich Record Office: Reg. 5/9: Register William Alnwick (Norwich), fos. 53v, 93; Ayscough was often in attendance during the Norwich heresy trials, 1428–31 (Tanner, *op.cit.*, *passim*). Also, it may be significant that Alnwick and Ayscough were ordained, respectively, acolyte and deacon, on 21 September 1415, by Bishop Fordham's suffragan. (Register Fordham (Ely), *ut supra*, fo. 265.)
122 See above, 4.
123 They frequently served on the same commissions and Alnwick joined Cromwell in the foundation of Tattershall College (*CPR, 1436–41*, 292).
124 *POPC*, III, 167.
125 *RP*, IV, 297–8.
126 *CCR, 1422–9*, 269.
127 Griffiths, *op.cit.*, 38. He includes, in this group of Henry's V's servants, Archbishops Chichele and Kemp, Bishops Morgan, Langley and Stafford (despite the latter's replacement as treasurer), the duke of Exeter, the earl of Warwick and Lords Cromwell and Scrope. I.e. almost all the regular Council attenders for this period!

COUNCIL MEETINGS, 1 – 4
HENRY VI (SEPTEMBER 1422 – AUGUST 1426)

1 HENRY VI (September 1422–August 1423)

	Days with meetings	Meetings at Wm	Meetings at FPL	Meetings elsewhere	Location unknown
Total number:	126	70	30	8	40
Attendance unknown:	40 (32%)	9 (13%)	0	0	33 (82.5%)
Attended by Alnwick:	58 (44.5%)	35 (50%)	20 (66.5%)	7 (87.5%)	4 (10%)

2 HENRY VI (September 1423–August 1424)

	Days with meetings	Meetings at Wm	Meetings at FPL	Meetings elsewhere	Location unknown
Total number:	82	65	1	0	17
Attendance unknown:	15 (18%)	5 (7.5%)	0	0	10 (59%)
Attended by Alnwick:	64 (78%)	59 (91%)	1 (100%)	0	5 (29.5%)

3 HENRY VI (September 1424–August 1425)

	Days with meetings	Meetings at Wm	Meetings at FPL	Meetings elsewhere	Location unknown
Total number:	26	18	0	1	7
Attendance unknown:	9 (34.5%)	4 (22%)	0	0	5 (71.5%)
Attended by Alnwick:	15 (57.5%)	13 (72%)	0	1 (100%)	1 (14.5%)

4 HENRY VI (September 1425–August 1426)

	Days with meetings	Meetings at Wm	Meetings at FPL	Meetings elsewhere	Location unknown
Total number:	60	19	5	28	11
Attendance unknown:	20 (33.5%)	2 (10.5%)	2 (40%)	9 (32%)	8 (72.5%)
Attended by Alnwick:	4 (6.5%)	0 (16%)	0	1 (3.5%)	0

TOTAL 1–4 HENRY VI (September 1422–August 1426)

	Days with meetings	Meetings at Wm	Meetings at FPL	Meetings elsewhere	Location unknown
Total number:	294	172	36	37	75
Attendance unknown:	84 (28.5%)	20 (11.5%)	2 (5.5%)	9 (24.5%)	56 (74.5%)
Attended by Alnwick:	141 (48%)	110 (64%)	21 (58.5%)	9 (24.5%)	10 (13.5%)

Wm: Westminster
FPL: Friars Preacher of London (i.e. Blackfriars)

N.B. The main evidence for attendance for 4 Henry VI is signatures on council documents so it is unlikely that the figure above is truly representative of Alnwick's regularity of attendance.

Religious Gilds and Regulation of Behavior in Late Medieval Towns

BEN R. McREE

In 1515, in the middle of an otherwise ordinary account roll, the clerk of the Gild of St. Anthony in Lynn reported a violent disruption at the organization's annual meeting. In the words of the clerk, two of the gild's members, William Spaldyng and Thomas Johnson, were '. . . cessid in the statuts of disobedients of the brethern in this gild', because they had '. . . violently usurpid in words and deds in the presence of the alderman sittyng on the generall day'.[1] Although the phrase 'violently usurpid in words and deds' is disappointingly vague, and the clerk's laconic report conceals the details of the incident, the causes of the disruption are not far to seek. Both Spaldyng and Johnson were officers of the gild in 1515. Spaldyng was an elector, one of those responsible for choosing officers for the coming year, while Johnson was an auditor of the gild's accounts. A disputed election or shady accounting might easily have provoked the outburst. On the other hand, according to the Lynn register of freemen, Spalding and Johnson were both butchers, so the dispute could also have grown out of a business misunderstanding.[2] Whatever the explanation, the alderman quelled the disturbance and censured the two upstarts. Spaldyng and Johnson later reconciled themselves with the gild and each paid a small fine. The episode did no permanent damage to either man's standing, and both went on to hold gild offices in subsequent years.[3]

It is easy to imagine that small-scale disturbances of this sort were common in medieval gilds. Documented cases, are, however, surprisingly rare. No doubt many incidents were too trivial to warrant a report, though any action that resulted in a fine ought to have found its way into the rolls. The rarity of violent disruptions was more likely a product of the pressure that many gilds placed on their members to conform to a common standard of behavior. Men and women who joined these organizations had to pledge themselves to a strict code of personal conduct. Some ordinances were intended to insure proper behavior at gild functions. Obedience to the alderman, attentive silence during meetings, and sober comportment during ceremonies insured the smooth operation of the gild. Other rules, however, extended gild authority into members' private lives.

Men were warned not to wander the streets at night or play games of chance, while women were admonished to avoid the company of suspicious men.[4]

At first glance, such regulations do not appear to require any explanation. Some of the by-laws were aimed at preventing the kind of disturbance that Spaldyng and Johnson caused at Lynn. Others fit comfortably with the upright, pious spirit that religious gilds claimed as their inspiration. It should not, after all, be surprising that organizations dedicated to the Virgin Mary or the Holy Trinity, organizations whose professed aims included the celebration of saints' days and the performance of charitable works, should have expected their members to meet high moral standards. It is, nevertheless, peculiar that organizations pledged to pious goals should have felt the need for stringent behavioral controls. Why were they so distrustful of their gild brothers and sisters?

Scholars have used the religious orientation of the gilds to answer this question. H.F. Westlake, writing in the early part of this century, fit ordinances governing behavior into his interpretation of the gilds as agents of a vigorous lay piety. Seeing no contradiction between the lofty purposes of the gilds and their needs to discipline their members, he viewed their behavioral rules as a natural outgrowth of their religious enthusiasm.[5] A more recent analysis followed a similar line. Susan Brigden presented gild behavioral regulations as examples of the influence that religious beliefs had on social behavior in sixteenth century London. The London gilds took special care, she found, to see that their members observed the Christian injunction to love their neighbors, in this case their gild brothers and sisters.[6]

Not every scholar has used religion to explain gild concern for behavior. However, in a study of social control, Sylvia Thrupp found the gilds to be effective enforcers of community standards of behavior. She based her judgement on the informal social pressure that gilds could exert on their members through gossip and control of neighborhood opinion.[7] Although the work of Westlake, Brigden, and Thrupp has helped to define the role of the gilds in regulating behavior, it has not adequately explained why the gilds took it upon themselves to become the guardians of social and religious order. Why did ostensibly pious organizations find it necessary to legislate against misbehavior by their members? The initiative taken by the gilds in this area can only be explained by a close examination of the kind of regulations passed and the organizations that passed them.

Religious gilds differed from the more well-known craft and merchant gilds of the medieval era in the breadth of their membership and the range of their goals. Merchant gilds were the oldest of the three types of organization, tracing their origin back to the twelfth century. They were urban associations, composed of a town's leading citizens, whose most important function was to regulate local trade. They decided who, for example, would be allowed to buy and sell in their town and how much they would have to pay for this privilege.[8] Craft gilds, which became prominent in the fourteenth century, were composed of practitioners of particular trades or groups of related trades. Their primary purpose was to oversee the conduct of their craft. They set quality standards, regulated apprenticeships, and decided who would be admitted as masters.[9] Both merchant and craft gilds supplemented their economic endeavors with social and religious activities. They heard masses together, distributed alms to the needy, and gathered for communal feasts.

The men and women who joined religious gilds, on the other hand, came from all walks of life. A single gild might contain drapers, grocers, shoemakers, chandlers, tanners, and smiths, as well as representatives of other trades. Although some organizations restricted membership to the inhabitants of a particular parish, others counted men and women from every quarter of their towns as members.[10] The primary purpose of these organizations was religious, not economic. They sponsored feasts, processions, and masses on the feast days of their patron saints; lit candles throughout the year in their parish churches; donated funds for the repair of these churches; and even provided proper burial services for their members.[11] Their popularity grew rapidly during the fourteenth century, and they appeared in towns and villages not only in England but all across Europe.[12] Until they were disbanded during the Edwardian Reformation in the 1540s, religious gilds remained a ubiquitous feature of English parish life.[13]

The responses that these religious gilds made to a royal inquiry during the last quarter of the fourteenth century provide the best sources for their history. A writ issued at the Parliament held at Cambridge in the fall of 1388 required that the masters of all religious gilds make a return to Chancery by the following February describing the nature of their organizations. Each return was to be a comprehensive summary of a gild's activities, including descriptions of the foundation, government, ordinances, privileges, land holdings, and annual income of the organization. Each master was further directed to include any oaths administered by his gild, any charters it had been granted, and a description of any common activities, such as meetings and feasts, that it sponsored.[14] Over five hundred of these gild returns survive, providing a solid foundation for comparative study.[15]

Along with stories of their foundations, descriptions of their activities, and copies of their charters, many gilds included in their returns a list of ordinances governing their members' behavior. The organization that trusted its members the least, the Gild of the Blessed Virgin in Kingston-on-Hull, provides an interesting starting point for the study of behavioral regulations. When the founders of this gild met to frame a set of rules for their association, they agreed to levy a fine on anyone who proved rebellious or foul-mouthed at gild meetings. Next, they specified a penalty for members who refused to honor their financial obligations to the gild. After this rather ordinary beginning, the founders went on to compile a frightening list of potential transgressions. They apparently considered their fellow members capable of a remarkable range of crimes. The ordinance read:

> Moreover, if any brother or sister be publicly and truly charged with articles of public fame or felony, such as robbery, homicide, arson, assault, plunder, rape, breaking prison, counterfeiting, forswearing the realm, conspiracy, treason, receiving thieves, outlawry, sorcery, heresy, or any other felony touching life or limb (which God forbid), then he or she should, without any delay, be put out of this gild. Also, if any man or woman of the gild shall ever be found to be a malefactor, lover of law-suits, libeller, bully, night-walker, destroyer of goods, liar, harlot, excommunicate, or guilty of any other crime injurious to the good name of the gild and its brethren, he or she shall, unless sooner punished by law, be put out of the gild.[16]

This statute, along with the other regulations of the gild, was to be read to new members when they joined the organization. The length of the ordinance alone insured that it would make an impression on those who heard it. Some of its clauses must have been intended, moreover, largely for rhetorical effect. This explains the lengthy list of felonies proscribed by the gild. The judicial system of medieval England had only one punishment for a felon: execution. Expulsion from the gild could not have mattered much to a convicted thief of murderer. Framers of the ordinance intended their imposing catologue of crimes to impress upon members their concern for honest behavior. After hearing the statute a new member may have forgotten its specific clauses, but he or she surely remembered that gild leaders were watching his or her behavior. Gild leaders may also have been seeking to protect the dignity of their organizations from the actions of felonious members. The ceremonial expulsion of a criminal insured that other members, as well as the public, knew that the gild did not approve of such illegal activities.

Although the criminal catalogue of the gild at Kingston-on-Hull was exceptional for its detail and completeness, its provisions were not unique. Moral and criminal transgressions worried the leaders of other gilds as well. Most issued blanket prohibitions of criminal activity, calling for the expulsion of members guilty of such behavior. The Gild of St. Thomas in Lynn, for example, threatened to expel anyone found to be a thief or to have committed any 'wrong on hand' against another.[17] Coventry's merchant gild was even less specific, prohibiting any crime that could be described as 'abhominable'.[18] Leaders of other gilds worried about violations of canon law. A Lynn gild, for example, forbade its members to do anything contrary to the law of the church while a Cambridge gild specified punishment for infractions by the court of the Bishop of Ely.[19]

Adultery and gambling were also popular targets of gild regulations. After proscribing criminal activities and rebellion against gild leaders, a Lincolnshire gild added sexual misconduct to the list of transgressions that merited expulsion. This provision, it should be noted, applied only to female members of the gild.[20] A Lancaster gild was even more restrictive, ordaining that no female member, single or married, was to keep company with known adulterers or receive them in her house. This statute, perhaps intended to keep prostitutes out of the gild, again applied exclusively to women.[21] Men, on the other hand, were more likely to run afoul of rules regarding gambling. The Gild of St. John the Baptist in Wisbech claimed that games of chance were a dangerous source of discord and forbade members to participate in them. Anyone who persisted after being warned to stop was subject to a heavy fine. Those still refusing to cooperate could, after several warnings, be expelled from the gild.[22] A Cambridge gild classed gaming with other disreputable activities such as wandering the streets at night and keeping suspect company. It decreed that any member caught playing chess or dice could be thrown out of the fraternity and turned over to the bishop for punishment.[23]

Most gilds contented themselves, however, with less sweeping prohibitions. They intended their regulations to help preserve harmony within the organization. Yet it was not always easy to maintain order when accounts were being audited or elections were being held. Nor was it easy to keep private squabbles between members from disrupting gild affairs. To avoid conflicts gilds repeatedly urged their members to treat gild brothers and sisters with respect. The Holy Trinity gild in Grimsby counselled its members to use only measured and reasonable speech at gild functions. They were especially to avoid bombastic or pompous language.[24] Great Yarmouth's Trinity Gild threatened to fine members who verbally abused their brethren, while it was the duty of one London gild master to control 'chydyng, brawlyng or any maner of striff or won to another any evyll wordes'.[25]

Language was not the only source of conflict. The Gild of St. John the Baptist in West Lynn refused, for example, to allow members to serve as pledges for one another's debts.[26] Leaders prudently reasoned that pledges forced to meet their fellows' obligations might harbor hostility that could explode at the next feast or meeting. Gilds also sought to maintain harmony by excluding quarrelsome individuals from their ranks. A London organization promised to expel any member who gained a reputation as a 'questmonger' or a maintainer of quarrels, while another gild fined members who showed excessive zeal in pursuing lawsuits.[27]

Lawsuits, in fact, were the subject of some of the most common restrictions. The Gild of the Assumption in London, for example, stipulated that arguments between members could not be taken to court until the gild had had an opportunity to intervene. Disputants had to submit their quarrel to the masters of the gild who tried to settle the matter. If they could not arrange an agreement, the dispute was put before a panel of gild members who strove to arrange a concord. Only if these two attempts failed could the disputants take their quarrel to court.[28] Restrictions on lawsuits remained popular in the years that followed. Wymondham's Gild of Our Lady's Light, an association that flourished during the fifteenth and early sixteenth centuries, put its policy this way:

> non of ye brothers and systers xall plete wt othyr for no manr of cawse tyll ye rewlers and hyr counsell hathe provyd to make an ende and unyte and love betwyne partyes and if yt may not make an ende thei may take ye comon lawe and ho deny thys xall pay iiij li. of waxe.[29]

The phrase 'unyte and love betwyne partyes' reveals this gild's motivation. Rather than allowing an outside agent like the court to decide the issue and risking the resentment of the loser, gild leaders intervened personally, seeking compromise and conciliation. They hoped for a settlement that would satisfy both sides and permit the gild to operate in peace.

Regulations controlling lawsuits could provoke the resentment of outsiders. In 1306 the citizens of York complained to the king that a gild of wealthy burgesses was operating there against the interests of the city. Although the principal charge concerned a conspiracy to avoid taxation, they also accused the gild of adjudicating disputes among its members, depriving city courts of the profits of justice. This was a charge that could have been made against many gilds later in the fourteenth century. The plaintiffs at York were apparently jealous of the economic advantage that private settlement of arguments entailed. They were also suspicious of the secrecy involved and wanted to know what the gild was trying to conceal from fellow townsmen. After hearing both sides, royal justices took the extreme step of disbanding the gild, concluding that its existence was contrary to the king's interests.[30] Despite this decision, the government did not adopt a policy of disbanding gilds that arbitrated members' disputes. The 1389 returns, in which so many gilds openly revealed their prohibitions against lawsuits, are suffiecient evidence of that. The harsh treatment that the York gild received was due primarily to its evasion of taxes. The original complaint that the citizens lodged against the gild reveals, nevertheless, considerable suspicion of gild attempts to keep their members out of court. Even if the justices were not disturbed by the gild's settlement of private disputes, other members of the community were.

Regulations concerning conduct at gild meetings and feasts suggest that the preservation of harmony was not always such a solemn business. Seats were the object of gild protection at Stratford-on-Avon where the Holy Cross Gild fined members a ha'penny for stealing others' stools during its meetings.[31] A number of Lynn gilds also had special regulations governing their annual feasts or drinkings. These rules were intended primarily to preserve order on what were potentially riotous occasions, but they also reflected the age's growing fascination with manners and polite behavior.[32] The ordinances of the Gild of the Conception were typical. All members had to arrive in proper attire. Entry was refused those who came dressed in only a tabard or a cloak, or those who presented themselves barefooted or bare-legged. The dean of the gild maintained order during the festivities and could fine those who celebrated too boisterously. Lazy members were admonished to pass the drinking cup briskly when it came around and were warned not to fall asleep at the table. The ordinances concluded by reminding members that when the alderman stood up and left, it was time for them to go as well, frustrating, no doubt, the plans of late-night revelers.[33]

From treason and murder at Hull to overindulgence at Lynn, this catalog of transgressions illuminates vividly the battle that gild leaders faced to maintain order in their organizations. But internal order was not the sole, nor perhaps even the principal motivation for these statutes. A close look at the language of several ordinances suggests that leaders saw discipline not as an end in itself, but as a means to a larger objective. The closing words of the Kingston-on-Hull statute quoted above reflected this objective. After naming some two dozen transgressions that could bring expulsion from the gild, leaders added a final clause to cover infractions they might have overlooked. They stretched their ordinance to include 'any other crime injurious to the good name of the gild and its brethren'.[34] Concern for the reputation or public image of the gild lay at the heart of leaders' concerns about behavior. A member who became a night-walker or who embarked on a crime spree ruined not only his own reputation, but that of his gild as well. Similarly, a noisy lawsuit between members could attract unwanted attention and damage the reputation of a gild, while news of a brawl during a meeting or of a riotous feast would surely be difficult to keep from fellow townsmen.

Other gilds shared these concerns. In Wisbech, for example, the Gild of the Holy Trinity fined members who played games of chance, engaged in malicious litigation, used foul speech, or, in a restriction similar to the Hull gild, did anything else that might bring scandal to the gild.[35] London's Holy Cross Gild used almost exactly the same phrase, threatening to expel anyone who brought scandal to the fraternity.[36] The statutes of yet another London gild contained an even more telling example. Members of this organization were not allowed to gamble while wearing the livery of the gild.[37] They could, in other words, go from the gild hall to a gambling den as long as they stopped to change clothes first. What the gild allowed them to do as private citizens, it prohibited when they appeared dressed as its representatives. Leaders of these gilds valued good behavior not for its own sake, but for the effect it might have on public perception of their organization.

This may explain why religious gilds seldom had to enforce their behavioral ordinances. Only isolated instances of misbehavior occurred among the East Anglian gilds whose account rolls and minutes I have examined.[38] The most serious incident took place in Norwich. Officers of the Gild of St. George expelled Walter Geffreyes from the organization in 1436 because he defamed several other members of the gild. Geffreyes had insulted them by declaring that they 'were the falsest that myght goo up on herthe'.[39] This was a serious charge. In a study of fourteenth century London slander cases, one scholar found that the insult that provoked the most litigation was calling someone a 'false man'. Those found guilty of this or other slanders, moreover, received stiff punishments. The court typically levied fines of £40 or imposed jail sentences of forty or more days on slanderers.[40] Although Geffreyes' outburst did not result in litigation, it did have serious consequences. Not only was he expelled from the gild, but the men he insulted were so angry that they 'her helpely handes of good and of fortheryng to the seid fraternite vtterly have withdrawen'.[41]

Acts of moral turpitude also demanded a stern response from gild leaders. When one of the members of Norwich's post-Reformation Company of St. George was found guilty of 'whoredom', for example, he received the usual public punishment from local authorities. As the Company's clerk reported, Nicholas Davy 'hath suffered the open shame of riding in a cart about this City for the abominable sin of whoredom'.[42] Leaders of the Company had no choice but to expel Davy. Their action indicates that shame was not merely individual or familial, but was corporate as well. The Company could not afford to keep a notorious sinner in its ranks if it wanted to preserve its image and retain its corporate honor.

The only other reports of misbehavior among the East Anglian gilds during the medieval period involved minor infractions such as being absent from gild meetings without a valid excuse.[43] Scholars working in other parts of the country have turned up only scattered examples of more serious violations. One London gild fined a member in the early sixteenth century for suing a fellow member without the association's permission. The same gild also levied a fine on another man for 'mysbehauing hym in wordis speking'. [44] The elite Trinity gild in Coventry expelled several of its members for adultery during the fourteenth century. [45] The scarcity of evidence does not mean that behavioral statutes were never violated. As long as gilds were more concerned with their public image than the actual behavior of their members, they did not need to concern themselves with transgressions that escaped public notice. Punishment would only be necessary when the actions of a gild brother or sister threatened to scandalize the gild.

Why were these gilds so sensitive about their reputations? A quantitative approach to the returns of 1389 suggests an hypothesis. Only about one-sixth of the gilds whose returns survive mentioned behavioral regulations. But these organizations had more in common than a desire to control their members' behavior. They shared a number of other characteristics that set them apart from gilds without behavioral statutes. Most of the examples in this study have been drawn, for instance, from urban gilds: London, Lynn, Cambridge, and so on. This is no accident of selection. Nor is it due to a shortage of rural gilds in the royal survey. Rules governing the behavior of members were an almost exclusively urban feature. Of all the gilds having behavioral regulations of one kind or another, eighty percent could be found in market towns or larger towns and cities. Even if the market towns are excluded, nearly sixty percent were located in cities such as Leicester, Norwich, London, and Canterbury. [46]

Geographical location was not the only feature that separated gilds with behavioral ordinances from those without them. Gilds concerned about behavior also tended to be wealthier. They owned property worth, on the average, more than three times as much as gilds without such provisions. As we might expect, they were more expensive to belong to as well, demanding an average entry fee of more than 5s. This was nearly twice as high as the typical fee for a gild without behavioral statutes and more than three times as much as the 20d. Brigden cited as typical for London gilds of the sixteenth century. [47] In the urban environment, where dozens of gilds existed, the higher fees undoubtedly influenced men and women of modest means to seek less costly organizations. Gilds with behavioral regulations must have had a wealthier, more exclusive membership than other gilds.

Gilds with behavioral statutes used their superior wealth to participate actively in the showy ceremonial life of the feast days of their patron saints. These processions were often elaborate affairs, mixing piety, bravura, and social promotion. In the march sponsored by the Gild of St. George in Norwich, for example, church bells rang, priests chanted, and poor men carried candles and banners before a parade of gild members outfitted in colorful red and white liveries. The event culminated in a dramatic confrontation between a man dressed as St. George and another who played a fire-breathing dragon.[48] Gild processions usually ended at a church where a special mass was said for the assembled members of the gild. After the service, many gilds held sumptuous feasts that featured mountains of roasted meat, barrels of ale, and entertainment by minstrel groups. Nearly all the organizations with behavioral regulations also required their brothers and sisters to join the funeral corteges of fellow members, accompanying the body to the burial ground in a grand show of solidarity. Table 1 summarizes these features.

TABLE 1
Behavioral Regulations and Gild Ceremony

	Gilds With Behavioral Regulations (%)	Other Gilds (%)
Processions	31	15
Liveries	24	7
Masses	55	47
Feasts	47	31
Funeral Services	95	63
N	78	398

Source: Gild returns of 1389: PRO C.47: bundles 38–46.
Organizations that were clearly craft or clerical gilds have been excluded from the analysis.

Gilds sharing these features enjoyed a high degree of public visibility. Processions, funeral marches, feasts, and worship services placed them squarely before the public eye. For the well-to-do men and women who joined these organizations, this was, no doubt, an attractive feature. It was a public signal that they had reached the pinnacle of urban society and now enjoyed the prestige and valuable social connections that membership conferred.[49] But public visibility could be a liability as well as an asset. When fellow members involved themselves in disreputable activities, their actions endangered the good name of the gild and its membership. Many of these organizations, consequently, found it prudent to protect their reputations by passing ordinances demanding good behavior from their brothers and sisters.[50]

A few gilds had even stronger reasons for watching the behavior of their members. Like the merchant gilds of the earlier Middle Ages, these associations played a signifcant role in the political life of their communities. They frequently numbered the mayor and his council, as well as a town's most prosperous merchants among their members. Indeed, in many towns, such gilds became an integral part of local government. In Norwich, for example, the outgoing mayor automatically became master of the Gild of St. George, an organization that already included the city's aldermen in its membership.[51] Coventry's Trinity Gild, the Holy Cross Gild in Stratford-on-Avon, and the Gild of the Holy Trinity in Wisbech followed a similar pattern.[52] For their members, a spotless reputation had special importance. No community would have sat still while its rulers, or those with whom its rulers associated, acquired a reputation for adultery, gambling, brawling, or litigiousness. Rumours of such transgressions would not only have undermined the social prestige of those involved, but would have threatened their political power as well. As moral watchdogs, these gilds performed important services for their members and for their communities. For members, they provided a check against behavior that could be socially or politically damaging. For the communities, they guaranteed that those who wielded power would lead an honest life or face punishment from their peers.

Not every gild with behavioral regulations was intimately involved with town government, of course. But even if they did not have a political position to protect, members of these organizations did worry about their social status. As part of the urban elite, they sought to protect their reputations in the same way that civic rulers did.

Gild behavioral statutes were part of a code of conduct that the upper ranks of urban society of late medieval England imposed on itself. The code was not particularly severe, nor was it original. The vices that gild regulations proscribed were the same kinds of transgressions that preachers regularly denounced and town nuisance statutes prohibited. But the upper strata of urban society, constantly in the public eye, felt that it was important that they adhere to this moral code. They knew that urban life had always been and would always be a game of appearances. Respectable behavior was simply part of the game.

NOTES

1 Details of the incident come from the gild's account roll, kept in the record office at King's Lynn (KL) Gd. 78. Spaldyng (alias Colvyle) joined the gild in 1508 or 1509 and Johnson joined in 1512.

2 Both purchased the freedom of the city as butchers in 1512–13. See A Calendar of the Freemen of Lynn, 1292–1836 (Norwich: Norfolk and Norwich Archaeological Society, 1913), pp. 78–9.

3 Spaldyng was an elector in 1514 and 1515 and a steward (echevin) in 1514 and 1516–22. Johnson was an elector in 1513, 1514, and 1516 and an auditor in 1515. KL Gd. 78.

4 See below for a more detailed discussion of these ordinances.

5 H.F. Westlake, The Parish Gilds of Mediaeval England (London: Society for Promoting Christian Knowledge, 1919), pp. 66–76. Westlake was responding to the secular interpretation of gild intentions put forward by nineteenth century writers such as Lucy Toulmin Smith and Lujo Brentano: Toulmin Smith, ed., English Gilds: The Original Ordinances of More Than One Hundred Early English Gilds, with an introduction by Lucy Toulmin Smith and a preliminary essay by Lujo Brentano, Publications of the Early English Text Society, orig. ser., no. 40 (Oxford: Oxford University Press, 1963; originally published 1870), pp. xi–cxcix.

6 Susan Brigden, 'Religion and Social Obligation in Early Sixteenth-Century London,' *Past and Present*, 103 1984, pp. 67–112. See especially pp. 96–98.
7 Sylvia L. Thrupp, 'Social Control in the Medieval Town,' *Journal of Economic History*, 1: supplement (1941), pp. 39–52. See especially pp. 41–42. She did not examine the behavioral ordinances that will be the topic of this paper.
8 The best general work on merchant gilds is still the nineteenth century survey by Charles Gross, *The Gild Merchant*, 2 vols. (Oxford: Oxford University Press, 1890). See particularly the first four chapters of the first volume. For the early medieval predecessors of these gilds, see E. Coornaert, 'Les Ghildes Medievales,' *Revue Historique*, 199(1948), On Anglo-Saxon gilds, see the work of Gross and the statutes published in *Diplomatarium Anglicam Aevi Saxonici*, ed. and trans. Benjamin Thorpe (London: MacMillan, 1865), pp. 605–17.
9 For the late appearance of the craft gilds, see Susan Reynolds, *An Introduction to the History of English Medieval Towns* (Oxford: The Clarendon Press, 1977), pp. 83–84, 165–67. For examples of craft statutes, see J. Malet Lambert, *Two Thousand Years of Gild Life* (Hull: A. Brown and Sons, 1891).
10 Even some of the so-called parish gilds looked beyond the parish boundaries when recruiting members. See, for example, the introduction to *Parish Fraternity Register: Fraternity of the Holy Trinity and SS. Fabian and Sebastian in the Parish of St. Botolph Without Aldersgate*, ed. Patricia Basing (London: London Record Society, 1982), p. xxi.
11 The best introduction to the religious gilds are the works of Westlake and Toulmin Smith.
12 The gild returns of 1389 (introduced below) testify to the popularity of these organizations in England. Jacques Chiffoleau found a similar growth in fourteenth and fifteenth century France: *La Comptabilite de l'au-dela: Les hommes, la mort et la religion dans la region d'Avignon a la fin du moyen âge (vers 1320–vers 1480)* (Rome: Ecole Française de Rome, 1980), pp. 266–74.
13 It is easier to define the differences among the three types of gilds than it is to recognize them in practice, largely because features often overlapped and surviving records are frequently incomplete. How, for example, should a gild composed of tanners be classified if it had no craft statutes and limited itself to religious activities? I would group such a gild with the craft organizations, but plausible arguments could be made for placing it among the religious gilds. Medieval record keepers do not offer a solution either. They did not differentiate among the various kinds of gilds, referring to all types interchangeably as gilds, fraternities, or brotherhoods. In the pages that follow, I have identified merchant and craft organizations as such where their characters can be established. Though I have not considered these gilds in detail, they often had behavioral ordinances. Their motives in this area are easier to understand, however, than those of the religious gilds. A merchant gild, composed of a town's leading citizens, or a craft gild, made up of practitioners of a particular trade, each had a corporate image to protect. A criminous craftsman, for example, threatened to bring all his fellow tradesmen into disrepute, damaging their reputations and their businesses.
14 For a translation of the writ, see Toulmin Smith, *English Gilds*, pp. 127–29. The reasons for the inquiry are not clear. The most likely explanations are that the king was suspicious of the political activities of the gilds or that he wanted to tax their property. A statute passed by Parliament in 1391 gives credence to the latter explanation. This statute extended the mortmain legislation of the previous century to include the property of the gilds. See Colin Platt, *The English Medieval Town*(New York: David McKay, 1976), p. 143.
15 The surviving returns are housed in the Public Record Office (*PRO*) in Chancery Lane, classification C.47, bundles 38–46. Many have been published. Those in English, along with translations of selected returns in Latin and French, appear in Toulmin Smith, *English Gilds*. Others may be found in the publications of local record societies. A useful tabular summary of the returns was printed as an appendix to Westlake, *Parish Gilds*, pp. 138–238. Since Westlake's book appeared, nine new returns have been discovered. All nine are in extremely poor condition. Although Westlake's summaries are generally accurate, they are inconsistent in the amount and type of information they provide. His appendix is thus not reliable for a comparative study of the gilds.

16 PRO C.47/46/451.
17 PRO C.47/43/271.
18 PRO C.47/46/439a,b.
19 The Gild of St. Leonard in Lynn: PRO C.47/43/260; the Gild of the Assumption in Cambridge: PRO C.47/38/5.
20 The Gild of St. John the Baptist in Boston: PRO C.47/39/76. The term sexual misconduct is not euphemistic here; the gild itself used vague language. It promised expulsion for a female member if she 'sit mala de corpore suo.'
21 The Gild of the Holy Trinity and St. Leonard: PRO C.47/39/69.
22 PRO C.47/38/39a,b. The fine was 10s.
23 The Gild of the Assumption: PRO C.47/38/5.
24 PRO C.47/40/116.
25 PRO C.47/45/372 for the Yarmouth gild. The quotation is from the statutes of a pair of London gilds dedicated to the Visitation of the Blessed Virgin cited in Brigden, 'Religion and Social Obligation,' p. 97.
26 PRO C.47/43/285.
27 The Gild of Our Lady, St. Joseph, and St. John: PRO C.47/46/465; and the Gild of St. Peter in Wisbech: PRO C.47/38/41.
28 PRO C.47/41/188.
29 Quoted in Westlake, Parish Gilds, p. 73. An account book for the gild, covering the period from 1442 to 1527, is kept in the muniment room of the parish and abbey church of Wymondham. A photocopy of the manuscript has been deposited in the local history collection at the city library in Norwich. Westlake does not state the source for his quotation and I have not found it in the account book.
30 The details of the incident can be found in George Sayles, 'The Dissolution of a Gild at York in 1306,' English Historical Review 55 (1940), pp. 83–98.
31 PRO C.47/46/440a and b.
32 On manners, see the courtesy books that gained popularity during the late Middle Ages. For example: William Caxton, Caxton's Book of Curtseye, ed. Frederick J. Furnivall, Early English Text Society, extra ser., no. 3 (London: N. Truebner, 1868), pp. 17–31.
33 PRO C.47/42/240.
34 PRO C.47/46/451.
35 PRO C.47/38/43.
36 PRO C.47/41/90.
37 The Gild of St. Mary of Bethleham: PRO C.47/42/202.
38 These organizations are the Gild of St. George in Norwich; the gilds of All Saints, SS. Giles and Julian, St. Anthony, St. Francis, Corpus Christi, St. John the Baptist, St. George, the Holy Trinity, and Trinity Merchant in Lynn; the Gilds of St. Mary, St. John the Baptist, All Saints, the Holy Trinity, and Our Lady's Light in Wymondham; as well as fragmentary records from gilds in Swaffham, Great Hallingbury, Bardwell, March, and Cambridge.
39 Grace, Norfolk Record Society, p. 39. The argument probably grew out of the troubled city politics of the 1430s; see William Hudson and John Cottingham Tingey, eds., The Records of the City of Norwich, 2 vols. (Norwich: Jarrold and Sons, 1906–1910), I: lxxxiii–xciii. Geffreyes had obtained the freedom of the city as a scrivener in 1433–34 and had joined the gild in the same year. A Walter Geffreyes appeared frequently in gild records between 1453 and 1470. It is impossible to say whether this was the same man. If he had been a city alderman, however, he would automatically have become a member again when the gild was linked with the city's government in 1452.
    The full text of the accusation against Geffreyes said that he 'hath conspired and comerously outered ongoodly language of worthi bretheren of the seid fraternite that is for to seyn of Sier Roger Pratte John Belhaghe Nicholas Mannyng and Roger Ward seyeng that thei were the falsest that myght goo up on herthe thurgh the which voys and slaundre the fraternite aboue

seid and the seid cite is gretly hyndred so that the forseid Sir Roger Pratte John Belhaghe Nicholas Mannyng and Roger Warde her helpely handes of good and of fortheryng to the seid fraternite vtterly have withdrawen. . . .' Geffreyes was, for good measure, also accused of 'dyuers resistens and rebellions ayens the seid alderman and bretheren at dyuers tymes.'

40   Carl Lindhal, 'Chaucer the Storyteller: Folkloric Patterns in the *Canterbury Tales*' (Ph.D. diss., Indiana University, 1980), pp. 168–71.

41   The accusation did not specify what aid the four victims had provided to the gild. They did remain members of the gild and some later held gild offices.

42   Benjamin Mackerell, 'Account of the Company of St. George in Norwich from Mackerell's History of Norwich, MS. 1737,' *Norfolk Archaeology*, 3 (1852), p. 344. The incident occurred in 1563 after the medieval Gild of St. George had been reorganized as a secular Company during the Reformation.

43   The Gild of St. Giles and Julian in Lynn, for example, fined two members for absence from a meeting in 1422: KL Gd. 37.

44   The Gild of the Assumption in 1520: Westlake, *Parish Gilds*, p. 73 and plate facing p. 74.

45   Charles Phythian-Adams, *Desolation of a City. Coventry and the Urban Crisis of the Late Middle Ages* (Cambridge: Cambridge University Press, 1979), p. 138.

46   Reliable information concerning the population of late medieval towns is notoriously difficult to come by. For the purposes of this study, larger towns and cities were those places where more than 1,900 individuals paid the Poll Tax of 1377. Figures were taken from Josiah Cox Russell, *British Medieval Population* (Albuquerque: University of New Mexico Press, 1948), pp. 142–43. With 1,900 taxpayers as the cutoff point, most of the country's urban centers fall under the heading of large towns or cities. Those having gilds that made returns in 1389 were: Cambridge, Leicester, Lincoln, Boston, London, Norwich, Lynn, Great Yarmouth, Oxford, Shrewsbury, Bury St. Edmunds, Coventry, Beverley, and Canterbury. Smaller towns, such as Ely, Stamford, Ludlow, and Kingston-on-Hull, fell into the market town category.

47   Gilds with behavioral regulations took in an average of 612d. (£2 11s. 1d.) in property rents each year while other gilds collected only 196d. (16s. 4d.). Similarly, the entry fees for gilds with such ordinances averaged 64d. (5s. 4d.) while those of other organizations averaged 39d. (3s. 3d.). PRO C.47/38–46. For the London gilds, see Brigden, 'Religion and Social Obligation,' pp. 98–99. With entry fees of only 20d., she concluded that most of the city's inhabitants could have afforded to belong to a gild. The 5s. fees of gilds with behavioral regulations in 1389 would obviously have been more restrictive.

48   Information about the Norwich procession can be found throughout the acount rolls of the Gild of St. George. These documents ran from the early fifteenth century through the Reformation: Norwich Record Office, 8/e and 8/f. See also the gild minutes printed in *Records of the Gild of St. George in Norwich, 1389–1547*, ed. Mary Grace, Norfolk Record Society, v.9 (Norfolk, 1937).

49   These gilds resembled the 'grander gilds' described by Brigden for London, not the simpler parish organizations: 'Religion and Social Obligation,' pp. 99–101. It is no coincidence that religious gilds with behavioral ordinances were those whose membership most closely resembled the merchant gilds. See above, note thirteen.

50   It was not uncommon for medieval elites to discipline their own to maintain their public image. Coventry's prestigious Trinity Gild, cited above, was one example of this. The same rule applied to rural settlements. In the village of Broughton, for example, Edward Britton found that presentments for adultery were far more common for high status villagers than for others: *The Community of the Vill* (Toronto: MacMillan of Canada, 1977), pp. 35–37.

     Why did rural gilds generally not have behavioral regulations to protect high status villagers? A typical village had only a single religious gild to which most of the adult population belonged. Drawing its members from all levels of village society, such an organization had no special status to protect. Urban settlements, in contrast, often had a dozen or more gilds. For rural gilds, see Gabriel Le Bras, *Institutions ecclesiastique de la*

Chretiente medievale, pt. 1 (Paris: Bloud and Gay, 1964), pp. 416–17. Also, by the same author, *L'Eqlise et le village* (Paris: Flammarion, 1976), pp. 162–64. Chiffoleau, *La comptabilite de l'au-dela*, p. 276, also argued for the open membership of rural gilds.

51   Hudson and Tingey, *The Records of the City of Norwich*, I:xcix–ci.

52   For Coventry, see Phythian-Adams,*Desolation*, pp. 118–121; for Stratford-on-Avon and Wisbech, see Westlake, *Parish Gilds*, pp. 104–116. Other examples can be found in the volumes of *Victoria County Histories*.

The Household as a Religious Community

R. G. K. A. MERTES

From the earliest days of Christianity, the domestic community has served as a unit of worship. The New Testament letters of Paul, and the writings of church fathers such as Augustine and Jerome, assume that religious training and celebration was based on the household. In the later middle ages, c. 1350 to 1550, the English aristocracy also accepted that their households should be religious as well as domestic communities, and took steps to see that this should be put into practice. The household, an amalgamation of servants, family, and followers, existed primarily to serve its master; and he had Christian duties to fulfill, whether through a sense of obligation, self-aggrandizement, or personal piety. Lords used their households to administer those duties. Thus the household paid out alms and annuities to religious foundations, saw to the arrangement of major festivals, and financed and organised a regular liturgical system.

Religious activity within the household probably increased throughout the late 14th and 15th centuries. The personalisation of Christianity, especially among the aristocracy – as expressed in the astounding increase in numbers of private books of hours, portable altars, statuary and relics owned by the laity – seems to indicate a general movement in religious feeling, towards a more intimate and personal relationship with God, perhaps in the face of preoccupation with death and concern with the afterlife, especially escape from purgatory, so prevalent in Europe during and after the great plague years.[1] The aristocracy used their households both as passive organisers of such practices as daily office, mass, and prayers for the dead, and also as active participants in these, adding their prayers and good works to the Lord's. In this manner the household could become not only a simple administrator of its master's pietistic duties, but in itself could function as a religious community for its own salvation and that of its Lord.

The 3rd Duke of Buckingham posited in his chequer roll of 1519 that all household members were to attend mass daily, as 'no good governaunce in politik rule may be had, without service to God as well'.[2] The 5th Percy Earl of Northumberland, in his book of household ordinance, expressed a similar sentiment; several 15th and 16th century royal ordinances, and most courtesy books for young courtiers, also echo this.[3] The difficulty lies in showing whether this ideal remained unfulfilled, or whether the mediaeval household did indeed have a specifically Christian as well as a domestic identity. In the end we have little unambiguous evidence; but we can examine the means of religious observance available in the household, and study some of the motivations to use these means, looking in particular at five families whose household records extend over several generations and who themselves cover a wide spectrum of the gentry and nobility: the Staffords, Dukes of Buckingham; the de Veres, Earls of Oxford; Ralph Lord Cromwell and his heirs the Radcliffes; the Luttrells of Dunster Castle, Somerset; and the Stonors of Stonor Hall, Oxon.[4]

In the nineteenth century morning and evening prayers were often said in the dining room, where family and servants could congregate most easily. In the middle ages, the gentry and nobility had far more elaborate accoutrements available: the buildings, the implements, the staff. Even Robert Melton, a wealthy yeoman farmer, had a small room set aside as a chapel for his tiny household;[5] one would be hard-pressed to find a gentle or noble establishment devoid of a building or room for worship. Technically, private chapels required a licence from a bishop before mass could be celebrated in them; but episcopal registers do not seem to be a very good guide to the existence of such chapels, as it seems that in many, mass was regularly held without any licence being purchased, or at any rate recorded. For instance, the Luttrells had two active chapels within the walls of Dunster Castle; but no licence for either is traceable in the near-perfect set of registers for the diocese of Exeter. Similarly, the earliest licence recorded for the Stonor family's chapel is for 1349, but mass was celebrated there as early as 1331, and the building style indicates that it probably dates from the mid 13th century, and is possibly even older.[6] Despite the relatively-low incidence of registered private chapels, therefore, one usually finds that aristocratic households contained at least one chapel, with all the liturgical paraphenalia for mass.

These chapels could be anything from a 'closet' or small room adapted as a chapel, to a separate building in the size and style of a parish church; and often, within a single castle or manor-house, there was more than one. The oldest are those in keeps, dating from 1100 to 1300 approximately, such as occur in Dunster Castle, Somerset and Castle Hedingham, Essex (a De Vere stronghold); they are largely similar in concept to those more well-known royal ones at the White Tower, London, and Castle Rising, Norfolk. The old chapel at Dunster was fitted into a small tower-room, over the entrance of the Norman shell-keep, and probably measured no more than 10 feet square.[7] Before 1350, some larger, generally wooden chapels were constructed in baileys; but it is generally after this date

(Stonor Hall, Oxon. being a pertinent exception) that large stone chapels were erected, such building being especially common during the 15th century. Often free-standing or partially attached to the main body of the dwelling, these are distinguished by their surprising size, comparable to a parish church. That at Stonor measures 57 feet long by 19 feet wide, and had at least three side-altars; that at Hedingham (now only the foundations are visible) as long and somewhat wider.[8] The size of these later mediaeval chapels may tell us something about mass attendance in the household; they coincide in date with the beginning of a steady increase in the number of household servants.[9] While the 5th Earl of Oxford in *c.* 1290 may have been able to fit his household of around 45 in the keep chapel at Castle Hedingham, the 120 employed by the 13th Earl in the 1480's would never have managed. The much-larger bailey chapel may have been built to accommodate a growing congregation. On the other hand, such chapels may be explained by a growth in personal religious practices; the prestige value of a new and obvious chapel; and/or the general domestic-building phenomenon of the 15th and 16th centuries which was marked especially by an increase in space and luxury.[10]

The older chapels were not, however, de-sanctified, but continued as active places or worship. In the same year (1405–1406) that he finished the new bailey chapel of St. Lawrence at Dunster, Sir Hugh Luttrell spent £21 7s. 5d. on the repair and refurbishing of the old keep chapel; he later supplied it with new vestments and plate.[11] Throughout the 15th century, other additional chapels, besides the old keep rooms and the new, larger buildings, were set up – many of them 'privy' chapels, such as that dedicated to St. George at Stonor, and the 'closet chapel' at Castle Hedingham, in which the Earls of Oxford said prayers with their chamber-servants or alone. In fact Castle Hedingham had, by 1513, at least four chapels in use, fully fitted with liturgical gear.[12]

As well as the physical means, the household also had the animate means for religious celebration. One would be hard-pressed to find a household document which does not mention at least one resident chaplain, and numerous '*clerici*'. The chaplain might have other priests and clerics to assist him; at least one sacristan, certainly, to look after the upkeep of the chapel and its accoutrements; and, in the largest households, a singing-school, comprised of both boys and men. Unfortunately, it is difficult to say a great deal about any household's clerical element. The incompleteness of episcopal registers (in themselves and as sets), the commonness of many names (such as Robert Kent, chaplain to the Luttrells in the 1430s – five of this name are listed in the Exeter registers), a lack of sureness as to where such clerics might have been ordained, and the generally-low social origins of many in orders, means that biographies can be compiled only for a very few. John Bacwell, another Luttrell chaplain (1405–1423), was clearly a priest;[13] his name is almost certainly a Somerset one, and his services are concentrated in that area; but no Bacwell is listed in any surviving West Country register, nor can his family be traced. Thus one can seldom determine with any surety if those household members called '*clerici*' in the service of the chapel or otherwise are in any kind of holy orders, unless good internal evidence survives, especially considering the 15th century trend to apply the term to lay accountants. We must not assume that any '*clerici*' were priests unless they are specifically designated as such.

Despite these reservations we often find households with more than one resident cleric capable of saying mass. In 1349 the Stonors were licenced to have six chaplains; in 1428 the Luttrells employed at least two priests; the de Veres and Staffords usually had about three; and in 1512 the 5th Earl of Northumberland employed as many as six chaplains, of whom one was designated as the 'Ladyemessepriest', as he was employed soley in the saying of masses to the Blessed Virgin.[14] These priests, whilst some were employed in accounting capacities,[15] were in the main hired to function as chaplains. As such, their duties were comprised of saying daily mass and perhaps divine office; such requiems, twelve-month-minds, and penitential services as the lord required, and constructing and directing these services in the chapel.[16] More generally, they seem to have been charged with the moral and spiritual welfare of the household community, especially that of other clerics in the household.

Household clerics must have posed something of a problem to bishops. They frequently moved around the country with their masters, in and out of dioceses, and hence in and out of the authority of their spiritual overlords. Those paid by benefice in the lord's granting must have required a perpetual leave of absence. Some evidence exists to show that, as far as the household was concerned, the senior chaplain had a special authority over other household clerics. The 5th Percy Earl's Dean of Chapel occupied such a position.[17] As well, in the Stafford chequer rolls for 1517 and 1519,[18] the servants are grouped in departments, within which they are ordered by rank; the clerics, of the chapel and of other parts of the household such as the kitchen, are all grouped together and are headed by the Dean of Chapel, who is placed in relation to them in the same way in which sub-heads of departments are placed in relation to their staffs. Thus it appears likely that the senior chaplain was recognised, within the household at least, as being in a special position of authority as far as other household clerics were concerned. The form this authority took is harder to determine, but practically, it probably involved much the same responsibilities attributed to the Dean of the Chapel Royal of Edward IV:[19] such things as seeing that clerics fulfilled their religious obligations, and that they did not become involved in scandal or commit gross theological errors. The senior chaplain may also have drawn upon non-chapel clerics for liturgical ceremonies such as chanting, reading the lesson, etc.

The chapel staff proper, however, could also contain laymen. Most households employed at least one sacristan or verger, usually classified as a valet or groom and often a layperson, who was charged with the upkeep and guarding of the chapel and its valuable goods. The Earl of Northumberland also had two 'yeoman pistelers' who were employed solely to read the lesson from the New Testament Epistles at daily mass.[20] In the greatest households, *scholae cantorum* in imitation of the Kings's chapel royal enriched the household's religious life. Such chapel choirs appeared in the royal household as early as 1135. The first instance of a singing school in a noble household, however, does not occur until 1360, when we find that Henry, Duke of Lancaster employed six adult singers in his chapel. Henry's son-in-law, John of Gaunt, also employed such a chorus, but with boys' voices as well. John Duke of Bedford also had a choir for his household chapel in 1435, as did Humphrey, Duke of Gloucester, who left annuities in his will to his numerous *schola* members, boy and man. Margaret Beaufort had a *schola cantorum* in the late 1480s, and may have had one earlier.[21] Edward, Duke of Buckingham, was almost certainly imitating her, his guardian and mentor, in his own *schola*, as he had imitated her household administration in other ways. Both Edward Stafford's and Margaret Beaufort's choirs consisted of about 12 boys and around 4 gentleman-singers under the direction of a master of the children of the chapel.[22] John, 13th Earl of Oxford, also employed a *schola* consisting of a master, 12 boys and at least two adult male voices, in 1490; by 1512, and probably earlier, the 5th Earl of Northumberland patronised a large household choir.[23] Cardinal Wolsey and Henry Fitzroy, Duke of Richmond, also had private choirs in the early 16th century.[24] Such choirs were obviously restricted to the greatest nobles, who alone had the wealth and prestige properly to support such schools of singing.

The choir members came from all classes of society. Unfortunately we have few names of the masters; but those whose identity is known seem to have been respectable musicians, even minor masters of the art of polyphony and the English melodic adaptation of plainsong. William Excestre, John of Gaunt's *magister* in 1393, became master of Henry IV's chapel royal, and probably wrote some or most of the pieces now known from the Old Hall MS.; Thomas Farthyng, Margaret Beaufort's choirmaster, has left numerous compositions which exhibit his skill and illustrate his importance to the development of English music.[25]

We know somewhat more about the singers than the masters. Those of relatively humble origins, such as the Duke of Buckingham's Roger Adamsey and the 13th Earl of Oxford's James Hoggys and Richard

Robkyn, perhaps showed youthful promise at a Cathedral school or other educational establishment, and were commandeered by their noble patron. Other 'children of the chapel', however, were actually henchmen, brought into the household as youthful servitors as an act of patronage; they came from well-established gentry families, often from those traditionally allied with the employing lord. Edward Stafford's *schola* included, in the years 1485 to 1521, several Brays, de la Mares, Pointzes, and other gentry family members from the Welsh Marshes, traditionally allied with the Dukes of Buckingham.[26] Along with the other henchmen of the household, these choirboys received a gentleman's education. For boys of lesser rank, their position in the *schola* could lead to a lifetime profession. Some, like 'litel Fraunceys', an otherwise unknown protege of the 3rd Duke of Buckingham, entered the University of Oxford and later the church with their patron's assistance.[27] Others, like the 13th de Vere Earl's choir boy, John Hewett, remained in the household on a gentleman's pay of 53s. 4d. *per annum*; some even formed the adult voice corps of the *schola* if their youthful promise persisted.[28] Some singers, however, entered the household choir as adults. Like their young colleagues they covered a wide social stratum, from the younger sons of gentry families to gifted commoners, who could have received their training in a Cathedral school or grammar school.

Obviously, nearly every aristocratic household, large or small, had the means for creating a religious community. However, our picture of 'the court' and 'courtly life' both royal and noble, is one of considerable worldliness, pomp, show and splendour. We may easily picture those Puritan households of such as Oliver Cromwell,[29] living a strict life of common prayerfulness; we have a harder time imagining that sort of religious community which might exist at Castle Hedingham, or the 3rd Duke of Buckingham's Thornbury, or Ralph Lord Cromwell's Tattershall. We need to look at the motivation present in such a household, which might, through the regular pattern of worship shared by the community, encourage the formation of religious zeal in individuals, and in the household as a whole; for the lord, and for his household members. A great deal depended upon the individual lord's or lady's sense of piety. Acts of charity were almost a social duty of the aristocracy, as were mass-attendance and the initiation of other religious services. Certainly chroniclers cite such pietistic practices as synonyms of good lordship; it is impossible to discover a noble or gentleman who never gave alms or endowed a chantry. But such activities could of course be largely external; or they could be expressed not only through but in the household.

We have already mentioned the intensely personal aspect of religious feeling in the later middle ages; a kind of mystical yearning for closeness to God which ran as an undercurrent through much of 15th century theology in particular. Few people, of course, had the spiritual concentration of St. Vincent Ferrer or the emotional violence of Jan Hus. But for nobles, in particular, the personalisation of religion helped to ameliorate the conflict between Christian humility and poverty and worldly display, by identifying Christ with themselves and their possessions. The personalisation of the sacred naturally encouraged the practice of piety in the household. To have one's own services, one's own priest, one's private liturgical adaptations and celebrations, was a way of controlling and coming closer to a distant Godhead. One could in a sense bring Christ into the living quarters, within the very heart of one's life, by the creation of a private chapel. Household members, as well as their masters, were susceptible to this religious trend. It may be posited that the sale of indulgences was the church's response to a genuine need in western Europe; that indulgences, 'relics', and rosaries, which were available to most people, were a way of 'crystallizing the image'[30] of God, of controlling and becoming one with God.

The importance of strongly personal religious feeling, then, could motivate closely-knit groups such as noble households to be drawn into their own patterns of piety, to which the individual could relate as part of a community. More practical motives, however, also encouraged the practice of religion in the household. We have mentioned the status-value of a new chapel; and certainly such magnificent buildings and their accoutrements were one way of advertising one's splendour. What better way for the noble further to exhibit his strength and munificence than by utilising religious festivals and processions to display his personal following? Such a display was thereby given an acceptable excuse, rendering it less likely to be inflammatory; politics was cloaked by piety. Certainly the third Duke of Buckingham's household expedition to the burial-place of Prince Edward, son of Henry VI, in April 1508 was a but-thinly disguised advertisement of his sympathies,[31] meant to remind Henry VII of his family's attachment to the Lancastrian cause.

Finally, the creation of the household as a religious community was of benefit to the household as an organisation. Lords recognised the value of group worship, and often left specific notices urging enforced mass-attendance.[32] As Paul V.B. Jones posits, 'Not a noble master, but felt that his control over his servants was fortified, and a difficult management made smooth, through the attendance of the entire house, compulsory if necessary, at religious services. . .'[33] For the sake of morale and what we would call 'teamwork', group worship must have been an ideal way of uniting the household and incorporating it into the hierarchical structure of society encouraged by mediaeval Christianity. The practical unification of the household was not just in the lord's interest, however, group worship was as much an expression of, as a causal factor in, household 'teamwork'. Any community of individuals wishes to express and confirm its unity through some kind of ritual; whether this be the crowning of a monarch, the yearly celebration of Mothering Sunday or a community street-party. Daily worship is one obvious ritual which expresses group unity. Individual household members may have been motivated to attend the household mass provided for them, because it re-affirmed each day their place in the community around which most of their lives centred.

Certainly motivation existed, therefore, for the creation of the household around its lord as a religious community. In each household, however, worship varied in terms of what was actually done, and how, depending on size, means and individual interests. Nobles and gentry largely confined themselves to the exercise of traditional forms of pious practice open to the layperson, but adapted these to suit the requirements of what Joel Rosenthal calls 'an individualised form of institutionalised religion'.[34] We can conveniently divide aristocratic household religious activity into four categories: daily worship patterns, observance of the liturgical year, generational ceremony, and charity. In these four spheres the lord acted through his household, which organised these events, and also in most cases participated in them.

While it seems likely that daily mass was supposed to be common in households, we cannot really be sure that it was in actuality celebrated daily, or whether, if so, individuals actually attended. We must remember that even weekly mass was beyond the religious exertions of many people. The general impression is that the aristocracy were fairly fastidious about their religious observances, either out of piety or duty. One feels that Thomas Stonor would hardly have paid for a licence to say mass before daybreak – presumably for when he would be journeying and wished to set out early – if he did not wish to avail himself of it.[35] Moreover, some useful economic evidence exists for supposing that daily mass was celebrated. Wardrobe costs in the Stafford, Luttrell and de Vere households[36] break down to reveal that nearly a third of the candles, torches, etc. used in the household were expended in the chapel. Since candles are an essential part of the mass and divine office, it seems reasonable to draw the conclusion that fairly regular services were held in these chapels. In the Luttrell household and in that of Henry Lord Stafford and Margaret Beaufort, this candle consumption continues even in the absence of the noble family. (Indeed the 'Ordinances of Eltham' of Henry VIII and 'The Northumberland Household Book' make provision for the keeping of community meals and daily mass in the absence of the lord.)[37] Therefore, one can probably assume that a daily mass was said in most chapels; and that the motivations previously described, and/or the insistence of the master, ensured some sort of congregation.

Several ordinances also specify other daily services: in particular the divine office and masses for the dead. The 5th Duke of Northumberland, and the governors of little Edward V when he was still a prince, both made provision for the chapel staff, including the *schola*, to say the office in part – probably lauds, terce and vespers – each day.[38] Edward V and his young henchmen were supposed to attend the office, but naturally the rest of the household was not expected to do so. They were of course too busy with their household duties. The same is true of requiem masses. In effect some lords endowed chantries in their private chapels, usually for the souls of their dead parents; but these were not intended as congregational masses, nor was the household community expected to attend.

Religiously-inspired abstinences and bounty were also regular observances that coloured the life of the household. In nearly every household account we find a scrupulous observance of the Friday abstinence from meat; in others, such as the Stafford accounts from the 2nd (Dowager) Duchess Anne's time onwards, and the (Percy?) household represented in the Cockermouth Roll also,[38a] abstinence on Wednesday and Saturday– recommended but not required by the church – was observed. In the 3rd Duke of Buckingham's household, one day a week – usually Friday, but occasionally Wednesday – a full fast may have been instituted; the accounts show that on one day a week, only about eight people on average took meals (the old, the young and the sick would have been exempted).[39]

The purveyance patterns of most households show that these penitential days were countered by a day of joy – Sunday. In the Luttrell, Cromwell and Stonor families, spending and consumption was particularly large on this day, increasing the total expenditure over a normal meat-day such as Monday or Thursday by as much as fifty percent.[40] Unusual or exotic foods also occur frequently on Sundays – herons in Ralph Cromwell's house, and wine, even for the lower servants, boars for the Radcliffes.[41] This Sunday pattern is less obvious in the de Vere and Stafford accounts, probably due to the size of the establishments, which depended heavily on the stock-piling of food, so that buying does not always exhibit a consumption pattern.

As well as these daily–weekly observances, the annual cycle of the church calendar probably exercised a strong influence over the life of the household. Of course, it can be argued that the liturgical year impressed itself on any medieval mind; but in the noble household, as in the monastery or convent, the church calendar was more intensely experienced. Much more than other laypeople, noble household communities were likely to be affected by the liturgical calendar, because there were both the means of responding to it, if such was the lord's desire, and the congregation. A look at the account books of most households shows that the major feasts of the year, what are now called solemnities, feasts and holy days of obligation, were almost without exception celebrated as feasts. The Annunciation is one of these, often occurring as a break in the austerity of Lent. Accounts all show conclusively that during Lent meat-abstinence was strongly enforced, though not extending to such items as eggs; a complete fast was observed on Ash Wednesday, Maundy Thursday and Good Friday.

Easter Vigil and Easter Sunday were solemnly celebrated at all the five households on which we are concentrating, with high mass and a banquet. Hugh and John Luttrell distributed largesse in honour of the day;[42] in the Stafford Household under Edward the third Duke, a preacher was invited to give a homily each Sunday in Lent, as well as Good Friday, Easter Vigil and Easter.[43] During Eastertide, Ascension Day, Whitsunday or Pentecost, Trinity Sunday and Corpus Christi were solemnly celebrated by all. The Birthday of St. John the Baptist, which coincided with midsummer, and the Assumption of the Blessed Virgin (29 June and 15 August, respectively) were the only common summer feasts. St. Michael the Archangel's feast (Michaelmass) was not only the beginning of the household's fiscal year, but was generally celebrated as a religious holiday, on 29 September. All Saints' and All Souls' (1 and 2 November) were kept with numerous requiem masses and the saying of the office for the dead.

Then, as now, Christmas – the whole season as well as the day – was probably the most important holiday of the year; not only religious, but as 'secularised' and commercial as a modern Christmas. Buying for it began in October and November: special torches and candles, fowl and stock cattle for fattening, and supplies of such dainties as figs, dates, and sugar are entered as Christmas '*empciones*' as early as 15 October in the Luttrell, de Vere and Stafford accounts.[44] Christmastide officially began at the first Sunday of Advent, but in fact the Immaculate Conception of the Virgin on 8 December marked the heightening of household preparations for Christmas, as yet more supplies were purchased and guests poured in for the holiday. Guests were an important feature of the Christmas season, especially relatives; Edward Stafford invited close on one hundred in 1507.[45] It was also celebrated with entertainments: waits, companies of players, 'clerks of St. Nicholas', musicians, gymnasts and fools; even the smallest households managed to import a peripatetic lutor.[46] Nevertheless it was not, certainly, devoid of religious sentiment; daily high mass, special preachers and solemn high office were also commonly celebrated. The Christmas holidays followed the traditional pattern of twelve nights in most households, from Christmas eve to Epiphany.

All these religious festivals were organised in and through the household; but also for and with householders. The best illustration of this can perhaps be found in the celebration of the presentation of Christ in the temple and the purification of the Blessed Virgin (2 February), on which feast candles were generally issued to every household member so that they could participate in the ceremonies, from the steward to the scullery boy.[47]

Each household, besides these main feasts, also had its own particular set of feast days which filled out the liturgical calendar. Patron Saints' days, dedication memorials, and other obscure solemnities with special meaning for the family were celebrated with high mass and a special meal. The variety of these feasts are endless, so it is best perhaps to recount the particular liturgical feasts of two families in order to give some impression of their private calendars. Our knowledge of these yearly cycles varies, of course, from family to family, depending upon the number of daily accounts surviving. These, by recording in detail expenditure, number of guests, and so on, tell us a good deal more about holidays than the yearly summaries.

The letters of the Stonor family also provide useful insights.[48] From the earliest to the latest letters (1370–1485) we find a particular devotion to the Holy Trinity. 'May the Trinity keep you' closes nearly every Stonor letter over one hundred years of correspondence. Their chapel was of course dedicated to the Holy Trinity, though whether this was the cause or effect of Stonor devotion is uncertain. Solemn celebrations were also held on the feasts of St. Anne (26 July) and St. Katherine of Alexandria (25 November), the patron saints of many Stonor women; and also St. George (23 April) to whom chapels in the house, and the church in the nearby town of Henley, were dedicated. The anniversary of the dedication of the private chapel of the Holy Trinity (somewhere between 22 October and 8 November) was also a cause for feasting and for high mass in the Stonor household.[49]

Ralph Lord Cromwell was particularly devoted to St. Winefride (8 November), St. Nicholas (6 December) and St. Thomas the Apostle (21 December), feasts kept by his servants even in his absence; his heirs the Radcliffes (through Ralph's nieces), also seem to have kept these feasts, especially that of St. Nicholas.[50] This gives us some conception of the variety of private calendars. One might note the persistence of days of patronage – chapel dedications, for instance, not only of the Stonors' Holy Trinity, but the de Veres' St. John the Evangelist, and the Luttrells' St. Lawrence. St. Thomas the Apostle may also have been the patron of Ralph, Lord Cromwell's private chapel. One wonders if these celebrations, which honoured the noble family involved, as much as the saint specified, had the same sort of meaning for the household as a whole. We cannot know, but the theory is a tempting one. In a household which functioned as a religious community, such patronage feasts could easily have been used to express, through religious ritual, the unity of the household; it is perhaps significant that Ralph Lord Cromwell's servants kept the family's traditional feasts even in the absence of the family.

Generational events marking the passage of a linear time, and involving church ritual, were often organised by and participated in by the household: in particular baptisms, marriages and funerals. These rites of passage were, for that matter are, highly significant occasions. Ritual allows one to control, understand and maintain continuity through unsettling changes in status. This is as true of Christian as it is of primitive or pagan ritual. We find continually that lords and servants participated in each others' generational rituals.

A Stonor paper of 1482 includes a list of directions for a christening, probably for the baptism of William Stonor's son John. This was organised through the household and took place in the chapel at Stonor. Of the twelve priests involved, several were household chaplains; and a number of other household servants, alongside relatives and influential local gentry, were involved in the ceremony – Christopher Holland, then household steward, held the basin and salt.[51] The inclusion of household members in the christening is perhaps significant; perhaps it symbolically pledged them to serve the heir of their master, providing a rationale for continuity between the generations. Certainly it worked in the opposite direction. Lords frequently stood as godparents to their servants' children, later acting as their patrons. The Dowager Countess of Oxford, widow of the 13th Earl, was godmother to Elizabeth daughter of Margaret and Nicholas Ryder, who had both served the de Veres for many years; the Dowager left the girl a substantial dowry.[52] Such godchildren often appeared in later years in the household service of their patrons.

Marriage must have affected household life and practices more immediately and distinctively than any other major shift in status; and we know, from the Stonor and also the Hoby letters, that it could create tensions in the household. Thus it is unfortunate that no household accounts, for the years of the marriages of any head of household, can be found to survive. We do have some information about the marriages of daughters. These often took place in the chapel of the bride's father, as in the double marriage in the Stonor chapel in 1331, the marriage of Hugh Luttrell's daughter Elizabeth at Dunster in 1406, and the rather late but particularly fully-documented marriage of the daughter of Sir William More of Loseley, Surrey, in 1567.[53] These were organised through the household, which handled the catering, entertainment and decoration; and John Bacwell, the household steward and chaplain, was involved in the negotiations over the marriage of Elizabeth Luttrell to William Harleston.[54] On the household's part in the actual ritual of marriage, however, we are sadly lacking in information. On the marriage of servants, on the other hand, we find that lords often attended the service, providing a substantial marriage-gift and sometimes a dowry for the bride.

The 13th Earl of Oxford in 1490 extended his patronage to the marriage of John Watson, one of his valets; the same Earl's dowager left dowries in her will to several of her maids.[55]

But it was in death that the household particularly involved itself in the rite of passage. For the servants, natural sorrow was accompanied by great insecurity as the household changed hands, even though many lords stipulated in their wills that their servants were to be kept on for at least six months after the funeral. Household members organised and participated in their masters' funerals, arranging for the procession, burial and largesse, and also for the wake afterwards, usually following the instructions in the will. Servants also normally took part in the procession, following after the chief mourners and in some cases carrying or leading the body. Their numbers were not restricted; all household members were issued livery and expected to join in the procession.[56] Through the funeral ritual servants were able to express their grief, perform a last act of service to their dead lord, and perhaps by their position in the ceremony identify themselves with the lord's heirs. The anniversary of the death was celebrated in the twelve-month-mind, which involved both a religious service and a feast. These were sometimes held by masters for servants: Elizabeth (Ryche) Stonor's chamberer, Richard, for example, was remembered by the household in this way in 1469.[57]

Our information on generational rituals is perhaps rather slender, but suggestive. Householders not only organised such rituals for their lord, but participated in them, with their masters, and he participated in theirs; intimating the importance of the householding institution as a crucial framework governing the lives of master and servant.

Apart from liturgical ceremonies, lords chiefly fulfilled their Christian duties by dispensing alms, and founding and supporting religious houses. When discussing the role of the household in charity, one may distinguish between the great, planned charitable actions and casual almsgiving. The former was largely organised through the lords's will, or through his receiver-general of estates. Casual almsgiving and largesse, however, involved the household. Though largesse was, at some religious feasts and celebrations, a set custom – the Staffords always donated a fixed amount to be distributed by the almoner at Easter and Christmas, and Joan (Belknap) Stonor, who died in 1425, was extremely explicit, in her will, about the alms to be distributed in twelve parishes after her funeral[58] – in essence most almsgiving was casual and spontaneous. Most lords and their households had certain biases in their almsgiving. The most frequent recipients of alms were friars of one sort or another. Hugh Luttrell and Humphrey Stafford were particularly fond of Franciscans; the third Duke of Buckingham had close ties with several Dominican houses, to whose members he often gave hospitality. William Stonor gave much largesse to

Oxford University students, as did Edward Stafford, the 3rd Duke of Buckingham, who was also particularly charitable to lepers.[59] Numerous 'powre men' met on the road and given alms are mentioned in nearly every daily account now survivng.

Such alms were generally financed by the household. Hospitality was paid for by the steward or almoner; simple alms were usually dispensed via chamber servants who accompanied the lord, but any nearby servant could be told to open his purse. The accounts of Elizabeth of York, Henry VII's queen, show her gentlewomen being reimbursed for providing her impulsive gifts, 'per mandatum dominae'. Many similar entries occur in the third Duke of Buckingham's private accounts.[60]

One occasionally finds, however, a dispensation of alms not given 'per mandatum domini', but 'pro', or 'in nomine, hospicii', such as that dispensed to lepers for the household of Edward Stafford in 1520, or that given to poor men of Minehead by the Luttrell household for the Christmas of 1405.[61] Moreover, the private accounts of the Stonor servants, and for Reginald Seynesbury, Hugh Luttrell's purveyor, enter in their discharges the casual dispensation of alms to beggars met in the course of their travels.[62] The evidence seems to suggest that household members, as a group and as individuals, had the right and duty to dispense charity. Finally, servants themselves could benefit from their master's charity through the household. Robert Draper was financed as a chantry priest for Hugh Luttrell by the latter's heir John when Draper left household service; John Glade, a servant of the third Duke of Buckingham, became a hermit, in which pursuit he was supported by gifts and, on feast-days, hospitality.[63] We can suggest the psychological effect upon the household member of the household's charitableness. He would have been aware that the establishment in which he lived gave as much and sometimes more than most religious houses; and some of this was distributed in the name of himself and his fellows, for whom it would reap a harvest of prayer. The fact that servants' own charitable givings could be claimed as expenses, moreover, probably both encouraged them to give the more readily and to think of their individual giving as an extension of household charity.

Much of the evidence available on household piety is ambiguous and uncertain. We know, from ordinances and chequer rolls that lords wished to see their households operate as a religious community, daily worshipping in a body; but such sources reflect the ideal, rather than the real, household, and we must use them with circumspection. The means for the existence of such a community were present, but how, and how much, these means were utilised is less sure. Implicit and explicit motivation for the formation of the household as a pious community can be argued, but is more difficult to prove concretely. Finally, the pious actions of households can in many cases be discerned, but the evidence of such action may be ambiguous, and its real significance – such as whether household members actually did attend the daily masses which were quite probably held in most households, and if so, why – is difficult, often impossible, to ascertain. In the end we must rely on quantity as much as quality of evidence; on the steady accumulation of information, which, though each item by itself is perhaps insignificant, achieves in toto a kind of persuasiveness. Few medieval households could have reached the ideal aspired to by such nobles as George, Duke of Clarence, who ordained:

> . . .sith that alle wisdom, grace, and goodnesse, procedeth of veray love, drede, and feythfulle service of God, withoute whose helpe and socoure no good governaunce ne politique rule may be hadde; it is ordeyned therefore,. . .one of the chapleyns shall be redy to saye matyns and masse to the householde, and also evensonge; and that every (one)... be at the seid dyvine service. . ..[64]

Behind this idealistic front, surely, lurked the less exalted motives of order and control, and the manipulation of religious spectacle for political purposes. Nevertheless, accumulated evidence seems to suggest that the noble household in the later middle ages was united under its lord as a religious community – not as a monastery, certainly, but as a reasonably cohesive body which attempted regular daily worship and frequent charitable practices as a 'familye (that) may live together in love and kindness'.[65]

NOTES

1 For an exposition of this subject, see T.S.R. Boase, *Death in the Middle Ages*, London, 1972, p.98.
2 Longleat ms. 457, m.1.
3 Thomas Percy, ed., *The Northumberland Household Book*, privately printed, 1826, pp. 332–333; see also Society of Antiquaries, eds., *A Collection of Ordinances and Regulations*, London, 1790, passim, and Frederick Furnivall, *Babees Book*, Early English Texts Society no. 32, 1868, passim.
4 R.G.K.A. Mertes, 'Secular Noble Households in England, 1350–1550,' Doctoral thesis submitted to the University of Edinburgh, 1980, gives in detail the ms. material available for these families and for other households in England.
5 Caroline Kerrison and Lucy Toulmin Smith, eds., *A Commonplace Book of the 15th Century*, London, 1886, pp. 10–12.
6 *Calendar of Patent Rolls* (CPR) 1368–1372, p. 290, and R.J. Stonor, *Stonor*, Newport, 1952, pp. 59 and 88.
7 H.C. Maxwell-Lyte, *Dunster and Its Lords, 1066–1881*, privately printed, 1882, pp. 1–10 and diagram 1.
8 Stonor, p. 88, and Severn A. Ashurst-Majendie, *Some Account of the Family of De Vere*, London, 1904.
9 See Mertes, ch. 3.
10 Margaret Wood, *The English Mediaeval House*, London, 1965, pp. 208–227.

11 Somerset Record Office (SOM RO) DD/L P37/7 and 10-A.

12 Ashurst-Majendie, p. 94.

13 See in particular SOM RO DD/L P37/9.

14 See Stonor, p. 88; Maxwell-Lyte, pp. 112–114; Essex RO D/DPR 137; Society of Antiquaries (Soc Ant) ms. 77 and Public Record Office (PRO) E 101 518/5 for the Staffords; and Percy, ed., p. 323.

15 The Luttrell's chaplain, John Bacwell, was also steward and treasurer, 1405–1423; see SOM RO DD/L P37/7, 9, 10-A and 10-B.

16 J.R.R. Tolkien, E.V. Gordon and Norman Davis, eds., *Sir Gawain and the Green Knight*, Oxford, 1967, pp. 2–3, 11, 37–84, shows an idealized version of household liturgical practices.

17 Percy, ed., pp. 322–325.

18 Longleat ms. 457, m.2, and *PRO* E 101 518/5, pt. 1.

19 A.R. Myers, ed., *The Household of Edward IV*, Manchester, 1959, pp. 133–135.

20 Percy, ed., pp. 325–326.

21 Frank L. Harrison, *Music in Mediaeval Britain*, London, 1958, pp. 17–25.

22 *Ibid*, pp. 25–30 and 172–174.

23 Soc Ant ms. 77, and Percy, ed., pp. 325–326.

24 Harrison, pp. 174–176.

25 *Ibid.*, p. 21, and Walter L. Woodfill, *Musicians in English Society*, Princeton, N.J., 1953, p. 166.

26 *PRO* E 36 220; British Library (BL) Royal ms. B XXXV D; and Staffordshire (Staffs) RO D 641/1/3/5–10.

27 BL Royal ms. B XXXV D.

28 Sir William H. St. John Hope, ed., 'The Last Testament and Inventory of John de Vere, 13th Earl of Oxford,' in *Archaeologia* vol. 66, 1915, p. 301.

29 H.F. Lovell-Cocks, *The Religious Life of Oliver Cromwell*, London, 1960, esp. pp. 20–23, 68–70.

30 Jan Huizinga, *The Waning of the Middle Ages*, London, 1979, p. 172.

31 *PRO* E 36/220.

32 See notes 2 and 3.

33 Paul V.B. Jones, *The Household of a Tudor Nobleman*, University of Illinois Studies in Social Sciences, no. 6, 1917.

34 Joel T. Rosenthal, *Nobles and the Noble Life, 1295–1500*, London, 1976, p. 49.

35 Stonor, p. 88.

36 See especially Staffs RO D 641/1/3/4 (1452–3), and BL add mss. Egerton 2208 (1438–9) and 2209 (1454–5), and SOM RO DD/L P37/7 (1405–6).

37 SOM RO DD/L P37/7, 10–12 (1422–1431); Westminster Abbey Muniments (WAM) 12185 (1468), Percy, ed., pp. 88–96, and Society of Antiquaries, eds., pp. 27–28.

38 Society of Antiquaries, eds., pp. 76–77.

38a Carlisle RO Cockermouth ms. – blind.

39 Staffs RO D 641/1/3/8 (1503–4).

40 For Instance, see SOM RO DD/L P37/7. The average Sunday total was 14s 7d; that of the next-greatest day, 9s 1d.

41 Kent RO Cat Mk U1475 A93 (1447), A92 (1475).

42 SOM RO DD/L P37/7.

43 *PRO* E 36 220 (1520).

44 SOM RO DD/L P37/7; Soc Ant ms. 77 (1490–1); Longleat ms. BPA 5949 (1506–7); Staffs RO D 1721/1/5 (1507–8).

45 Staffs RO D 1721/1/5.

46 See especially SOM RO DD/L P37/7 and PRO C47 37/2 (1432–3).

47 BL Add ms. roll 3962 (1444–5) and PRO C47 37/4/12–14 (1474–75).

48 Charles Lethbridge Kingsford, ed., *The Stonor Letters and Papers*, Camden Society Third Series, vols. 29 and 30, 1919. (*SL & P*).

49 See Stonor, pp. 80–88; also *PRO* C 47 37/7 (1478).
50 Kent RO Cat Mk U1475 A93 and A92.
51 *SL & P*, 30, no. 358.
52 N.B. Lewer, ed., 'The Testament and Last Will of Elizabeth, Widow of John De Vere, 13th Earl of Oxford,' in *Transactions of the Essex Archaeological Society*, vol. 20, 1933, pp. 7–16.
53 Stonor, p. 80; SOM RO DD/L P37/7; and John Evans, 'The Wedding of Richard Posted and Elizabeth, Daughter of William More of Loseley', in *Archaeologia*, vol. 36 (1), 1855, pp. 35–52.
54 SOM RO DD/L P37/7.
55 Hope, pp. 278–80; Lewer, pp. 7–16.
56 Hope, p. 278.
57 *PRO* C 47 37/3/30–33.
58 *PRO* E 36 220, especially, and *SL & P*, 29, no. 47.
59 *PRO* E 36 220; *PRO* E 101 631/20 (1513–14); BL Royal ms. 7f XIV, ff. 1–19 (1518–1519); Staffs RO D 1721/1/10 (1547; *SL & P* 29, p. xlvii.
60 N.H. Nicolas, *Privy Purse Expenses of Elizabeth of York and Wardrobe Accounts of Edward IV*, London, 1830; *PRO* E 36 220.
61 *PRO* E 36 220; SOM RO DD/L P37/7.
62 SOM RO DD/L P37/9 (1421–2) and *PRO* C 47 37/5/1–9 (*tempus* Edward IV).
63 SOM RO DD/L P37/11–12 (1428–1431); and *PRO* E 36 220 and BL Royal ms. 7f XIV, ff. 1–9.
64 Society of Antiquaries, eds., p. 89.
65 Jones, p. 186.

Law and Arbitration in Nottinghamshire 1399–1461

SIMON J. PAYLING

Recent work on the problem of disorder in fifteenth-century England, particularly that of Dr Edward Powell, has led to a marked change of emphasis in the way in which this problem is viewed. No longer is it fashionable to stress the apparent ineffectiveness of the sophisticated judicial machinery of the crown but rather the emphasis has shifted towards an appreciation of the self-regulating properties of local communities through the extra-judicial process of arbitration. In his study of the last major perambulation of the king's bench, which took place in the summer of 1414, Powell concluded that the maintenance of the king's peace, far from depending on the exemplary punishment of those of baronial and gentry rank whose disputes were a genuine threat to public order, was based 'upon a fragile consensus in local society, promoted by arbitration and conciliation'.[1] Underlying this conclusion is a major reassessment of the nature of royal justice. The traditional assumption that law and order was most effectively imposed from above by a strong king has been rejected, stress being laid instead on the responsibility that the local communites themselves bore for the maintenance of a public order that ultimately depended not on the law courts but on the attitude of individuals towards their neighbours.[2] It is not my purpose here to discuss whether the later middle ages saw a general breakdown in the administration of royal justice which, in effect, threw the responsibility for maintaining social peace on to extra-judicial conciliation within the local communites. Dr Powell has already argued persuasively, if not conclusively, against this view. My aim is the much more limited one of examining the situation as it existed in the county of Nottinghamshire during the Lancastrian period, concentrating largely on the gentry and magnate crime which constituted the greatest threat to public order.

The starting point must be to ask how effective was the crown in the punishment of crime, particularly among the local aristocracies. It had long been realised that the justices of the peace were ineffective in this rôle for not only were the justices themselves often involved in the very disorder they were commissioned to suppress but the jurors, on whom the justices were entirely dependent for indictments, were overwhelmingly of sub-gentry status and unwilling to indict their social superiors.[3] Of no greater value in the suppression of aristocratic violence were the justices of assize and gaol delivery: the goal delivery justices could only be concerned with those already in custody as a result of indictments in local courts, usually before the justices of the peace, and were dependent on the verdict of petty jurors often loth to convict,[4] while the criminal jurisdiction of the assize justices was confined to those cases referred to them from king's bench, again from local courts in the first instance, and had the same dependence on local petty jurors.[5] Much more effective, although by no means free from local restraint, were the general commissions of oyer and terminer and enquiry through which the crown was able to take a direct interest in local disorder. Indeed, once the king's bench had become stationary at Westminster, no longer acting as a court of first instance in its visitation of particular counties, these commissions were the most potent means by which the crown could intervene in local affairs.[6] Such commissions were issued for Nottinghamshire twice during the Lancastrian period: in 1414 and 1440. The first illustrates the system at its most impartial, as an effective method of suppressing local disorder; and the second at its most partial with the commission reduced to a tool of political faction just as the more limited special oyer and terminer had been before it fell out of use early in the fifteenth century. Both are worth examining in detail for they illustrate not only the problems that faced the crown when it attempted to intervene in local affairs but also the close connection that existed between the formal machinery of the law and the informal machinery of arbitration.

The first, issued during the course of Henry V's second parliament held at Leicester, was part of a much wider campaign to restore peace to the localities, headed by the king's bench perambulation of Leicestershire, Staffordshire and Shropshire.[7] The last years of Henry IV had been characterised by a series of disturbances in the midlands and elsewhere, and the new king was determined to put an end to this disorder before embarking on his French conquests. It is probable that the three petitions presented in the Leicester parliament against the oppressive activities of the powerful Nottinghamshire knight, Sir Richard Stanhope, were the immediate pretext for the issue of the Nottinghamshire commission of enquiry on 14 May,[8] but the presentments later made by the county jurors show that the enquiry is to be seen against the wider background of disorder in the county dating back to the summer of 1411, and for which Stanhope, although predominent in it, was by no means solely responsible. Much of this disorder was occasioned by a land dispute between two minor gentry, Alexander Mering and the Stanhope follower, John Tuxford, which came to involve not only Stanhope but other leading county knights.

The story of this dispute can be partly reconstructed from the even-handed presentments made before the commissioners by the county grand jury.[9] In so far as a failed arbitrement led to violent recriminations, it bears a striking resemblance to the Erdswick/Ferrers dispute which precipitated the king's bench visitation of Staffordshire.[10] In August 1411 a loveday held to reconcile the competing claims of Mering and Tuxford, and involving six leading county gentry as arbiters, floundered on Mering's refusal to come to terms. In response, Tuxford, through the maintenance of Stanhope, who had acted as an arbiter for him at the loveday, and Stanhope's young brother-in-law, Ralph Cromwell (not yet the third Lord Cromwell), forcibly expelled Mering from the disputed lands. Mering, in turn, with the equally powerful maintenance of Sir John Zouche and Sir John Leek, both of whom had earlier acted as his arbiters, raised a large force to make a forcible re-entry. A dangerous conflict was averted only by the timely arrival of William, Lord Roos of Belvoir, at that time the leading magnate landholder in the county.

While this riot was the subject of the main presentments made by the grand jury it also made several other presentments against the county élite. Both Stanhope and Zouche were indicted as common maintainers and sustainers of quarrels and for other trespasses unconnected with the Merring/Tuxford dispute, while Cromwell was indicted for felony.[11] Taken together with the presentments made by the lesser wapentake and borough juries, what appears to be a fairly complete list of the recent criminal activity of the county aristocracy was returned. The crown itself must take much of the credit for producing this desirable state of affairs. During the Leicester parliament, which ended just before the commissioners sat, Stanhope had been committed to prison to answer the petitions laid against him,[12] an essential preliminary to an objective enquiry, while the crown had also acted wisely in its choice of commissioners. Henry chose to avoid the appointment of local magnates and gentry instead relying on men personally connected with himself. The commission was headed by his Chamberlain and one of his closest intimates, Henry, Lord Fitzhugh of Ravensworth, and the comptroller of the household, Sir John Rothenale. In these circumstances it is not surprising that the county community should have cooperated, the leading gentry, with the exception of those involved in the recent disorders, proving their loyalty by serving as jurors and producing a balanced catalogue of recent offences.

Indeed this commission shows royal intervention in local affairs at its most effective, at least as far as eliciting indictments was concerned. But how successfully did it fulfil its purpose? If this was the exemplary punishment of the indicted it failed badly. The issue of the illegally comprehensive general pardon of December 1414, available *de cursu* from the chancery, on the payment of 16s. 4d. and a few other incidental payments, effectively alowed nearly all those who had been indicted during the wider campaign against lawlessness, of which the Nottinghamshire enquiry was but a small part, to escape conviction and punishment.[13] This has led Dr Powell to conclude that this campaign was never intended to punish crime but was rather an exercise in political management, not primarily designed to secure convictions but to resolve or at least defuse existing disputes amongst the county aristocracies before the king departed for France. This view tallies well with the Nottinghamshire evidence where the aim of the enquiry appears to have been to deter the leading gentry from further maintenance of the Mering/Tuxford dispute, which was not yet concluded but had now moved into the royal courts, and to serve as a warning to Stanhope that the new king would not tolerate his illegal activities. There is nothing to indicate, as there is for Shropshire and Staffordshire, that the king took large securities of the peace, additional to the much smaller securites that had to be found as a condition of the granting of a pardon, form those indicted in Nottinghamshire, but the success of the enquiry is to be measured by the fact that the Mering/Tuxford dispute was brought to a peaceful conclusion two years later and no further compaints about Stanhope were received. His restoration to the county bench in November 1417 marks the completion of his rehabilitation.

The lack of partisanship demonstrated in the presentments made before this 1414 commission is not matched in 1440, a commission issued in very different circumstances. Although it was in the form of a general commission of oyer and terminer with a mandate to enquire into all offences, it was issued not directly on royal initiative but in response to a private petition to the council by the Derbyshire esquire, John Statham, and on payment of a mark into the hanaper. He complained of attacks on him and his property by Henry, Lord Grey of Codnor, and requested an oyer and terminer on the grounds that Grey had been guilty not only of offences against him but also against many others in the county.[14] It is remarkable how quickly the crown acted on this petition: only four days elapsed between the last attack complained of and the issue of the oyer and terminer commission.[15] This suggests that the petition had a powerful sponsor and subsequent events as well as what is known of Statham show that this was so. Statham was one of the leading members of Cromwell's Derbyshire affinity,[16] and Cromwell was at this time at the height of his influence both locally and nationally. A long serving councillor, he had been treasurer since 1433 and, over the previous decade, chiefly through his acquisition of the Belers and Heriz inheritances, he had acquired extensive estates in both Nottinghamshire and Derbyshire to supplement the ancient lands of his family in these counties. Moreover, his local influences had been augmented by grants of local office; from 1434 he was constable of Nottingham Castle, keeper of Sherwood Forest and the royal parks of Bestwood and Clipstone, offices once held by Grey's father.[17] Indeed, by the early 1430s he had supplanted Grey as the leading magnate in the area, and his appointment to the oyer and terminer commission, together with that of the two leading Nottinghamshire knights closely connected with him, Sir Thomas Chaworth and Sir William Babington,[18] and a long-time rival of Grey's in Derbyshire Sir Richard Vernon,[19] implies that this commission, mandated to enquire into all offences not only in Derbyshire but also in Nottinghamshire, was never going to be impartial.

Since the original indictments no longer survive, the presentments made before these commissioners have to be reconstructed from the rex section of the king's bench plea roll.[20] It is not possible to say what proportion of the total number of indictments those found on the plea roll represent, but in view of their number and the duplication between them (inevitable since most of the offences involved large groups of men) it is probable that it is a substantial one. This impression is strengthened by the fact that, at some unknown date, all the records of the commission were called into king's bench by *mandamus* and that very few of the indicted were tried before the commissioners although some made fine.[21] It is hence particularly striking that all but one of the plea roll entries relate to the crimes of Grey, his tenants and servants, over a hundred of whom were indicted. If these indictments are to be taken at their face value, Grey himself was guilty of a great number of offences, including incitement to murder and abusing his position as a justice of the peace in both counties. But most significant are the indictments concerning his campaign against Cromwell's followers. Lengthy presentments were made concerning the attacks on Statham and his manor of Morley which had taken place on 6 and 7 July 1440, while other presentments related to the attempted ambush of Thomas Darcy, a leading member of Cromwell's affinity in both Nottinghamshire and Lincolnshire, and the vandalism of the property of James and Thomas Stanhope, the stepsons of Cromwell's sister.[22] Most revealing of all is a presentment made by a Derbyshire jury concerning a raid on Cromwell's park at West Hallam, which had taken place on 19 August, more than a month after the commission had been issued and a few weeks before the commissioners sat. The raiders, identified as followers of Grey, had killed a deer, torn out its internal organs and deposited them at the gates of the park, *in despectu* of Cromwell.[23] It is tempting to think, in view of the imbalance of these presentments, that they reflect only one side of a dispute, and that similar offences committed by Cromwell and his supporters against Grey went unreported.[24] This is the more likely since the sheriff, who empanelled the indicting juries was Cromwell's neighbour, John Cokfeld, a man who had much benefited from his patronage in the past.[25] Moreover, while the composition of these juries is unknown, two releases of attaint and *decies tantum* from known followers of Grey to one Nottinghamshire and one Derbyshire jury enrolled on the close roll give an indication of the composition of the petty juries which tried the private bills presented before the commissioners, and both strongly suggest that the juries were rigged. The Derbyshire jury was headed by none other than Statham himself and his two sons, and the Nottinghamshire jury by Darcy, a servant of his named Richard Burgh, who had complained before the commissioners that Grey had falsely imprisoned him, and John Stanhope, a kinsman of Cromwell's whose uncle's lands had been vandalised by Grey's servants.[26] The empanelling of such juries and the presentments made are not the only indications of partiality for we also have the testimony of Grey himself.

Statham's petitions immediately provoked the crown into taking strong measures against him. On 16 July, just five days after the issue of the commission, he was ordered under pain of one thousand pounds to surrender himself to the Tower, and, although released a month later, it was only on condition that he moved no more than three miles from London.[27] He was thus absent from Derbyshire when the commissioners took the presentments against him and his servants, and was probably still in London in the following March when he petitioned the king for a general pardon. This was granted when Cromwell's old adversary Humphrey, duke of Gloucester, interceded on his behalf, but only on condition that he find security of the peace in £1000. Soon afterwards he presented a further petition complaining about Cromwell's role as one of the commissioners. He claimed that Cromwell was his mortal enemy and a biased judge, and asked that he be ordered to attend no further sessions.[28] His request was granted, but the damage had been done. His position in local politics was fatally undermined. Many of his supporters had been outlawed, and while he was able to free himself from the presentments made against him by pleading his pardon in king's bench in Trinity term 1442,[29] his outlawed supporters had to wait until the general pardon of 1446 before they could reverse their outlawries, by which time Grey was dead.

Not content with bringing the formal judicial machinery of the crown against Grey, Cromwell had also used his powerful position in local politics to harness the informal procedure of arbitration to further humiliate his rival. On 28 August 1441 Grey had made a feoffment of his valuable manors of Hoo in Kent and Toton in Nottinghamshire to a group of Cromwell's nominees. The condition attached to this feoffment was that Grey and his servants should stand to the judgement of Maud, countess of Cambridge, William, bishop of Lincoln, and three of the oyer and terminer commissioners, John, viscount Beaumont, Sir Thomas Chaworth and Sir William Babington, in all matters hanging between them, on the one part, and Cromwell, Darcy and Statham, on the other. Less than a fortnight later, these arbiters returned their award: Grey was to find security of the peace in chancery or before the Nottinghamshire justices of the peace in the sum of eight hundred pounds.[30] This Grey failed to do, and hence the manors, which represented about a quarter of his landed income remained in the hands of Cromwell's nominees not only up to Grey's death in July 1444 but also throughout the minority of his son and heir. It was not until 1455 that Cromwell gave instructions that they should be restored.[31] In short, not only had Cromwell, with ruthless efficiency, destroyed his only serious rival in local politics, but he had also exploited the situation to increasse his own landed income by about one hundred and thirty pounds per annum. The award returned by the arbiters was wholly superfluous in view of the large security of the peace Grey had already had to find as a condition of his pardon, and it is hard to avoid the conclusion that Cromwell orchestrated the whole affair with the aim of depriving Grey of valuable lands.

The Nottinghamshire evidence reveals the limitations of the oyer and terminer and enquiry commission as a means of controlling aristocratic disorder. Not only was it at best an occasional expedient, it was also totally dependent on the cooperation of presenting juries susceptible to local influence. When the crown was strong, as in 1414, the local gentry were generally prepared to return a fairly complete and balanced picture of recent criminal activity, but when the crown was weak, as it was throughout the 1440s and 1450s, oyer and terminer could too easily be reduced to a tool of political faction exploited by men of local and national influence to obtain indictments against their local rivals. Moreover, even disregarding the dependence of the crown on the cooperation of local juries, which was by no means assured even when the crown was strong as illustrated by the failure of the commission sent to Devon in February 1414, there was a further more serious limitation to oyer and terminer and crown prosecution of gentry and magnate crime in general, namely that the crown depended on those very gentry and magnates whose disputes were the raw material of public violence for the administration of the counties. In this situation, the stringent punishment of those involved in local disputes could only serve to disturb the equilibrium of local political communities, which, as recent gentry studies have shown, were tight-knit and independent-minded and often resented direct royal intervention in their affairs. Resentment would have been far greater and hence cooperation far less if such intervention had resulted in severe punishments. Furthermore, since the crown lacked the means to enquire adequately into the truth of the indictments made by presenting juries, and was dependent on the verdict of petty juries, which were open to the same local influences, such punishments of the indicted were generally inappropriate.[32] Indeed, as Dr Powell has pointed out, the problem of maintaining public order in the later middle ages was, from the crown's point of view, as much political as judicial. Emphasis had to be laid on the restoration of social peace through the reconciliation of disputing parties rather than on the punishment of those parties for past crimes against the king's peace. Since aristocratic violence was rarely motiveless, being frequently the product of local property disputes, with the forcible entries and riots these entailed, it was right that this should be so. While at its best oyer and terminer could deter those in dispute from resorting to further violence and force them into the courts, it could do no more. Moreover, it would be unrealistic to imagine that, once in the courts, the machinery of the common law should unfailingly have been able to end these disputes by judgement. Nor was this principally because of the much debated weaknesses of this machinery; the ineffectiveness of mesne process in personal actions, the delays involved in securing the appearance of petty juries, the Fabian tactics allowed to the defendant, or even the depen- dence of this machinery on that most corruptible of local officials, the sheriff. But rather the chief cause lay in the fact that the law was an antagonistic process, verdict and judgement leading to a complete victory or utter defeat for the litigant. There was no room for compromise in this rigid system, and yet it was in compromise that the best opportunity for lasting peace lay. To find these solutions, local gentry communities had to look inwards to the informal judgement of their peers and immediate feudal superiors rather than outwards to the royal courts. As Dr Wright has pointed out, the infrastructure of kinsmen and neighbours provided an alternative and older system of justice to that imposed by central government.[33] Conciliation and arbitration within this infrastructure had significant advantages over litigation; it could, at its most effective, quickly and cheaply produce compromise solutions acceptable to both disputing parties, circumventing the expenses, delays and inflexibility of the common law, and ensuring that the solution fitted into the social and political context of the environment in which it was made, namely that of the local landed community.

The Mering/Tuxford dispute is a well-documented example of this process at work. I have described how this dispute escalated into violence after a failed loveday, but this was only the beginning. Having failed to oust Tuxford by violence, Mering resorted to litigation.[34] In January 1412 he sued out a writ of novel disseisin, but, unfortunately for him, the taking of this assize was much delayed by the tenurial interest of the crown in the disputed lands. An unlicensed feoffment made by Tuxford resulted in their seizure into the king's hands only a few days before the assize was first scheduled to be heard, while, at this hearing, Tuxford ingeniously, but fraudulently, pleaded that the crown was seized of the reversion under an entail of 1369. Consequently the unfortunate plaintiff was left to sue for royal licence to proceed with the assize, and it was probably this delay that led Mering to agree to a second attempt at arbitration, sponsored by William, Lord Roos, who had intervened to end the riot of 1411. In October 1412 both parties entered into mutual recognisances in 500 marks to abide by the arbitration of Roos himself, William Gascoigne, the chief justice of the king's bench, and Robert Tirwhit, one of the justices before whom the assize was pending.[35] Clearly a lesson had been learned from the failure of the first attempted arbitration and local gentry were not to play any part in the award. Nevertheless, despite the high rank and legal expertise of the arbiters, no settlement was reached, and Mering subsequently petitioned for the resumption of the assize. A later petition presented on his behalf by the commons in the parliament of March 1416 gives details of the verdict. It was found that Mering had indeed been disseised and the jury awarded him the not inconsiderable sum of 50 marks in damages. However, a clerical error by the clerk of the justices had prevented judgement being given, and it was to remedy this error that the petition was presented.[36] The crown assented to the amending of the clerk's record, but it seems probable that pressure was exerted on Mering in parliament not to proceed to the rendering of the judgment. The evidence for this can only be circumstantial. Very shortly after his successful petition Mering non-suited in the assize, despite the fact that he already had a verdict in his favour, and two knights, Sir Thomas Rempston of Nottinghamshire and Sir John Assheton of Lancashire, who had been MPs in this parliament, were appointed to arbitrate.[37] They returned an award which, while it favoured Mering, ensured that Tuxford was not left empty-handed for he was given what amounted to a life estate in a moiety of the disputed lands with reversion to Mering and his heirs.[38]

The story of this dispute amply illustrates the advantages of the arbitration process over litigation. Despite the delaying tactics employed by Tuxford he was, in the end, unable to prevent the total defeat of his weaker claim in the assize with heavy damages being assessed against him. However, the implementation of his verdict would have offended powerful local interests, in particular those of Sir Richard Stanhope, the dominant landholder in that part of the county in which the disputed lands lay. The arbiters' award ensured that Tuxford avoided this complete defeat, and yet, at the same time, that the lands would eventually become reunited in the hands of the Merings. This was appropriate since Tuxford's title, although weaker than Mering's, was not entirely frivolous, being based on an entail made in 1369 by Mering's elder brother, whose widow Tuxford had married.

In view of the advantages of arbitration as a method of dispute settlement is it not surprising to find the crown, principally through the equitable jurisdiction of the chancellor, actively engaged in encouraging it. Dr Powell had pointed out that a comparison of the early chancery proceedings with the bonds of arbitration entered on the dorse of the close rolls reveals many examples of chancery cases referred by the chancellor to the award of arbiters. The Nottinghamshire evidence provides a parallel example, but in this case with the chancellor acting upon a petition to the minority council rather than to the courts of chancery. The prior of Blyth complained that, on 27 March 1428, an armed body of 400 men, led by the gentleman Hugh Cressy of nearby Grove, had thrown down several of his houses and driven away his tenants.[39] This offence was also the subject of a presentment made on the following 20 April before the Nottinghamshire justices of the peace under the provisions of the 1411 statute of riots, and a few weeks later a royal commission was issued for the arrest of Cressy and 29 others, including two local esquires, John Gaitford and Hugh Hercy.[40] This commission, issued as it was to the two JPs who had taken the presentment, was probably the council's first response to this presentment and the prior's petition that had preceded it, but the matter was also referred directly to the chancellor, John Kemp, archbishop of York. While Kemp was on his way north to York late in the following July he stopped for a few days at his archiepiscopal manor house at Scrooby, just a mile from the priory, and from here he actively intervened to reconcile the prior and the local gentry. On the 28th he took conditional bonds in 500 marks from the prior, on one part, and Cressy, Gaitford and Hercy, on the other. The condition was that both parties should abide by the award of the two JPs, Sir Richard Stanhope and Sir Henry Pierpont, before whom the presentment had been made, together with two south Yorkshire esquires and two local lawyers. If these six arbiters, three acting for each side, failed to make an award, the parties were to abide by the award of Cromwell and the archbishop himself.[41] Unfortunately, the terms of this award are unknown, but since no more is heard of the dispute we may assume that it was brought satisfactorily to a conclusion. The chancellor's arranged arbitration no doubt proved a far more effective method of achieving this end than would have the simple punishment of the local gentry and their followers under the provisions of the statues of riots[42] since we are not dealing here with a motiveless act of vandalism but a symptom of some wider dispute between the priory and its neighbours. There had been tension in this area for some years previously with the prior and the local gentry and their followers being involved in suit and counter-suit in common pleas for debt, assault and close breaking.[43] Only with the underlying cause of this tension removed could peace be restored: arbitration was a means to this end, punishment of the rioters was not.

However, although the chancellor was involved in encouraging arbitration at the local level in those disputes which came before him, a more immediate and hence more effective part in the furthering of extra-judicial dispute settlement was played by local magnates. Drs Post and Rawcliffe have shown that baronial councils exercised an equitable jurisdiction similar in type, if not in scale, to that of the chancellor himself.[44] This is hardly surprising since the more immediate interest of magnates in the affairs of their own localities, together with their personal and political ties with local gentry, gave them a particular interest in settling disputes within their own areas of influence, especially those within their own affinities. As Dr Wright has pointed out, the affinity provided a ready-made umpire in its lord, while the lords themselves saw the maintenance of peace within their own affinities as one of the obligations of lordship.[45] Even a magnate of such poor reputation as George, duke of Clarence, was active in this rôle.[46] No doubt that system worked both ways, with lords sometimes using their authority to impose settlements on their dependants, and at others the dependants appealing to their lords for an authoritive award. Moreover, it may not only have been the retainers of a lord that looked to him to settle their disputes, a lord of sufficient influence and with a reputation for fair-mindedness might act as an arbiter within the wider local community, witness, for example, Lord Roos's attempt to end the Mering/Tuxford dispute in 1412.

After Roos's death in 1414, no great lord had any particular interest in Nottinghamshire affairs until about twenty years later when Cromwell began to increase his landholding in the county at the same time as he rose to national prominence with his appointment as treasurer in 1433, and it is from his period of dominance in county affairs that the best Nottinghamshire evidence for the rôle of magnates as arbiters comes. There can be no doubt that Cromwell took his responsibilities in this direction very seriously. In the late 1440s or early 1450s he wrote to two members of his Norfolk affinity, who were at odds, urging them to do no more to further their quarrel until they had discussed the matter with him, ending his letter with a warning, 'ye faile not herof, as I may do anything for you heraftir'.[47] In similar circumstances he intervened to end a dispute between two of his Nottinghamshire affinity, Richard Sutton and Thomas Nevill, in July 1447. So tangled was this dispute that he had at the outset to call on the legal advice of John Portington, a justice of the common pleas and one of the assize justices for the county, but, even with this learned assistance, the matter proved beyond immediate resolution. In the final award it was determined that Nevill should pay £10 to a servant of Sutton's who had been assaulted in the course of the dispute. For the rest Cromwell found both parties equally blameworthy, and referred the matters remaining to Portington and his fellow justice of assize, William Ayscogh, because, in his words, 'it is a matere longinge to the lawe which is diffuse to determyne withoute counsell lerned'.[48] There could be no better indication of Dr Powell's contention that arbitration served as an adjunct to the law rather than stood in its place.

The same theme is illustrated in a different way in an award that Cromwell did successfully return, an award that brought an end to an altogether more important dispute for it involved members of one of the leading county families, the Willoughbys of Wollaton. It is of particular interest not only because it shows the necessity of confirming by collusive litigation the terms of any award that concerned itself with title to real property, and the consequent indispensability of common lawyers, and even royal justices, to the arbitration process, but also because it demonstrates the failure of the land law to deal unaided with the increasing sophistication of family settlements made possible by the feoffment-to-use.

For these reasons the background of what is a complicated dispute is worth recounting in detail. It had its origin in the over-generous provision made by the wealthy Sir Hugh Willoughby for his children by his second wife; such provisions made at the expense of the common law heir, were a frequent cause of strife in fifteenth-century England. When Sir Hugh drew up his will in September 1443 he was at the head of a very large family;[49] by his first wife he had two surviving sons, the eldest being Richard, while by his second wife, the wealthy heiress Margaret Freville, he had no less than five boys and five girls, eight of whom remained unmarried when the will was drawn up. In these circumstances it is understandable that he should wish to make some provision for these younger children, and any such provision was bound to be to Richard's disadvantage. The issues of two thirds of the Nottinghamnshire manors of Bradmore and Willoughby, along with the Lincolnshire manors of Dunsby and Wigtoft, and the Leicestershire manors of Cossington and Hambleton, were to provide the considerable sum of 200 marks for each of the children that remained unmarried at this death and to keep his sons at grammar school. Moreover, Hugh's feoffees were to make estate of these heavily encumbered manors not to Richard but to his step-mother, Margaret, for her life and subsequently to her executors for variously two or three years after her death. Only then were they to come to Richard. The chief manor of the Willoughby inheritance, Wollaton, on which no charges were placed, was also to remain in Margaret's hands and those of her executors for three years before reverting to Richard. Even more alarmingly for Richard, all the Willoughby lands in Wollaton, not parcel of the manor there, together with the neighbouring manor of Sutton Passeys and a sub-manor of Willoughby were settled on Margaret with remainders over to her issue by Hugh and her own right heirs. Most of the rest of the Willoughby lands were assigned as Margaret's dower, while certain small scattered estates were to provide for her sons by Hugh. In short, Richard was to inherit nothing until after her death and even then his expectations would be much reduced. He had every reason to feel deeply aggrieved at the settlement, especially since Margaret was little older than himself and had valuable lands in her own right from which she might be expected to make at least some provision for her many children by Hugh.[50]

In this situation, it is not surprising that Hugh should have anticipated that his eldest son would not acquiesce in the settlement, and that given freedom of action he would attempt to overturn it at law: an attempt that would have had every chance of success since much of the Willoughby inheritance, including the manor of Wollaton, had been tailed to the main line by the founder of the family's wealth by fines levied in the 1330s.[51] Hence Hugh added a clause to his will that Richard should find security to Margaret within a year of his death that he would not in any way hinder the performance of the will. If he would not do this, the whole of the Willoughby inheritance was to go to Margaret and her heirs by Hugh. As death approached, Hugh took a firmer measure to secure obedience to his wishes. On New Year's Day 1448 he forced Richard to swear an oath before Cromwell, three leading local knights, including Sir Thomas Chaworth and Sir Richard Vernon, and two spiritual representatives, the abbot of Welbeck and a friar, that he would allow both Margaret undisturbed possession of the manor of Wollaton and Hugh's feoffees to dispose of the other lands according to the terms of the will.[52]

Hugh died in the following November, and Richard, immediately disregarding his oath, began a subtle campaign to win his father's lands. By labouring the jurors in the inquisitons taken on his father's death he sought to have it returned that all the Willoughby lands were held in fee tail. This was true for the bulk of it, but not for the manor of Sutton Passeys, the lands in Wollaton and the sub-manor of Willoughby, which had been permanently alienated from him in his father's will. To circumvent this inconvenience, he prevailed upon the Nottinghamshire jurors fraudulently to return that these lands had been jointly settled by deed on Hugh and his first wife, namely Richard's mother, and their issue.[53] As a result of the returned inquisitions, Richard was able to sue out of the king's hands all his father's lands, save those to be assigned in dower.[54] Clearly the situation was now even more fraught with difficulty than it had been at Hugh's death, and it was at this point that Richard and Margaret agreed to arbitration, whether of their own volition or at Cromwell's insistence is unknown. On 11 September 1449 they entered into mutual bonds in the large sum of 1000 marks to be bound by Cromwell's award, whereupon Cromwell, who was plainly prepared to disregard the oath Richard had previously taken before him, called to his assistance the formidable legal expertise of the chief justice of the king's bench, Sir John Fortescue, and the common pleas justice who had previously been associated with him in the Sutton/Nevill award, John Portington. They returned their award in London on 15 November, a year to the day after Hugh's death.[55]

Inevitably the main part of the award was concerned with the division of the estates and its terms can be briefly described. Richard was to have immediate possession of the manors of Wollaton, Sutton Passeys and the other lands in Wollaton, while Margaret was to have as her dower the manors of Willoughby and Cossington, and, above her dower for life, the manor of Hambleton and the sub-manor of Willoughby, all of which were to revert to Richard or his heirs immediately after her death. In recompense for the loss of Sutton Passeys and the other lands alienated to her in Hugh's will, she was to have the Lincolnshire manors of Dunsby and Wigtoft to her and her heirs. Both parties had reason to be content with the settlement. Richard gained immediate possession of a compact and valuable estate just north of Nottingham which ensured him of his rightful place amongst the shire élite. The price he had to pay was the permanent loss of the two outlying Lincolnshire manors, but this was greatly preferable to losing Sutton Passeys and any of the Wollaton lands. Indeed, the most unfortunate provision of Hugh's will was that those lands permanently alientated from the common law heir lay at the heart of the Willoughby inheritance, a provision to some extent forced on him by the fact that these were the only lands he held in fee simple. The arbiters noted the undesirability of this provision in their award when they stated that Richard was to have the main Nottinghamshire lands of the inheritance, either in possession or reversion, 'for his great ease and quiet and to that end that no other person but he shall have interest in the said towns of Wollaton, Sutton and Willoughby'. For her part, Margaret too had little reason for complaint. She could not reasonably expect to hold on to all she had gained under the terms of her husband's will, and yet, from the award, she gained much more than her common law dower entitlement while the two Lincolnshire manors were to be permanently alientated to her and her heirs. Together with the considerable estates she held in her own right, principally the Warwickshire manor of Middleton, this made her a very rich widow. Moreover, under another of the provisions of the award, the burden of providing for her many children was to fall partly on her stepson who was to pay £20 p.a. for five years towards the marriages of his half-sisters.

Having settled the estates in a satisfactory manner it remained to the arbiters to ensure that the settlement would withstand any subsequent challenge at law, particularly urgent was the need to insure Margaret's heirs against a challenge by Richard or his heirs for the two Lincolnshire manors, both of which had been entailed to the main Willoughby line in the fourteenth century. To solve this problem the arbiters chose to break the entails on all the Willoughby lands. The award provided that Richard and Margaret should jointly enter the inheritance and suffer a common recovery with single voucher. The two clerks who thus recovered the lands were then to settle them according to the terms of award by deed enrolled in common pleas. It is an interesting sidelight on this award that the common recovery was early in the following century to become much used for the breaking of entails to effect just the sort of settlement envisaged by Sir Hugh. The recovery prescribed in this award is a very early example of this collusive form of action.[56]

Taken as a whole, the returned award was a masterly document, clearly drawn up by lawyers, if not Fortescue himself. Every possible cause of future dissension was dealt with, down even to provision for the keeping of the crops harvested at Wollaton in the previous year and the payment of any fines later to be incurred for any unlicensed alienations made by Sir Hugh. Most elaborately of all, further complex collusive litigation was to be undertaken in common pleas at Margaret's expense to secure the title of her son, Baldwin, to the small manor of Car Colston. This potentially highly devisive inheritance dispute was thus brought peacefully to a conclusion.

Cromwell himself must take much of the credit for, although he probably had very little to do with the actual drafting of the award, except perhaps as it related to the actual division of the inheritance which was not made on common law principles, it seems likely that it was his authority in the county that resulted in the dispute being settled by arbitration rather than forcible disseisins. All that is known of him as an arbiter suggests that he was fair and effective in this rôle, prepared to expend time and energy in the maintenance of peace within his own areas of landed influence. Moreover, even though he was ruthlessly efficient in the protection of his own interests, as witnessed by his destruction of Grey's influence in 1440–1 and his winning of the Heriz inheritance against the rightful heir ten years before, he appears to have rarely resorted to violence, preferring instead to employ legitimate manipuation of the legal machine to his own advantage. These two factors, together with the success his endeavours enjoyed, do much to explain why he was able to recruit such a large following amongst the Nottinghamshire gentry during the 1430s and 1440s. His success in this respect finds an instructive parallel in the career of Humphrey, duke of Buckingham. Dr Rowney has argued that Buckingham's failure as an arbiter, the result of his tendency to place short-term political expedience above justice, prevented him from creating a loyal following amongst the north midland gentry during the same period.[57] It thus seems reasonable to conclude that successful lordship lay in the provision of good justice rather than in the exploitation of the arbitration process for factional gain, although Cromwell himself, as in his dispute with Grey, was not above such exploitation.

Before we leave the Willoughby dispute there are some further conclusions to be drawn from it about the particular rôle of arbitration in fifteenth-century society. It is significant that a dispute of this nature, resulting as it did from the provisions of a will breaking earlier entails, would have been most uncommon before the fourteenth century, when feoffments-to-use first became commonplace, and rarer still from the early sixteenth century when it was well-established that entails could be broken by common recovery. However, in between these times with the aristocracy increasingly employing the use to devise land by will and with a large proportion of aristocratic land bound by earlier entails, such disputes were very frequent. Furthermore, they had potentially serious consequences for public order since they often occurred within the leading magnate and county families. The story of the dispute between Ralph, second earl of Westmorland, and his uncle (of the half-blood), Richard, earl of Salisbury, is too well known to need repetition here, but it is worth mentioning that Ralph's chagrin at his disinheritance was exacerbated by the fact that some of the lands settled on his uncle had earlier been entailed to him.[58] A similar, if less dramatic example, is the dispute within the Talbot family after the first earl had attempted the partial disinheritance of his common law heir.[59] Although this dispute was eventually peacefully settled, it is interesting to reflect on the very serious repercussions it would probably have had if John, Lord Lisle, the main beneficiary of the resettlement of the Talbot estates, had not died with the first earl at Castillon. A closer parallel with the Willoughby dispute is to be found in the feud that arose within the wealthy Warwickshire family of Mountford in the 1450s.[60] Sir William Mountford attempted to disinherit his son by his first wife in favour of his son by his second. Such an arrangement was bound to cause trouble, but the more so because the lands concerned were entailed to the main Mountford line.[61] On William's death, an attempt at arbitration between the two rival heirs failed because of the competitive maintenance of the earl of Warwick and the duke of Buckingham: maintenance which was doubly dangerous because it not only threatened public order in Warwickshire but also reflected and deepened the national divisions which eventually contributed to the fall of Lancaster. In this context, Cromwell's achievement in peacefully bringing to an end the dispute within the equally important family of Willoughby is the more impressive. These reflections suggest that the apparent increase in the use of arbitration in the fifteenth century may owe something to the inability of the common law to resolve disputes arising from unusual *post mortem* family settlements made through feoffements-to-use, and that hence it paralleled the developing equitable jurisdiction of the chancellor.

So far we have looked at arbitration as something either imposed from above or else appealed to from below, and while the role of both the chancellor and local magnates was important in furthering arbitration, of more importance was the arbitration of disputes within the confines of gentry society itself. Dr Wright in her study of the Derbyshire gentry has pointed out how frequently they looked to their fellows to act as arbiters in their disputes, and that even those with magnate connections did not necessarily employ these lords to arbitrate, preferring instead to settle matters within their own gentry circle.[62] In another gentry study, of the somewhat atypical county of Cheshire, Dr. Bennett has described a quite remarkable example of the self-regulating properties of a gentry community. At Macclesfield church in April 1412 more than sixty Cheshire gentry assembled to witness the formal settlement of a property dispute between two of their colleagues.[63] Nottinghamshire provides a parallel if less spectacular example, of interest both for the way in which the arbiters concluded the dispute and the number of them involved. In September 1408 the last direct male representative of the ancient family of Cressy, Hugh of Hodsock, died seised of a considerable but scattered inheritance.[64] Provision for the division of this inheritance had been made by fine as early as 1401: one moiety settled on Hugh's sister, Katherine, her first husband, Sir John Clifton, and their issue, and the other on a justice of the common pleas, Sir John Markham, and his issue by Hugh's other sister, Elizabeth, who was already dead by the time the fine was levied.[65] However, beyond stating that the inheritance should be divided evenly no more specific provision was made, and in view of the wide distribution and uneven value of the component manors this was a potential source of dispute. The death of Clifton at the battle of Shrewsbury in 1403 and Katherine's subsequent marriage to an outsider from county society, the Derbyshire esquire Ralph Makerell, added a further dimension. The divergent social status of her new husband and the widowed Markham may partly explain why the partition of the inheritance proved so difficult at Hugh's death. According to the final award, the two parties had been unable to agree 'tractatus et colloquium', and it was into this deadlock that the kinsfolk of the Cressy family and the leading gentry of the Bassetlaw wapentake, in which Hodsock lay, intervened. Eight arbiters are named in the award, four local knights and four local esquires, headed by Hugh's cousin, Sir Henry Vavasour, and Sir Richard Stanhope. But if the words of the final award are to be taken literally these men were not the only ones involved for it was said that the award was made, 'per consilium aliorum plurimorum de consanguinitate et affinitate' of both parties. The witness list of the award tends to confirm this for it lists not only the eight named arbiters, but thirteen other gentry of the Bassetlaw wapentake.[66]

The award itself is interesting not so much because of its terms but because of the manner in which these terms were made. The arbiters decided that the division should be accomplished by the drawing of lots, two bills each naming certain manors of the inheritance. So widespread were the Cressy manors that the logic of estate management did not demand that any in particular should be kept together, so all that remained for the arbiters to decide was how to ensure that each bill described lands of roughly equal value. With a little to-ing and fro-ing this they eventually managed and the two bills were then concealed in balls of wax, which were, in the words of the award, to be as identical as humanly possible. Since Katherine had been the elder of Hugh's sisters she was now to have first choice. After the bills had been drawn both parties swore not to make any claim to the manors assigned to the other, and the division of the inheritance thus made endured for several centuries in the families of Clifton and Markham.

This dispute is a clear example of the operation of kinship and local ties in bringing competing parties together. It was unusual in that each party, having agreed to arbitration, did not choose two or three arbiters to act on their behalf, as, for example, in the first Mering/Tuxford arbitration, but agreed to abide by the award of a large body of arbiters, indifferently selected between them. This suggests that in this case at least the award came about as a result of informal social pressures exerted through these local and kinship ties rather than through a decision taken by the two parties at their own initiative. It is not possible to say from the Nottinghamshire evidence whether this was typical or not, and, even when final awards survive, it is often impossible to discern the motivating force behind them. However, it may be suggested that the form of words often employed in these documents, that the award came about 'by the mediation of the friends of both parties for perpetual peace and friendship between them' is something more than a form of words: it is a fair summary of the nature and purpose of fifteenth-century arbitration.

NOTES

All manuscript references are to documents in the Public Record Office, Chancery Lane, unless otherwise stated.

1 E. Powell, 'The King's Bench in Shropshire and Staffordshire in 1414', in *Law, Litigants and the Legal Profession* (1983), ed. E. W. Ives and A. H. Manchester, 102. For a more general statement of the same author's views: 'Arbitration and the Law in England in the Late Middle Ages', *Transactions of the Royal Historical Society*, Fifth Series, xxxiii (1983), 49–67; 'Settlement of Disputes by Arbitration in Fifteenth-Century England', *Law and History Review*, vol. 2, no. 1 (1984), 21–43.

2 M. T. Clanchy, 'Law, Government and Society in Medieval England', *History*, lix (1974), 75–6, 77–8.

3 This is not to say that the jurors were very humble men, but simply that it was rare for members of knightly and esqure families to serve: E. G. Kimball, 'Some Sessions of the Peace in Lincolnshire', *The Lincoln Record Society*, vol. 49 (1955), xxxix; J. B. Post, 'Some limitations of the medieval peace rolls', *Journal of the Society of Archivists*, vol. 4 (1970–3), 635; N. Saul,

Knights and Esquires: the Gloucestershire Gentry in the Fourteenth century (1981), 170. Several Nottinghamshire peace session jury lists survive amongst the ancient indictments, and only one of these juries, headed by a knight, contains such men: KB9/188, m. 21; 207/2, m. 38. This peace session was quite exceptional, held before the two assize justices for the county in the wake of the 1414 commission of enquiry. Much more typical juries, containing no gentry, are to be found in : KB9/199, ms. 45, 46; 219, ms. 21, 23: 230B, ms. 181, 239; 231/1, ms. 25, 35, 38; 251, m. 40; 256, m. 39; 278, m. 59; 289, m. 78.

4   Gaol delivery conviction rates were very low: for the 1400–30 period, the conviction rate for Derbyshire was 14.5%, for Leicestershire 12.5%, and for Warwickshire 14% (ex. inf. E. Powell). The rate was even lower for the far northern counties: C. J. Neville has calculated one of only 5.3% for Northumberland, Cumberland and Westmorland between 1439 and 1459 ('Gaol Delivery in the Border Counties, 1439–59: Some Preliminary Observations', *Northern History*, xix (1983), 59).

5   None of the Nottinghamshire criminal cases referred from king's bench to the assize justices between 1399 and 1461 resulted in conviction: KB27/554–799.

6   J. B. Avrutick, 'Commissions of Oyer and Terminer in Fifteenth-Century England', unpublished London University M. Phil'. 1967, *passim*.

7   E. Powell, 'The Restoration of Law and Order' in *Henry V: the practice of kingship*, ed. G.L. Harriss (1985), 53–74.

8   For the petitions against Stanhope: *Rotuli Parliamentorum*, iv, 29, 30; SC8/97/4081 (PRO31/7/114 is a copy of this now only partially legible original; it is unclear why it escaped enrolment on the parliament roll). The commission was enrolled under 22 May on the patent roll, but was dated at Leicester on 14 May: *CPR, 1413–16*, 222; KB9/204/2, m, 2.

9   KB9/204/2, ms. 6–7.

10 E. Powell, 'Public Order and Law Enforcement in Shropshire and Staffordshire in the Early Fifteenth Century', unpublished Oxford D. Phil., 1979, 293–5.

11 According to the grand jury, he had forcibly rescued a felon in the custody of the coroner.

12 He was imprisoned in Kenilworth Castle, but his incarceration was a brief one for he was free by 23 June 1414 when he appeared in king's bench at Shrewsbury to plead a pardon in answer to the indictments laid against him before the enquiry commissioners: SC8/97/4801; KB27/613, rex rot. 9d.

13 All the leading Nottinghamshire men indicted later came into king's bench to plead pardons taken out under the general pardons of either April 1413 or December 1414: KB27/613, rex rot. 9d; 614, rex rots. 9, 12; 615, rex rots. 21, 41; 616, rex rots. 17d, 28d. For the cost of general pardons: M. Hastings, *The Court of Common Pleas in Fifteenth Century England* (1947), 180.

14 C81/1545/79.

15 This commission was enrolled under 10 July on the patent roll, but the endorsement of Statham's petition shows that it was issued on 11: *CPR, 1436–41*, 450; C81/1545/79. The last attack complained of had occurred on 7.

16 In 1446–7 and 1451–2 either he or more probably his son, another John, was Cromwell's receiver in Derbyshire: HMC, *De L'Isle*, i, 216, 230. The son was later one of Cromwell's feoffees: *CPR, 1452–61*, 200, 341. It is this connection with Cromwell that explains the grant of the keeping of the royal castle of Horston to the two Johns, made in December 1439 when Cromwell was treasurer: *CFR, 1437–45*, 115.

17 *CPR, 1436–41*, 19.

18 For Chalworth's connection with Cromwell, which dated back to 1423: *CFR, 1422–30*, 59; *Cal. Docs. Relating to Scotland, 1357–1509*, no. 929; HMC, *De L'Isle*, i, 217; Magdalen College, Misc. 250 (in 1431 he was one of Cromwell's feoffees in the Heriz manors); CCR, *1441–7*, 351; Nott. Univ. Library, Mi D 1624. Sir William was also one of Cromwell's feoffees in the Heriz manors. His sons, William, Thomas, and Norman, had similarly close connections with Cromwell: e.g. *CPR, 1429–36*, 147; *1452–61*, 341; *CFR, 1445–52*, 25; HMC, *De L'Isle*, i, 18; SC11/822 (William the son was Cromwell's deputy as constable of Newark Castle).

19 S. M. Wright, *The Derbyshire Gentry in the Fifteenth Century* (1983), 66, 114.
20 For these presentments: KB27/724, rex rots. 8, 9, 30; 725, rex rots. 4, 5, 25d; 727, rex rots. 3d, 17; 728, rex rots. 2d, 23d, 34, 34d; 729, rex rot. 1d; 731, rex rots. 5, 5d; 741, rex. rots. 1, 2; 742, rex rots. 39, 40, 40d.
21 Avrutick, *op. cit.*, 199–202. She was able to make use of an unlisted king's bench process file relating to the Nottinghamshire indictments made before these commissioners. Unfortunately this can no longer be produced since Meekings's death prevented it ever being listed.
22 KB27/741, rex rots. 1, 2; 742, rex rot. 39.
23 KB27/741, rex rot. 1.
24 In Hilary term 1441 Grey sued Statham, three of his sons and two of his servants, for trespass; KB27/719, rot. 71.
25 CFR, *1437–45*, 120. His daughter and eventual heir, Agnes, married John Tailboys, one of Cromwell's Lincolnshire retinue: CP25(1)/186/39/20.
26 *CCR 1441–7*, 30, 37–8.
27 *Ibid.*, *1435–41*, 384, 388.
28 E28/67, 7 and 16 March; *CPR, 1436–41*, 507.
29 KB27/725, rex rots. 4, 5.
30 C139/116/35.
31 Magdalen College, Misc. 356(2).
32 K. B. McFarlane, *England in the Fifteenth Century* (1981), xx.
33 Wright, *op. cit.*, 199.
34 For what follows: *CCR, 1413–19*, 50–4; *Calendar of Inquisitions Miscellaneous*, vii, no. 443: *CPR, 1408–13*, 431–2.
35 *CCR, 1409–13*, 397.
36 *Rotuli Parliamentorum*, iv, 73.
37 *CCR, 1413–19*, 373–4
38 *CPR, 1416–22*, 54–5; CP25(1)/186/38/6.
39 SC8/84/4181.
40 KB27/671, rex rot. 4; *CPR, 1422–9*, 466.
41 *CCR, 1422–9*, 409–10
42 The rioters did not, however, entirely escape punishment for 38 of them, including Cressy, made fine of a mark each in Easter term 1429, while three others were summarily convicted on a default after first appearance: KB27/671, rex rot. 4; 672, Fines rot.
43 e.g. CP40 656, rot. 261d; 663, rot. 244d; 664 rots. 356, 384.
44 J. B. Post, 'Courts, Councils and Arbitrators in the Ladbroke Manor Dispute, 1382–1400' in *Medieval Legal Records Edited in Memory of C. F. A. Meekings*, ed. R. F. Hunnisett and J. B. Post (1978), 292–7; 'Equitable Resorts Before 1450' in *Law, Litigants and the Legal Profession*, ed. E. W. Ives and A. H. Manchester (1983), 70–8; C. Rawcliffe, 'The Great Lord as Peacekeeper: Arbitration by English Noblemen and their Councils in the Later Middle Agtes', in *Law and Social Change in British History*, ed. J. A. Guy and H.G. Beale (1984), 34.54. See also: J. Wormald, 'Bloodfeud, Kindred and Government in Early Modern Scotland', *Past and Present*, vol. 87 (1980), 72, where she speaks of the Scottish lords having 'a strong awareness of their responsibility, not to keep their men free from the consequences of their crimes, but to involves themselves personally in, and provide a solution to, disputes between their followers'.
45 Wright, *op. cit*, 125; J. G. Bellamy, *Criminal Law and Society in Late Medieval and Tudor England* (1984), 78–9.
46 M. A. Hicks, 'Restraint, Mediation and Private Justice: George, Duke of Clarence, as 'Good Lord", *Journal of Legal History*, vol. 4, no. 2 (Sep. 1983), 56–71.
47 *Paston Letters and papers of the Fifteenth Century*, ed. N. Davis, ii. 110.
48 Leicester Record Office, DE221/1/1/68; I. Rowney, 'Arbitration in Gentry Disputes of the Later Middle Ages', *History*, lxvii (1982), 368–9.
49 For this will: Nott. Univ. Library, MS F6, no. 14. It is imperfectly calendared in *Testamenta Eboracensia*, ii (for 1855), 130–4, with the codicil concerning the settlement of the Willoughby lands omitted.

50 Margaret had been born in c. 1402 and lived on until 1493: CCR, 1419–22, 48;
    Calendar of Inquisitions Post Mortem, Henry VII, i, no. 865. Richard's mother had died in
    1417, leaving three sons who survived into adulthood, while Richard himself
    predeceased his step-mother by more than twenty years: *Transactions of the Thoroton
    Society*, vi (1903), 51; C140/41/37. For the substantial Freville estates that Margaret
    brought to the Wlloughby family: Nott. Univ. Library, Mi M 214.
51 CP25(1)/286/38/198 (*inter alia* the manors of Willoughby, Bradmore and Wollaton);
    185/29/174 and 179; 185/31/286; C139/135/37.
52 Nott. Univ. Library, Mi D 1624.
53 C139/135/37. There is no record of any such settlement in the cartulary relating to the
    Willoughby lands in Sutton Passeys and Wollaton: Nott. Univ. Library, Mi Dc3.
    Moreover, no deed was shown to the jurors in evidence as was usual in such
    circumstances: C139/135/37.
54 *CFR, 1445–52*, 119, 131.
55 Both halves of their indented award survive: Nott. Univ. Library, MS D 4662 and 4763.
56 'The Reports of Sir John Spelman', ed. J. H. Baker, ii, *Selden Society*, xciv (for 1977),
    204–5.
57 Rowney, *op. cit.*, 374–5; cf. Rawecliffe, *op. cit.*, 38, 39, 44–5.
58 K. B. McFarlane, *The Nobility of Later Medieval England* (1973), 67–8.
59 For an interesting discussion of this dispute, which lasted from 1453 to 1466: A. J.
    Pollard, 'The Family of Talbot, Lords Talbot and Earls of Shrewsbury in the Fifteenth
    Century', unpublished Bristol University Ph. D., 1968, 51–62.
60 R. Griffiths, 'The Hazards of Civil War: the Mountford Family and the 'Wars of the
    Roses", *Midland History*, v (1979–80), 1–19; C. Carpenter, 'Law Justice and Landow-
    ners in Late Medieval England', *Law and History*, vol. i. no. 2 (1983), 219–25.
61 Griffiths's discussion of the dispute is marred by his belief that Sir William's action 'was
    quite legal in common law': *op. cit.*, 3. But a parliamentary petition, probably of
    1461–2, claims that the main Mountford manors of Coleshill and Ilmingdon had been
    entailed to the main line, 'as by severall gyftes by fynes and deds therof made redy to be
    shewyd more openly appereth': Birmingham Public Library, A 590, printed by
    Griffiths, *op. cit.*, 14–5. This was certainly true for Coleshill entailed by fine in 1371:
    'Warwickshire Feet of Fines, 1345–1509', *Publications of the Dugdale Society*, xviii
    (1943), no. 2188.
62 Wright, *op. cit.*, 124.
63 M. J. Bennett, 'A County Community: Social Cohesion amongst the Cheshire Gentry,
    1400–25', *Northern History*, viii (1973), 25–8.
64 C137/67/30.
65 CPR, 1399–1401, 411; CP25(1)/290/59/24.
66 The award is Nott. Univ. Library C1 D 674.

Kings, Continuity and Ecclesiastical Benefaction in 15th Century England

JOEL T. ROSENTHAL

The English kings of the 15th century, considered as a group, were active ecclesiastical patrons, benefactors, and founders. Though the Lancastrian kings (including Henry VII) were more prominent than the Yorkists, the collective royal record is an impressive one. It is made even more impressive if we keep in mind a number of related factors as we proceed to examine royal activity (and its tangible products) in some detail.

One consideration is that while royal activity remained significant through the century (from 1399 through 1509), comparable aristocratic activity declined, or rather continued a decline already well marked by the last 2 or 3 decades of the 14th century. The secular peers were no longer founding or refounding regular houses, friaries, or even large colleges and hospitals, and after 1399 the aristocratic record, beyond chantry chapels, secular colleges, and an occasional hospital or alms house, was distinctly on the thin side.[1] Consequently, sustained and flamboyant royal endowment – whether by design or by happy coincidence – served as a kind of separation activity between the kings and their cousins and erstwhile political rivals. Kings acted in a distinctive royal fashion as they took up the threads of an older monarchical tradition that had given the realm innumerable regular houses and such quasi-public monuments as Westminster Abbey. The nobles, on the other hand, were failing to emulate their predecessors who had built Cambridge halls and colleges or charterhouses in the 14th century, Benedictine and Austin foundations in the 12th and 13th centuries.

A second consideration in assessing royal activity is the degree of continuity and common purpose that seems to link the kings and their enterprises. Some of this was the obvious and direct link we would expect to find in an elaborate project that a father proposes, a son continues, and a grandson perhaps completes. But there was also the cultivation of dynastic myths and continuities, and there were efforts to show a royal sense of purpose across dynastic lines and political upheavals. The crown of England rocked far too often between Richard II's deposition and Henry VIII's quiet accession for any of its wearers to turn his back on traditions or projects that might prove helpful.

An assessment of a king's activity as an ecclesiastical patron is, of course, a standard topic when assessing his *res gestae*, and is treated by both contemporary and modern biographers. What biographers have not done, however, is to consider the kings in aggregate, and to look for indications of general or sustained patterns of activity. Scholars have been more concerned to judge the zeal and generosity of separate monarchs and to discuss whether royal piety was 'forward looking' or fixed rather upon traditional pre-reformation forms of expression and behavior. Thus we have a good record of the various ecclesiastical enterprises that attracted royal interest and funds, and we know a lot about the separate kings as founders and builders. What we propose to do here is to explore the themes of continuity and tradition between the kings and their projects. Such themes are not hard to find. They tell us something about 15th century monarchy, both as a hard-nosed political construct and as a branch of the larger and older tree of sacred and sacral kinship. Royal gifts to the church were a form of good works, a link in the chain of reciprocity between the sinner and his salvation, and a highly public and useful form of conspicuous expenditure. That almost all the kings played the game, at a serious and costly level, should indicate that the gifts were seen as an important investment.

The easiest explication of royal activity is by a chronological survey, from Henry IV's accession through Henry VII's death. In the mere circumstances of his accession, Henry Bolingbroke may have had some reason for a troubled conscience, and he talked much of turning to the church and good works for solace and forgiveness. If this surmise about Bolingbroke's uneasy sleep is reasonable, the events of his reign were not likely to be comforting. By the time he dictated his will, he was expressing himself in the morbid phraseology we characterize as typical of the 'waning of the middle ages': 'my sinful soul, the whiche had never be worthy to be man but through hys mercy and hys grace; whiche lyffe I have mispendyd . . .'[2] It was Henry's intention to make a pilgrimage to Jerusalem and to found 3 regular houses in England. The package was part of the concord Henry had arranged with Gregory XII in 1408, but it must also have carried some hopes of personal peace. For his well-publicized good intentions Henry received much sympathy. Once again, however, his intentions outstripped his resources, and he ended his years with neither the time nor money to honor his commitments. Upon his death in 1413 the foundations were as yet unfounded, the pilgrimage untaken. What J.H. Wylie says, referring to Henry's niggardly behavior towards a proposed college in Shropshire, can be applied to his activity *in toto*: 'But another evidence of how he managed to give to the Lord of that which cost him next to nothing.'[3] And yet we should note that the idiom in which Henry chose to express himself was that of ecclesiastical foundation, whatever actually came of his grandiloquent plans.

Henry V was more deliberate than his father, as well as more generous. If nothing could glamorize the throne like a foreign war, insular triumphs could likewise be yoked to celestial ones. Accordingly, the king followed his father's footsteps and founded the 3 proposed regular houses. Henry also lavished gifts and tangible affection upon Westminster Abbey: the reinterrment of Richard II was but part of his effort to turn The Confessor's church into the English counterpart of St. Denis. Regarding the new regular houses, Henry's interest in slightly 'off beat' orders helped make them stand out in the public eye. The sites were all in the neighborhood of Sheen, by Richmond, previously associated with Richard II's palace but now a Lancastrian preserve.[4]

The 3 proposed houses did not share a common history or fate. The Celestine house, launched in 1414 or 1415, was begun but never completed. During his short reign Henry V authorized something in excess of £600 for its construction. However, the times were not propitious for the introduction of an unfamiliar order with French roots, and the work languished. We have no record of a specific decision to abort the project, and the chances are that it just ground to a halt, as so often happened with ambitious designs. In fact, what is so striking about so many of the royal foundations of the century is that they were eventually completed.

Henry's second project was a Carthusian house. After corresponding with the prior of the Grand Chartreuse regarding his intentions (and those of his late father's), he moved to build a large house at Sheen, the House of Jesus of Bethlehem at Sheen of the Carthusian order.[5] It was intended for 40 monks, though no more than 30 ever seem to have been resident. The church itself was so grand that the nave alone ran over 100 feet in length (while that at Mountgrace was but 40). Work begain in 1414, and soon royal gifts – mostly from the lands of confiscated alien priories – came pouring in.[6] By 1419 the king had spent over £600, and in his will (of 1422) he left a bequest of 1000 marks, as he did to the nearby Bridgettine house, 'nostra foundationis'. In addition he gave the Carthusians money for 'certain books and things . . . in part payment of a greater sum'.[7]

The idea of introducing the Bridgettine order to England arose through royal links with Sweden, where it had originated. Henry, lord Fitzhugh, the king's friend and chamberlain, had been impressed by the mother-house at Vadstena which he had seen when he accompanied the king's sister Philippa to her wedding with Eric XIII back in 1406.[8] Fitzhugh had whetted Henry IV's interest, and when Henry V reopened the issue the idea of an English house had been in the air for a decade. The ultimate result was a large house, known as the Abbey of St. Savior in Syon, or the Monastery of Mt. Syon of Sheen, or the Monastery of the Holy Saviour, St. Mary the Virgin, and St. Birgitta. Swedish enthusiasm out-stripped their actual contribution, but 7 women and 2 men were sent to England to help start the house. The project took root, and the Order was pleased to honor Henry and his father in pompous eloquence: "As Solomon magnificently consummated the Temple which David his father had planned to build, so also may the merciful integrity of your majesty bring to fulfillment a monastery of this kind, which the devout intention of your generous father, hindered by death, could not achieve."[9] Henry subsidized the house more handsomely even than his Carthusian creation, and by 1420 he had spent over £850 in cash: there would also be the testamentary bequest of 1000 marks.[10] By his death the house contained 27 sisters, 5 priests, 2 deacons and 4 lay deacons. If well below the original projection of 60 sisters, 13 priests, and 12 deacons, it was still a very large establishment. It was moved to an adjacent site in 1426, and rebuilding progressed slowly, eventually to be supplemented by the support of Henry VI and completed by Edward IV. Edward also renewed the exemptions from taxes and the annual gift of 4 tuns of gascon wine. He restored lost properties, and eventually the obit list was expanded to hail him as a second founder, "who restored possessions which had been taken away unjustly."[11] By Edward's death the kings had spent some £4100. Henry V's other great ecclesiastical pet was Westminster Abbey. Within its confines he had Richard II reburied, and he himself was ultimately laid to rest in the new chantry chapel he had built east of the high altar.[12] The new work on the fabric, begun by Richard II, was languishing and Henry channeled money for 6 more bays of the nave. His help with construction, plus the miscellaneous grants and privileges, cost the crown in excess of £4000.

Henry VI is the feeblest king and the greatest patron. This inverse relationship is probably a good indication of his priorities, though it is hard to escape the view that Eton and King's College, Cambridge were substitutes for the king's 'real' business. But Henry would have concurred with, and no doubt gloried in, John Blakman's appraisal: 'Like a second Job, a man simple and upright, altogether fearing the lord God, and departing from evil. He was a simple man, without any crook or craft or untruth, as is plain to tell.'[13]

If not the man to win an Agincourt, he certainly labored to give his people his own version of royal triumphs. By 1440 he was interested in creating a new college at Cambridge.[14] The original proposal, for St. Nicholas College with a rector and 12 scholars, was soon left far behind. By 1443 – when the king reached age 21 – the original proposal was greatly expanded, and by 1444 or 1445 he was moving towards a foundation of 70 scholars. The king himself laid the first stone of the great chapel in 1446. Then followed a flood of privileges and endowments, including exemptions from feudal aids and tenths and fifteenths and the right to 'set up gallows upon the soil of their land'.[15] Between 1446 and 1453 Henry bestowed 15 manors and 3 rectories upon the college, plus the £1000 *per annum* he authorized for construction. The cash came largely from Duchy of Lancaster estates, which means in effect that it was from his private income. As such, it was a gift from the king for his people's collective spiritual betterment. The royal will of 1448 spells this out and gives us a glimpse of Henry's own vision of the enterprise. He was not indifferent to the creation of a cult of personality: 'I have devised and appointed that the same church shall containe 288 feete of assise in length . . . and all of the wideness of 40 feete, and the length . . . shall containe 120 feete . . . and I will that the edification proceed in large forme of my said college cleane and subst-antiall'.[16] After Henry's deposition Edward IV was rather cool to the project. But he soon relented and bestowed new lands and advowsons on the unfinished enterprise. In his short reign Richard III also poured some £1000 into Henry's college, with a special concern for the stained glass of the chapel. When Henry VII belatedly visited Cambridge in 1506 he too became concerned, and his gifts finally allowed the work to be completed. He gave £100 on the spot, £350 in 1507, and another £400 in 1509, and this generosity helped cover the 7 bays which had been standing bareheaded. By the time his executors paid his testamentary bequests he had devoted almost £12,000 to King's. This was in addition to Henry VI's £15–20,000, Edward IV's £1000–2000, and Richard III's lesser gifts.

Like King's, Eton College evolved, between 1440 and 1446, from a modest idea into a vast creation. Again, Henry VI had originally looked to found a 'college of a provost, fellows, priests, clerks, and boys and poor and indigent scholars and other poor men and a master of grammar', and the boys would perhaps go on to King's.[17] But very soon he was again thinking in terms of his 70 scholars, and royal enthusiasm funnelled men, money, and privileges to build and endow on an appropriate scale.[18] The royal will of 1448 talked of the project: 'That the edification of my said college of Eton procede in large fourme, clene and substancial, wel replenysshed with goodely wyndows and vautes leying a parte superfluite of to grete curiouse werkes of entialle and besy moldying.'[19] The endowments included the leper hospital of St. James, Westminster, with its lucrative annual fairs. Papal support was enlisted: Nicholas V offered pardons and indulgences to those who made a remunera-tive visit during the founding festivities or on the feast of the Assumption. In another of his self-conscious moves Henry bestowed royal arms, 'that we may impart something of royal nobility, which may declare the work truly royal and illustrious'.[20] His support ran to some £1200 *per annum* for the last 15 or 20 years of his reign.[21] Despite this the work was unfinished at his deposition and Edward IV – who had to be talked out of a plan to merge Eton College with St. George's chapel at Windsor – gave more money, as in turn did Henry VII.[22] It was the latter king who once more brought an 'inherited' royal and family project to completion.

The house of York, despite its short tenure, also contributed to our tale. Edward IV, as we have seen, became tolerably positive about the projects he assumed as part of the crown's unfinished agenda. He was less innovative on his own. He moved to found a house of Observant Franciscans at Greenwich in 1480.[23] After obtaining a bull for foundation from Sixtus IV in 1481 he donated a plot near the royal palace. His sister, Margaret of Burgundy, may have been the moving force in this, and we still have an illuminated gradual she gave the new house (British Library, Arundel Ms. 71). Observant Franciscan houses were not intended to have a lavish endowment, and Edward was quite good about not tempting the friars: he only gave them some land.

Edward IV's own project was the chapel of St. George at Windsor. Here his enthusiasm and generosity began an enterprise – again completed by the early Tudors – that ranks with Henry VI's two chapels among the architectural jewels of the century. The razing of older structures at Windsor began in 1473, and by 1477 enough had been cleared for the new work to commence. The king steered £1000 *per annum* towards it, much of the money coming from aristocratic lands in royal hands because of minorities and political vicissitudes.[24] Though new chapter houses for the canons and the vicars choral were completed in Edward's day, the monumental tomb he proposed for himself was never built. He bestowed upon the dean and chapter the alien priory of Brimpsfield, the free chapel of St. Anthony, London, the priory of Goldcliff in North Wales, plus numerous advowsons and privileges. Though account reckoning is always uncertain, a recent biographer estimates that Edward alone spent at least £6–7000 on the chapel.[25]

Henry VII picked up Edward IV's interest in the Observant Franciscans, and he subsidized construction at Greenwich.[26] When completed the house contained a warden and 12 brothers, and Henry's efforts represent a link between the first Tudor and his father-in-law. The new king was frank about his role: in the endowment he pointed out that he was 'bearing in mind Edward IV's pious intention'.[27] In his will he left the friary £200, 'for the closying of their gardyne and orcharde with a brikwell'.[28] The money was to be held in trust by the London Charterhouse, for the brothers had been 'many times in peril of ruin for lack of food'.[29] When the house was finished in 1495 the bishop of Rochester granted an indulgence to those giving alms. Henry's personal ties with the house were strong: sons Henry and Edmund were christened there, and Henry VIII gave his marriage vows to Catherine of Aragon within its walls in 1509.

Moved by his success and pleasure in the Greenwich foundation, Henry VII sought to become the general patron of an English branch of the Observants. He pushed to have the older friaries at Southampton, Canterbury, and Newcastle on Tyne converted to the more rigorous branch of the order. He supported the foundation of a house at Richmond, in 1500, and at Newark in 1507, and he left £200 in his will to the latter foundation, 'that by his succour and aid was newly begun'.[30] The Canterbury house received 100 marks and had an additional £200 deposited for its use with the prior of Christ Church. These efforts are the closest anyone came in this period to planting a new order upon English soil.

Henry's most famous ecclesiastical project is Westminster Abbey, and the work he supported culminated in his own giant chantry chapel. By his death the Abbey stood, unambiguously, as the English house of kings: it held Richard II, Henry V, and eventually Henry VII, along with his queen and his mother. The great new royal chapel, to the east of Henry V's earlier monument to self, was begun in 1502. By 1509 Henry had authorized the expenditure of some £15,000, money that could tie up a work force of 120–200 men at a time. His executors spent a sum about equal to that of his lifetime, and by 1515, when the new addition was in its final stages, the figure for royal support was at or beyond £30,000. Henry spent another £500–600 for some adjacent almshouses, designed for a priest and 2 poor men.

The last Henrician foundation is the Savoy hospital. Though a conventional foundation, it was an exceptionally large and costly one. Built on the site of John of Gaunt's vast palace (burned by the rebels in 1381), it was to contain beds for 100 transients and indigents. It employed a staff that included a master, 4 chaplains, 2 priests, 4 altarists, a matron, 12 sisters, a clerk of the kitchen, a butler, 2 cooks, 2 door keepers, and a gardener. Staff and inmates were to wear red and gold costumes, with a Tudor rose upon the breast emblazoned with the message also conveyed in the inscription above the entrance; 'Henry the seventh to his merite and honor This Hospital foundyd, poore people to socor'.[31] The 1508 grant of £523 was supplemented by an immense testamentary gift of 10,000 marks. The money went to erect the largest hospital of medieval England, with a main building alone that ran over 300 feet in length.

These houses comprise the bulk of the relevant enterprises, though a fuller list of the recipients of royal benefaction and endowment could be offered to bolster our thesis of sustained activity as a deliberate way of separating the monarch from the rest and of creating a sort of special and highly visible position. Apart from the institutions mentioned, Henry V was a patron-founder of the brotherhood or fraternity of St. Giles at Cripplegate. He contributed to his uncle's college of All Saints at Fotheringhay, usually seen as a Yorkist project (wherein Edward IV reburied his father and brother), as well as to collegiate churches at Higham Ferrers and at Tong, Shropshire. Had the king lived longer he probably would have put his yearly gifts to the London Dominicans and to the friars in the university towns on a permanent basis. Henry VI gave Pembroke College, Cambridge, land previously held by Linton priory, plus a cell at Isleham and 105 acres.[32] Both he and his father were donors to Christ's College, Cambridge, mainly with lands from the alien priories. Edward IV proposed a college of some stature for Towton, as a thanksgiving for his victory there. He obtained spiritual privileges for pilgrims, but he was slower to provide worldly aid. Though the college was never built, Richard III thought it a viable project and instructed the receiver at Pontefract to advance £40 annually for its 'building and edification'.[33] Edward founded chantries at All Hallows, Barking, and he steered alien priory lands into the coffers of Queen's College, Oxford. Richard III had his own favorite, Middleham College, and again it was an early royal death that kept it from reaching its fullest and most ambitious scope.[33a] Henry VII expressed an interest – not realized because of death – in building hospitals at Coventry and York to parallel his lavish foundation at the Savoy.[34]

In the full tale of royal support the queens and royal ladies, as well as the kings, hold a place of honor. Margaret of Anjou was a generous patron of Queens' College, Cambridge. She helped raise an endowment of £200 *per annum*: her efforts were, at least in part, for the 'laud and honneure of sex feminine'.[35] Elizabeth Wydeville contributed to the same college, and for her aid was hailed as a 'vere fundatrix.' She endowed a chapel, in honour of St. Erasmus, in Westminster Abbey.[36] Either Anne Neville or Richard III on her behalf, lent further support to Queens' College. Henry VII's mother, Lady Margaret Beaufort, by far the most generous of all these women, left endowments for the university lectureships in divinity, the founding of St. John's College, Cambridge, and gifts to Christ's College, Cambridge, where she wished to be remembered as 'heir to all Henry VI's godly intention'.[37] Though it is hard to calculate the sums authorized or actually spent by the women, we can again see a similar pattern of continuity between one generation and dynasty and the next.

If we look at all this activity we observe a policy – often implicit, sometimes explicit – of continuous enterprise and involvement. It constitutes, in aggregate, an important element of royal efforts towards self-exaltation and socio-political separation. Furthermore, the foundations of this policy lie, not in theories about the constitution and regality wherein we often search, but rather in the realm of behavior and action. Let us set the royal record against the comparable activity of the secular peers. The aristocratic record was one of regular support for chantries, collegiate churches, hospitals, and alms houses. But through the entire course of the century no English peer founded a regular or mendicant house. Though they collectively endowed more than 100 chantry chapels, not even the greatest aristocratic creations carried the grandeur or the spiritual impact of a new foundation. Nor was money alone the answer, for many of the nobles were more than open handed. The de la Warre college at Manchester had an annual income of £211, according to the valors of 1535, while the Cromwell college at Tattershall could boast of £348 *per annum*. But such creations still belonged, along with the de la Pole college and almshouse at Ewelme and scores of lesser establishments, to that 'new' world of privatized religion. These impressive creations were giant family chantries, for all their variety of form, scope, and cost. They were *sui generis*, rather than English branches of orders scattered throughout Christendom. Nor, as colleges could they compete – in splendour or location – with those erected by the kings.

From this vantage point the gulf between royal and aristocratic activity is very wide. Kings and nobles were going separate ways. We may find a few, well favored peers participating in the endowment of a royal house. Lord Fitzhugh was instrumental in bringing the Bridgettines to royal attention, and he gave them money. But this was an exceptional inititive, and it only came from a man on close personal terms with the king. For his efforts, including his bequest of £40, he was recognized in the Bridgettine obit list: 'primus qui introduxit hanc religionem in Regnum Angliae'.[38] Henry V's brother, John of Bedford, was a benefactor of Syon. Cardinal Beaufort, Henry VI's uncle left money for King's College and Eton, as did the duke of Suffolk. But these few men were close, in blood and/or comradeship, to the king who had launched the project to which they were now contributing. The general picture is that secular peers did not try to curry favor by poaching on royal enterprises. One contributed to ones own favorites, rarely to those of others. Great cathedrals may have been collective endeavors where aristocratic support merged with that of the bourgeoisie. But regular houses and friaries and colleges on the scale of Eton or Windsor grew mainly from the zeal of one man, or one woman, and their descendents. And princes, above all others, were jealous parents.

The sites of the foundations are also worth noting. Except for Henry VI's great college at Cambridge and those Observant friaries that Henry VII wished to scatter throughout the kingdom, the foundations were located along the length of the Thames valley. From Eton and Windsor to Greenwich, royal philanthropy and piety high-lighted the idea of the river as *the* royal highway, lined with royal ecclesiastical, educational, and spiritual foundations as well as residences and places of business. When we add the Tower of London and the palace of Westminster to our ripuarian list – the friary at Greenwich, the Tower, the Savoy hospital, the Abbey and ajdoining palace, the royal buildings and monasteries at Sheen, and then Eton and Windsor – we have a most impressive necklace.[39]

In addition to the map we can take the royal account book into consideration. From Henry V through Henry VII the kings altogether spent something in the neighborhood of £100,000, if not more, on these building projects. Henry VI's vision of 'edifications and other workes of bridges, conduicts, cloysters, and other thinges begoun and advised by me' sums it up.[40] It also bespeaks a costly vision: nothing deferential here. Royal houses and foundations were meant to be special, in size, in wealth, and in public esteem, and they were. In the evaluations of 1535 the Carthusians at Sheen showed an annual income of £880, the Bridgettines of Syon £1731, the College at Eton £1101, King's College at Cambridge £752, and the Savoy hospital £567. The Syon nunnery was the richest nunnery and the richest non-Benedictine house in the realm, and for the 5 houses – even without St. George's chapel at Windsor – we have an average annual income of £990. To call this princely is to turn a figure of speech into a quantitative assessment. Such a level of sustained expenditure, beginning with Henry IV's proposals and only ending with the work of Henry VII's executors a century later, may have been beyond sensible royal means, but it was possible. It surely helped publicize the gulf between kingly and baronial magnificence.[41]

Historians commonly survey this activity, but in piecemeal fashion, i.e. in terms of each separate monarch and his projects. We explain so much costly support as an example of 'conventional religious beliefs and (the) superstititions of his era', or as typical of 'the king's piety', the efforts of a 'conservative and observant' man.[42] This is too simple. The continuous tale, along with our estimate of the aggregate sums, might warn us that something larger is at issue. The continuity of endeavor and of expenditure surmounted both dynastic changes and the long durations always demanded by major building projects. When Edward IV resumed support for the house at Syon, he saw himself as a bridge between the two houses. He made bequests for prayers to bring *his* family into the affair: 'specially for the happy estate of the king and of Elizabeth, his consort, and Cecilly his mother, and for the souls of the same after death, and for the souls of Richard, late duke of York, the king's father'. But he was also at pains to indicate that he was regranting 'all the liberties granted by king Henry VI'.[43] Henry VII had more obvious ties with Henry VI, but he too made the link explicit, the glory shared: the supervisors of King's College were instructed, 'Incessauntly to persever and contenue till it be fully fynisshed and accomplished after like fourme and entent as it was ordered and devised by his saide uncle'.[44] And while the bridge between Lancaster and Tudor was a natural one, that between York and Tudor was also worth emphasizing, as when Henry VII turned to the Franciscans at Greenwich: 'accepimus qualiter Edwardus nuper Rex Angliae quartus antecessor noster carissimus.[45]

These royal foundations are but one chapter in the larger tale of royal legitimation, continuity, and separation. In these years kingship was bolstered by a whole arsenal of political propaganda. Ceremony and pageantry played their role in the great drama. Special royal genealogies, taking us to Uther Pendragon and Arthur, were used by the Yorkists as well as by the 'Welsh' Tudors.[46] The search for an English royal saint could even lead to Henry VI as the proper candidate.[47] New royal titles and modes of address were coming into use, part of the impulse to turn from the quasi-egalitarian terminology of feudalism to one reflecting a wider division between subject and sovereign.[48]

In the royal foundations – safe from the lewd hands of the peers – the ends of holy church were easily coupled to those of monarchy. The liturgy used in the royal foundations could raise the founder to a position somewhere between that of secular donor and patron saint. Today the evensong service of King's says, 'We give Thee hearty thanks for Thy servant King Henry VI, our founder, by whose bounty we are here brought'.[49] But compare this tepid reciprocity with the partisan passion of 15th century liturgical formulation, 'Ora pro nobis, beate Henrice, ut dignis efficiamur promissionibus Christi'.[50] The genesis of a royal cult, and the creation of monarchical propaganda, was a serious industry, an art form that became a powerful mode of public discourse. And if we count all those involved in various aspects of the discourse – from the anonymous workmen atop the scaffolding to the artists, heralds, poets, lawyers, priests, and political pamphleteers — it was hardly an insignificant industry, as measured by the size of its work force, its economics, or its impact.[51]

This picture of kingship gives the kings credit for the sagacity to develop a glorious if costly set of monuments in which the sacred and the secular were inextricably woven. By building and by identifying themselves with the new foundations the kings were showing a sensitivity to a special royal role that could elevate the crown. The game they were playing was both costly and serious. Kingship, in a period that opens with the deposition of the Lord's anointed, was not an intellectual chess match. It was about power, a power that could be magnified, manipulated, and preserved in no small part through a creative use of benefaction as spectacle. In this drama of separation and exaltation the kings themselves played the leading man. They knew of historical precedents, and they knew that ecclesiastical benefaction was what good kings had always cared for. When Joinville listed the accomplishments of the great St. Louis of France – from whom the English monarchs were proud to trace descent – he elaborated thusly: 'He provided for the brothers of Carmel, and bought them land . . . and caused a house to be built for them . . . And after he provided for the brothers of St. Augustine, and bought them the grange . . The brothers of the 'Sack' he provided for and he gave them a site . . . And the king bought them (the while Mantles) a house . . . And he lodged them (The brothers of the Holy Cross) in a street . . . Thus did the good king surround the city . . . with people of religion.'[52]

This kind of visible activity perhaps counted for more, in the eyes of the laity, than did the treatises on kingship that we are inclined to take from the hands of John of Salisbury or Sir John Fortescue. It was none other than Henry VI, the least assertive of monarchs, who discussed how benefaction and construction coupled the royal son to the heavenly father: 'Forasmuch as it hath pleased our Lord God for to suffer and grunte me grace . . . After that I by his blessed sufferaunce tooke unto my self the rule of my said realmes, for to erect, found, and stablish . . . my two college Roiall.'[53] Wherever the money came from, there was a public willingness to believe that tall buildings must have been the progeny of tall men.

NOTES

1   J.T. Rosenthal, *The Purchase of Paradise* (London, 1972), for aristocratic activity of this sort.
2   J. Nichols, *A Collection of All the Wills . . . of the Kings and Queens of England* (London, 1780: reprinted, New York, 1969), 203; K.B. McFarlane, *Lancastrian Kings and Lollard Knights* (Oxford, 1972), 112; Francis C. Hingeston, ed., *Liber de Illustribus Henricis per Johannem Capgrave*, Rolls Series, 7 (London, 1858), II, 124.
3   James H. Wylie, *The History of England under Henry the Fourth* (London, 1884–98), III, 243; for Henry's promises and commitments to the church, *Ibid*, II, 36/51–52; David Knowles, *The Religious Orders in England* (Cambridge, 1955), II, 176–77. Two Bridgettine monks arrived in 1408 and remained homeless for almost a decade.
4   J.H. Wylie, *The Reign of Henry the Fifth* (Cambridge, 1914–29), I, ch. 15, with Wylie's usual detail on royal activities. Also, *VCH, Middlesex*, I, 182–89; H.M. Colvin, *The History of the King's Works* (London, 1963–), I, 265–67; Knowles, *op. cit.*, II, 175–84; Frank Taylor and J.S. Roskell, ed. & trans., *Gesta Henrici Quinti: The Deeds of Henry V* (Oxford, 1975), appendix II, 186–87, 'Henry V's Monastic Foundations.' For Henry as a general reformer of monastic order, Knowles, *op. cit.*, II, 183–84; E.F. Jacob, *The Fifteenth Century* (Oxford, 1961), 196–98. For Capetian and Valois use of burial as ceremonial, E.A.R. Brown, 'The ceremonial of royal succession in Capetian France: The double funeral of Louis X,' *Traditio*, 34 (1978), 227–71, and 'The ceremonial of royal succession in Capetian France: the funeral of Philip V,' *Speculum*, 55 (1980), 266–93.
5   *CPR, 1416–22*, 87; Thomas Rymer, *Foedera* (London, 1760 edition), IV, 138: '. . . nostrae Cartusiensium . . . quae vocatur Bethleem.'
6   Knowles, *op. cit.*, II, 164–65, on the royal use of the possessions of the suppressed alien priories. On construction at Sheen, John Cloak, 'The Charterhouse of Sheen,' *Surrey Archaeological Collections*, 71 (1977), 145–98, with a map of the royal endowments (pp. 147–48).
7   Rymer, *Ibid*, and Alec Myers, *English Historical Documents, IV, 1327–1485* (London, 1969), 786–87, quoting from Thomas Walsingham's *St. Albans Chronicle*: '. . . The two convents ought to have, according to the rule, sufficient endowments for the maintenance of the religious and their servants and the support of the burdens of the monastery, so that in sterile years as well as fertile ones they may exist sufficiently and quietly.' Taylor and Roskell, *op. cit.*, 146: the Sheen Charterhouse is referred to as 'proprie domus sue.' Frederick Devon, *Issues of the Exchequer* (London, 1835), 340

8   On Fitzhugh, A. Compton Reeves, *Lancastrian Englishmen* (Washington, 1981), 65–138.

9   Margaret Deanesley, *The 'Incendium Amoris' of Richard Rolle of Hampole* (Manchester, 1951), 104. Henry IV had planned to give the order the decayed hospital of St. Nicholas, York, but once again the plan never materialized: Knowles, *op. cit.*, II, 177.

10 Harold F. Hutchison, *Henry V: A Biography* (London, 1967), 77: a piece of needlework given by the king to the nuns is now in the Victoria & Albert Museum. Patrick and Felicity Strong, 'The last will and codicil of Henry V,' *English Historical Review*, 96 (1981), 79–102, especially 92–94, for Henry's relevant bequests. Syon was to keep the books he had deposited, except for 'our' great bible which had come to him from his father and which was now to go to the infant Henry VI.

11 *VCH, Middlesex*, I, 188.

12 *Devon, op. cit.*, 328: a London joiner was paid £2 'for making and providing a 'horsebere', a coffin and other necessary things for the carrying of the body of Richard, late king of England.'

13 M.R. James, *Henry the Sixth: A Translation of John Blackman's Memoir* (Cambridge, reprinted 1955), 5. H.M. Colvin takes a dim view of a king whose main achievements are architectural: *op. cit.*, I, 268, 278. For a more positive assessment, Bertram Wolffe, *Henry VI* (London, 1981), 135, 145; Ralph A. Griffiths, *The Reign of King Henry VI* (Berkeley & Los Angeles, 1981), 242–46. Typical of the kinder treatment, p.243: Henry 'regarded the foundation [of Eton] as his first major independent act of initiative as an adult.' On the reliability of Henry VI's biographer, Roger Lovatt, 'A Collector of Apocryphal Anecdotes: John Blacman revisited,' in *Property and Politics: Essays in Later Medieval English History*, ed., Tony Pollard (Gloucester, 1984), 172–97.

14 On Eton and King's, Colvin, *op. cit.*, I, 268–92; R. Willis and J.W. Clark, *The Architectural History of the University of Cambridge* (Cambridge, 1896), vol. I, passim; H.C. Maxwell Lyte, *A History of Eton College, 1440–1910* (London, 4th ed., 1911); *VCH, Cambridge*, III, 376–90; Wolffe, *op. cit.*, 135–45; Griffiths, *op. cit.*, 242–48.

15 *Calendar of the Charter Rolls, VI (1427–1516)*, 68–69, for a grant made on 3 March, 1446.

16 Nichols, *op. cit.*, 302.

17 *CPR 1436–41*, 455; William Dugdale, *Monasticon Anglicanum* (London, ed., of 1817–30), VI, 1434.

18 Myers, *op. cit.*, 917–19.

19 Nichols, *op. cit.*, 296; Colvin, *op. cit.*, I, 288.

20 Maxwell Lyte, *op. cit.*, 54; Mabel E. Christie, *Henry VI* (London, 1922), 126–27.

21 Wolffe, *op. cit.*, 144–45, estimates that by 1461 some £15–16,000 had been spent on Eton. Between 1442 and 1444 some one and a half million bricks had been ordered and delivered (though not yet, by 1444, put into place).

22 Cora Scofield, *The Life and Reign of Edward the Fourth* (London, 1923), II, 435–38, for the king's reaction and then his mellowing. He ultimately expressed a wish 'to see the furtherance of the work begun upon the Church of our Blessed Lady of Eton,' and he gave land in the London parish of St. Martin Vintry. He pardoned all debts and gave lands previously held by Goldcliff priory: *CPR 1476–85*, 121, 334. He promised 100 marks, and eventually contributed about £1000 to King's between 1479 and his death in 1483. Charles Ross, *Edward IV* (Berkeley & Los Angeles, 1974), 269: 'His vindictive antipathy towards these institutions because of their Lancastrian associations came near to wrecking their future.'

23 *VCH, Kent*, II, 194–95.

24 Colvin, *op. cit.*, II, 870–82; Ross, *Edward IV*, 271–76. The work at Windsor was so extensive that it required the supervision of a clerk of the works, a master mason, a master carpenter, a master carver, a master smith, and 2 purveyors.

25 *CPR 1467–77*, 461, 484, 551; *CPR 1476–85*, 142, 172, 219–20, 333; Ross, *Edward IV*, 276. On the religiosity of the Yorkist dynasty, D.A.L. Morgan, 'The king's affinity in the politics of Yorkist England,' *Transactions of the Royal Historical Society*, 5th series, 23 (1973), 21–22.

26 Colvin, *op. cit.*, III, 187–213.

27   A.R. Martin, *Franciscan Architecture in England*, British Society for Franciscan Studies, xviii (1937), 235.

28   *Ibid*, 236.

29   T. Astle, *The Will of Henry VII* (London, 1775), 30–31.

30   *VCH, Nottinghamshire*, II, 478; *VCH, Hampshire*, II, 93; A.G. Little, 'The introduction of the Observant Friars in England,' *Proceedings of the British Academy*, 10 (1921–23), 455–71, and *Ibid*, 27 (1941), 155–58; Knowles, *op. cit.*, II, 12–13, on Henry's scorn for the general condition of the established Franciscan houses in his realm. For a general treatment of Henry VII and the church, Anthony Goodman, 'Henry VII and Christian renewal,' *Studies in Church History*, 17 (1981), 115–25; and on Henry and reform in the Cistercian order, Derek Baker, 'Old wine in new bottles: attitudes to reform in fifteenth century England,' *Studies in Church History*, 14 (1977), 193–211.

31   Colvin, *op. cit.*, III, 199; *passim*, 196–99, on the hospital.

32   *VCH, Cambridge*, III, 347: 'The grants gained for Henry VI the title of the second founder of the College, but they did not really amount to very much.' Also, Griffiths, *op. cit.*, 257, on Henry's re-endowment of St. Bernard's College, Cambridge.

33   Colvin, *op. cit.*, II, 292; *Calendar of the Papal Letters, XII (1458–72)*, 623.

33a   For Middleham, and Richard's endowments in general, Charles Ross, *Richard III* (London, 1981), 130–33.

34   J.H. Ramsay, *Lancaster and York* (Oxford, 1892), I, 307–08.

35   *VCH, Cambridge*, III, 408.

36   *Ibid*, 409. For Richard III, especially his bequests to King's and Queens' colleges, Cambridge, and his proposed collegiate foundations at Barnard Castle, Middleham, and York Minster, Charles Ross, *Richard III* (London, 1981), 128–32.

37   *VCH, Cambridge*, III, 430; Nichols, *op. cit.*, 356–402.

38   Deanesley, *op. cit.*, 95.

39   Ross, *Edward IV*, 273–74, on Edward's love of the Thames valley.

40   Nichols, *op. cit.* 294.

41   For miscellaneous royal grants, J.L. Kirby, ed., *Calendar of Signet Letters of Henry IV and Henry V, 1399–1422* (London, 1978), 832; *Calendar of the Charter Rolls, VI (1427–1516)*, 68–69, 91–94, 206–07; *CPR 1416–22*, 34, 87; *CPR 1422–29*, 341, 380; *CPR 1441–46*, 256; *Calendar of the Papal Letters, XII (1458–71)*, 341.

42   S.B. Chrimes, *Henry VII* (Berkeley & Los Angeles, 1972), 304; R.B. Mowat, *Henry V* (Boston, 1919), 320; Knowles, *op. cit.*, III, 3, on Henry VII: 'He was a representative, almost a survival, of the last generation of simple medieval orthodoxy.' Francis Bacon, *History of the Reign of King Henry VII*, ed. J.R. Lumby (Cambridge, 1902), 205, 212; Polydore Vergil, *Anglicana Historia, A.D. 1485–1537*, ed. & trans., Denys Hay, Camden Society, third series, lxxiv (1950), 145–47. For the work force on various projects, Colvin, *op. cit.*, I, 273–74, III, 189. Ross, *Richard III*, is being complimentary when he says of Richard: '[his] devotion to religion . . . apparently genuine and personal rather than merely politically-inspired . . .' (p.132).

43   *Calendar of the Charter Rolls, VI (1427–1516)*, 206–07. A grant of June, 1465 bestowed the right to acquire land of the annual value of £20, in mortmain, and to exchange land up to the value of £40 *per annum*.

44   Colvin, *op. cit.*, III, 188.

45   *Archaeological Journal*, 23 (1965), 65. When the earls of Salisbury and of Warwick took Henry VI prisoner they pledged, 'in order to gain his goodwill,' that they would hasten the completion of his church and the royal buildings in Cambridge: Colvin, *op. cit.*, I, 275; I, 278.

46   S. Anglo, *Pageantry and Early Tudor Propaganda* (Oxford, 1969), and 'The British History in early Tudor Propaganda,' *Bulletin of the John Rylands Library*, 44 (1961), 17–48: pp. 46–48, for manuscripts containing genealogies of Edward IV and the House of York. E. Kantorowicz, *Laudes Regiae: A Study in Liturgical Acclamations and Medieval Ruler Worship* (Berkeley & Los

Angeles, 1946), 173, quoting Geoffrey of Monmouth. Also, A. Allan, 'Yorkist propaganda: pedigree and prophecy, and 'The British History',' in *Patronage, Pedigree and Power*, ed., Charles Ross (Gloucester, 1979), 171–92.

47 Ronald Knox and Shane Leslie, *The Miracles of King Henry VI* (Cambridge, 1923); John W. McKenna, 'Piety and Propaganda: The cult of King Henry VI,' in *Chaucer and Middle English Studies in Honour of Russell Hope Robbins*, ed., Beryl Rowland (London, 1974), 72–88.

48 J. Bodds, *Dei Gratia in Royal Titles* (The Hague, 1971), 104; Edward IV was hailed at 'most high and mighty prince.' For usages on coins in France, by English kings, Kantorowicz *op. cit.*, 223.

49 As per Argo Record, RG 99, 'Evensong as sung in King's College Chapel, Cambridge.' The chapel bookstall sells items that affirm the links with the founder: John Saltmarsh, *King Henry VI and the Royal Foundations* (Cambridge, 1972), a scholarly if pietistic pamphlet, along with a postcard depicting parliament petitioning the king, who is meanwhile praying to The Virgin and St. Nicholas for the college (Postcard 19, illuminated from the College charter manuscript of 16 March, 1446).

50 Knox and Leslie, *op. cit.*, 7: further prayers, pp. 7–16.

51 S.B. Chrimes, *English Constitutional Ideas in the Fifteenth Century* (Cambridge, 1938), 7.

52 Joinville, *Chronicle of the Crusade of St. Lewis*, trans., F. Marzials (London, 1908), 318.

53 Nichols, *op. cit.*, 293. Henry VI said, 'We also, who, by disposition of the same King of Kings have now taken into our own hands the government of both our realms, have from the beginnings of our riper age carefully turned over in our mind how . . . or by what royal gift, according to the measure of our devotion and the example of our ancestors, we could do fitting honour:' Maxwell Lyte, *op. cit.*, 5.

A Conflict of Interest?
Chancery Clerks in Private Service

CHARLES W. SMITH

In the last decade of the fourteenth century, both the nobility and the crown made more extensive use of chancery personnel than ever before; by 1413, however, chancery clerks had ceased to appear as major administrative officers and influential councillors in private bureaucracies. Familiarity with the instruments and procedures of the common law and with the secretarial and administrative processes of the central government made the senior members of the chancery's staff a reservoir of knowledge which many noblemen were eager to tap. Professor Wilkinson identified a number of liaisons between chancery personnel and the magnates of the realm in the reign of Edward III, and it is apparent that contemporaries saw nothing improper in such service. As a natural consequence, during the reign of Richard II, chancery clerks were hired to more demanding positions in private administrations that brought them into more intimate contact with members of the nobility. This type of service survived the usurpation of Henry Bolingbroke only to disappear at the beginning of his son's reign. The obvious question is why; and the simple answer is that such service had been outlawed in 1406. But this does not explain what had occurred to make contemporaries see the employment of chancery clerks by private parties as a situation that should be avoided. Nor can it be said that the clerks had changed: the intervening years had witnessed no revolution in the organization of the chancery and, though individuals had come and gone, Henry V's clerks were men whose training and background differed little from those of Richard II. Consequently, the reasons for the end of this practice that had provided capable servants to the English nobility must be sought in changes in the political and social circumstances that occurred in the reign of Henry IV or Henry V.

As Professor Tout noted, 'In the fourteenth century it was both easy and customary for one man to serve two masters'[1] – the ambiguity of such a dual allegiance was not at all obvious to the men of that period. The oath of 1346 and the ordinances of 1388 required chancery clerks to conceal any secrets they learned while working for the king, but neither forbade the clerks to take service with anyone. Some of the greater magnates of England had been casually employing chancery clerks as attorneys, feofees, and business agents since at least the beginning of that century, and the dukes of Lancaster had recruited them as senior administrators since the middle of it. Prior to the reign of Richard II, however, we have no firm evidence that noble families other than that of Lancaster were hiring chancery clerks as feed retainers, but given the scarcity of records which would allow the study of private administrations in the fourteenth century, it is impossible to state that this was not already a longstanding practice. Certainly, based on the regularity with which some Edwardian clerks associated with certain nobles, it is possible to suggest that these clerks had indeed been retained, but there is no proof of this, and neither Wilkinson nor Tout made such a case. Beginning in the 1390s, however, references in the *Calendars of the Patent and Close Rolls* show that several noblemen were retaining chancery clerks as councillors.

In November, 1391, Richard II confirmed the private letters patent of Thomas Lord Clifford dated 1389, by which Clifford had granted John Scarburgh (or Scardeburgh) an annuity of £2 'for service done and to be done and for being of the grantor's council'.[2] Scarburgh was a clerk of the royal chancery from Yorkshire who had held the office of underclerk of parliament since 1385.[3] There is little else on the rolls to connect Clifford and Scarburgh. Earlier in 1391, it is recorded that Clifford appointed Scarburgh to be one of his general attorneys, but a single such reference would not ordinarily imply any close relationship between two men: chancery clerks were often chosen for such service because they *were* chancery clerks, but a man might appoint one clerk one year and another the following.[4] It was only because Clifford had died and his lands had escheated to the crown that his letters patent came to the king's notice (probably through a petition from Scarburgh) and were enrolled among the royal letters patent. More than anything else, this demonstrates the limitations of royal records in researching private administrations.

For the more respectable sum of £20, Thomas Overton, who began signing royal chancery writs at least as early as 1386, became a clerical retainer of Roger Mortimer.[5] Mortimer was not only the earl of March, of course, but heir presumptive, and therefore a singularly important individual. He appointed Overton to be one of his general attorneys annually from 1394 until his death. This office should have kept Overton in England where he and the other general attorneys would have looked after the earl's interests. However, in 1396, Overton was summoned to Ireland to carry a dispatch from the earl back to the king and his council in England; and, in 1398, shortly before the earl's death, Overton was again in Ireland where, as a member of the earl's council, he witnessed the indenture of another man entering Mortimer's service.[6] The previous year, Richard II had confirmed Mortimer's private letters patent granting Overton the £20 annuity and had them entered on the royal patent rolls.[7] After the earl's violent and untimely death, Overton served as one of Mortimer's executors with Edmund Mortimer and Henry Percy.[8]

The year of Mortimer's death, Thomas Mowbray, then duke of Norfolk, was sentenced to exile and obtained royal licence to appoint a 'continual council' to look after his estates. One of that council's members was John Rome, a Yorkshire clerk and notary public who had been associating with other chancery personnel since 1379 and who had probably been in Mowbray's service long before 1398.[9] In 1383, Rome was named to a commission of sewers in Lincolnshire whose members also included the then earl of Nottingham, Thomas Mowbray. At the earl marshal's castle of Framlingham in 1393, the chancery clerk received the acknowledgements of two parties to a charter in which Mowbray was not involved. This suggests that Rome was at Framlingham for other purposes, perhaps already as a councillor to the earl, and that the parties to the charter simply found it convenient to acknowledge it there rather than make a trip to London as they would normally have done.[10] The following year, Rome appeared as a general attorney of the earl.[11] In 1397, at the London inn of the earl, Rome became a member of a syndicate that obtained eighteen manors belonging to the earl of Warwick that were to be held as a surety for payments totalling £5,000 that Warwick owed Nottingham.[12] But it was not until Mowbray's exile – an extraordinary event – that the royal rolls identified Rome as his councillor. On Mowbray's death six months later, Richard II granted Rome £40 and named him clerk of the parliament, one of the most important offices a chancery clerk could hold.[13]

Other chancery personnel associated with various noblemen. Nicholas Bubbewyth served as a general attorney of Thomas Mortimer in 1392, of Roger Mortimer in 1396, 1397, and 1398, and of Roger's widow in 1399. Though he would eventually become the bishop of Bath and Wells, at this time Bubbewyth was merely another Yorkshire clerk of chancery, albeit a master after 1396.[14] Roudon, a Yorkshire man who became a master in 1394, was often involved in the business of Henry Percy, earl of Northumberland, from the mid-1390s.[15] Simon Gaunstede, a more junior clerk, had higher connections: he served as the general attorney of several royal family members. In the last five years of Richard II's reign, he acted for the earl of Rutland, and in the same period he had several associations with the Holland brothers and their families.[16] Lesser figures also had their chancery connections: Thomas Lord Morley was often a business partner of James Billyngford, a Norfolk man and a clerk of the crown in chancery from 1385; Reginald Lord Grey of Ruthin employed as his general attorney

Henry Maupas, a clerk from Yorkshire apparently serving in the chancery's rolls office at this time; and Sir Bernard Brocas and his family had a longstanding relationship with John Chitterne, who was from Wiltshire and became a chancery master in 1391.[17] These were all longterm and undoubtedly important relationships for the clerks, but there is no evidence that any of them involved annuities or indentures, and only Scarburgh, Overton, and Rome were called 'councillors'.

They were probably members of a 'council learned' – a type of body becoming more common among the nobility in the later middle ages. Although still a vague entity in the late fourteenth century, a council learned tended to be composed primarily of lawyers who advised their lord on legal matters touching his estate. According to Carole Rawcliffe, some of the council's members were temporary, hired for specific purposes, whereas others were more permanent and also filled posts as estate staff. The temporary councillors often had more than one master. Rawcliffe was also careful to distinguish between the council learned and the attorneys employed by many noblemen to oversee business in the courts of London and Westminster. This latter group of lawyers, whose members *usually* served more than one noble, sometimes formed a subsidiary staff to the council learned located in Westminster and occasionally headed by an attorney-general.[18] It is probable, then, that Scarburgh, Overton, and Rome were originally hired for their connection to the chancery and belonged to the Westminster staffs of their various masters. Later, having proven their worth, they became members of the council learned proper. So, even though they continued to have other casual employers, they became more closely attached to the interests of Clifford, Mortimer, and Mowbray.[19] None became a private administrator, however, as did some of those clerks hired by the duke of Lancaster.

When the county palatine of Lancaster was reconstituted for John of Gaunt in 1377, the duke, like his father-in-law, chose one royal chancery clerk, Thomas Thelwall, to be his chancellor and another, Peter Barton, to be a member of his council and his attorney in the royal chancery. John of Yarborough, the duke's personal chancellor (1375–83) and a man with no connections to the royal chancery, figured only as a minor character in the county palatine.[20] On Thelwall's death in 1382, the duke brought in Thomas Stanley from the royal chancery to watch over the palatinate chancery until the new chancellor, John Scarle, was appointed.[21] Scarle was a respected member of the royal chancery whose abilities would take him far. From 1384, in addition to his duties as chancellor of the county palatine, this Lincolnshire man served as the clerk of parliament – a crown appointment. He held both offices until his 1394 promotion to the keepership of the rolls, the chief clerkship of the chancery.[22] Thus, it appears that Lancaster's connections to the royal chancery were older but not much more extensive than those of any other noble, prior to the 1390s.[23]

There was one difference, however. Thelwall, Barton, and Scarle were all masters or clerks of the first form of chancery before they entered Lancastrian service; Scarburgh, Overton, and Rome were clerks of the second form while they served as councillors. John of Gaunt's wealth and the vice-regal nature of the county palatine were undoubtedly responsible for this in part. After the death of the Black Prince, the administration of the county palatine was more prestigious and more autonomous than any other except that of the king himself. It was only natural that Gaunt decided to imitate the royal chancery and chose royal chancery masters – who oversaw much of the royal bureaucracy's routine business – to achieve that end. Perhaps Gaunt also saw the chance to improve his connections with the central government by hiring royal clerks: the increasing number of clerks serving in both the Lancastrian and royal chanceries in the 1390s seems to support the idea that John of Gaunt may have been pursuing this as a conscious policy.

Aside from John Scarle and Peter Barton, there were at least five, and possibly eight, clerks serving simultaneously in the chanceries of Richard II and the duke of Lancaster during the 1390s; and several other royal clerks came from Lancashire or had close connection to the duke in that period.[24] John Wakeryng entered Lancastrian service by 1393, became keeper of the duchy's privy seal (and therefore the duke's personal chancellor or secretary) by 1394, and succeeded Scarle in the chancellorship of the county palatine in 1394 or 1395. Like Thelwall and Scarle, Wakeryng was a master of chancery and was destined for a distinguished career.[25] The signatures of Henry Kays, John Lilleston, John Shelton, and Simon Gaunstede appear on instruments prepared in both chanceries during the 1390s, and the surname 'Hunte' that occurs in the records of both in that period plausibly refers to the same man.[26] John Thoralby and William Aghton, who later became masters in the royal chancery, were clerks of the duke's chancery in the 1390s and probably members of the crown's as well; Aghton at least was a king's clerk in the 1390s.[27] Finally, five other men whose names indicate a northwest origin were serving in the royal chancery but had no visible connection to the Lancastrian chancery in the 1390s: Robert Faryngton, Thomas Stanley, John Cliderhowe, Henry Maupas, and John Brokeholes. By the middle of that decade, Faryngton was probably the most senior master in the chancery and Stanley was the keeper of the rolls from 1397.[28]

Consequently, by the end of Richard II's reign, a quarter or more of the forty-eight clerks of the royal chancery were either serving the duke of Lancaster or had strong ties to Lancashire. Seven of these men began signing duchy or county palatine writs in the early 1390s, and two others served consecutively as keepers of the rolls from 1394. Furthermore, when the king decided to reorganize his Irish bureaucracies prior to his expedition, and when it became necessary to appoint a new treasurer of Calais, Richard II chose chancery clerks associated with Lancashire: Robert Faryngton and Thomas Stanley, respectively.[29] These facts support the idea that Gaunt was trying to build a clique within the royal chancery and they fit grander, contemporary accusations that Gaunt's power at court was overwhelming all others by the end of his life. The fear of his younger brother, Thomas of Woodstock, and Gaunt's politic absences during the turbulent 1380s had caused the heart of the English nation to feel more good will toward the third son of Edward III. Richard II looked to his eldest uncle for guidance and sometimes even wore the duke's livery.[30] John of Gaunt could rightly expect later generations to remember him as 'time-honour'd Lancaster'.

However, a cautionary note should be sounded in favor of theories put forth by Professors Tout and Wilkinson and Dr. Michael Bennett. All of these men describe connections between the house of Lancaster and chancery (and elsewhere in the central government) beginning much earlier than the 1390s. Bennett presented a history of what he called the 'Winwick circle' – named for John Winwick of Lancashire who entered royal service in the 1330s and became very important in both the chancery and the privy seal office. According to Bennett, Winwick probably procured places in the king's service for a number of fellow clerks from the northwest, including Henry Haydok, Thomas Thelwall, Robert Faryngton, and Thomas Stanley. These men, in turn, could have introduced those Lancashire clerks who entered chancery in the 1390s. The increase in the number of northwesterners could then be explained as the result of a snowball effect – one man brought in two clerks, these two each brought in two more, and so forth. This theory in itself would be no hindrance to the idea that Gaunt's hand was also behind the entry of these men, but Bennett, like Tout and G.P. Cuttino, stressed the independence of these clerks and noted that their experience and talents were the key reasons for their appointments and that they 'were able to serve the realm, and themselves, unhindered by the vicissitudes of national politics'.[31]

Nevertheless, the very sudden appearance of so many northwesterners in both chanceries remains suspicious. Explaining this trend by pointing to a small cadre of Lancashire clerks earlier in the fourteenth century fails to take into account the much larger clique of 'Yorkshire' clerks which had dominated the chancery throughout that century. This group, whose members were actually from Lindsey and northern Nottingham as well as the east riding of Yorkshire, had recruited agressively from its home ground and managed to control the keepership of the hanaper from 1298 until 1399. It is, of course, possible that the Lancastrians were simply more effective than the Yorkshiremen at procuring chancery positions in the last decade of the fourteenth century. And the northeastern group had faded from dominance in every central bureaucracy except the chancery by the later fourteenth century.[32] But no mechanism – except Gaunt – presents itself to show why this should have been so. Moreover, events after 1399 which will be dealt with below show that some chancery clerks could become quite attached to their lordly patrons. Finally, even if the rise in the number of Lancashire-connected clerks was not the result of Gaunt's efforts, he could hardly have been sorry to see the trend and would certainly have encouraged it.

And what Gaunt found convenient, his son must have counted a blessing indeed, for, as Professor A.L. Brown has shown, when Henry Bolingbroke became King Henry IV of England, he was sadly lacking an 'estblishment' – a group of magnates who might have helped him govern. The greater part of the English nobility was either too amiable to Richard or unusable because of infirmities or youth. Only four earls could be relied upon to support the new king, making him more dependent on lesser men: barons, knights, gentry, and even bureaucrats.[33] This dependence was highlighted when Henry chose as his first chancellor of England none other than John Scarle, an old and trusted Lancastrian servant. Scarle was well-qualified administratively, but he was a curious choice. Other than the occasional layman, Scarle was the first non-episcopal chancellor since John Offord in 1345; and Offord had at least been the dean of Lincoln. Scarle apparently held only canonries. Moreover, Scarle was the first clerk of chancery to be promoted to the chancellorship in a half-century, the last having been John Thoresby in 1349. The new chancellor probably understood the ins and outs of his office better than most of his predecessors (or successors), but he had no other prestigious title or lineage with which to overawe his lordly petitioners and hence never delivered a sermon to parliament or involved himself in the other courtly rituals proper to his station; these were seen to by Archbishop Arundel and others.[34]

On the whole, the new king's affiliations with chancery personnel before and shortly after the usurpation are obscure, but apparently they were not extensive. Based on the records of the duchy of Lancaster and the accounts of Henry's treasurer, no chancery clerks seem to have been in the king's personal service for any great length of time before 1399.[35] Like Mowbray, Henry did appoint two chancery clerks to be general attorneys during his banishment, but Thomas Stanley and John Wakeryng were members of a twenty-member board including four earls, the archbishop of York, and two other bishops.[36] Furthermore, Stanley was the keeper of the rolls, the royal chancery officer most often appointed by any lord leaving England, and Wakeryng was the chancellor of the county palatine of

Lancaster, the inheritance Henry expected to obtain during his exile – they could hardly have been left out. After 1399, Henry wanted to keep his private estates separate from those of the crown and so he had Henry Kays, an official serving the royal and county palatine chanceries, draw up the great charter of the duchy of Lancaster. However, for the first years of his reign, the king placed his own men into the duchy's offices. John Wakeryng, who may have been John of Gaunt's personal chancellor as well as chancellor of the county palatine, did not become chancellor of the duchy, that office went to William Burgoyne. Subsequently, Henry saw the light and, after 1402, the office of chancellor of the duchy of Lancaster was subsumed by the chancellorship of the county palatine, thus making control of the Lancastrian chanceries by royal personnel complete because, although he had not used king's clerks in the duchy, the king had not disturbed their hold on the county palatine.[37]

Wakeryng remained chancellor of the county palatine until 1405 when he was promoted to the keepership of the rolls of the royal chancery. He was succeeded in office first by Thomas Stanley (1405–10) and then John Spryngthorpe (1410–13).[38] Stanley's connections to Lancastrian administration went back many years; his service as the interim head of the palatinate chancery in 1382 has already been mentioned. He was a *former* keeper of the rolls of the royal chancery (1397–1402) who had been dismissed from the latter office over a dispute involving the statute of provisors; but his abilities were too great and his family too important for him to stay long out of service.[39]

Spryngthorpe was a lesser man, but still a master of chancery since 1405, and an experienced Lincolnshire clerk who had been in royal service for more than thirty years when appointed chancellor.[40] Other familiar royal chancery names continued to appear in county palatine administration and were soon supplemented by others. Henry Kays and John Thoralby were joined by John Kirkeby. John Mapilton, and Richard Bolton.[41] Kirkeby was a highly experienced clerk from Lincolnshire who had seen service in Ireland under Robert Faryngton and had succeeded Faryngton as keeper of the rolls in the Irish chancery.[42] Mapilton and Bolton were much younger men who entered royal service in the 1390s.[43]

Furthermore, in addition to Scarle, other members of the chancery's staff were utilized elsewhere in the king's administration. Nicholas Bubbewyth proved to be a multi-talented minister for the crown and, although he has been mentioned in connection with the Mortimers in the late 1390s, he may also have had a relative in Lancastrian service: a Henry Bubbewyth was feodary of the duchy in Yorkshire in the 1380s. Nicholas served as the royal secretary from at least May until September, 1402, and may have obtained that office after Thomas Langley's promotion to the privy seal in 1401. From 1402, Bubbewyth was the keeper of the rolls of the royal chancery; in 1405, he was promoted to the privy seal, again following Langley; in 1406, he received his first episcopacy (London); in 1407, he became the king's treasurer; and, from 1408, having traded up to the bishopric of Bath and Wells, he retired from ministerial office. He would, however, remain a councillor of the house of Lancaster until his death in 1424.[44] When Bubbewyth moved out of the signet office he was replaced by John Brokeholes. Brokeholes did not become the king's secretary, but he did apparently serve in the signet office for much of Henry IV's reign and his purpose there may have been to act as an advisor on method and procedure in the newly reorganized office. Brokeholes was from Lancashire and had entered the royal chancery in the early 1390s.[45]

The king even seems to have encouraged his family to make use of royal chancery clerks in their private bureaucracies. Queen Joan's chancellor until 1410 or 1411 was John Kyngton, the royal notary or prothonotary of chancery.[46] As notary, Kyngton was appointed to the chancery from the outside and, hence, did not have much chancery experience – the usual lure of a chancery clerk. He was unusual in that he at least attempted to learn the course of the chancery and his signature appears on chancery documents of a relatively routine nature that were unconnected with the largely diplomatic mission of his office.[47] In 1409, John Hertilpole, a master of chancery from Lincoln diocese, was mentioned as the 'warden' of the king's son, Humphrey. Since Humphrey must have been in his very late teens at the time, the exact nature of Hertilpole's service is unclear; but, Hertilpole had been a master for fifteen years and may have been instructing Humphrey in the common law.[48] Whatever the case, a year later Hertilpole became the chancellor of Thomas of Lancaster, Henry IV's second eldest son, and accompanied his new lord to Ireland.[49]

Initially, Henry IV made no effort to prohibit chancery clerks from seeking employment with other lords. Given the hectic nature of his early reign this hardly seems surprising. Chancery clerks continued to serve those lords – and the families of those lords – with whom they had earlier contact. In November 1399, Simon Gaunstede acted as an attorney of the widow of the Holland earl of Kent, and, in 1400, John Rome helped the widow of Thomas Mowbray obtain the remaining goods of her husband and a royal grant of £1000.[50] Most of the connections between chancery personnel and the nobility in this period tended to be of this apparently benign nature. According to the royal rolls, the chancery clerk who remained in most intimate contact with the family of his old lord was Thomas Overton. He continued to serve as an executor of the late earl of March in the early years of the new dynasty.[51] Because of unrest and rebellion, however, it quickly became obvious to contemporaries that there was a conflict of interest involved when a chancery clerk served in a private bureaucracy. The first casualty of this new thinking was William Roudon.

The usurpation had not disturbed Roudon's service in the royal chancery. He received royal confirmation of his estate in the rectory of Stoke Bruerne, Northamptonshire, in October 1399, and the rolls show him to be involved in typical chancery business in the first four years of the reign of Henry IV. But sometime between 20 April 1403 and 4 May 1404, he was dismissed from the chancery.[52] For a chancery clerk, especially a master, to lose his place in the bureaucracy was highly unusual, and the timing of Roudon's dismissal leaves little doubt that the root of the problem was his connection to the Percy family: it was in the late spring and early summer months of 1403 that the grievances of the Percies built to the crescendo that ended in July at Shrewsbury. Although the chancery rolls of Henry IV do not record any liaisons between the Yorkshire clerk and the Percies, his close association with them and their property in the latter years of Richard II has already been mentioned above. There was no acrimony involved in the king's treatment of his former clerk: on 4 May 1404, Henry IV granted Roudon an annual tun of Gascon wine 'in consideration of his good service to Edward III, Richard II, and the king'. But it was to William Roudon, 'late' master of chancery that this boon went, and the clerk must have found his cup filled with sour grapes indeed.[53]

Roudon's case had been serious, but it had been handled in house, by the king or the newly appointed chancellor, Henry Beaufort. A similar episode involving Thomas Overton and the Percy family was the true turning point for popular opinion on chancery clerks in private service. Like Roudon, Overton spent the first years of Henry IV's reign quietly serving in the chancery. In 1402, he was named to a commission to hold Lesnes abbey with John Scarle, Thomas Stanley, Nicholas Bubbewyth, and others.[54] The following year, the king appointed Overton to audit the accounts of Robert Faryngton for those years the latter clerk had served as treasurer of Ireland.[55] But unlike Roudon, Overton did not involve himself – or was not known to be involved – in the first Percy rebellion that resulted in the death of Henry Percy and the execution of Thomas, earl of Worcester. It is possible that Overton had not yet entered the service of the Percy family, but, as an executor of Roger Mortimer, he had already been in contact with Edmund Mortimer and Henry Percy *pere*, earl of Northumberland, who were co-executors. Probably as a result of this relationship, Overton was drawn into the affairs of Northumberland and shared in the earl's condemnation at the parliament of 1406.

The chancery clerk had no part in the insurrection of Archbishop Scrope and as late as 9 February 1406, Overton was present in the royal chancery. On that date he signed a summons to the parliament that was to meet in March, 1406; the second session of which would declare Henry Percy a traitor.[56] Overton's movements in the days immediately after 9

February are uncertain, but he apparently joined the earl of Northumberland who fled to France early in the year: a pardon granted to Overton in 1408, after the earl's death at Bramham Moor, excused the chancery clerk for having adhered to and counselled Northumberland.[57] But the damage had already been done. In the same session that condemned the earl in 1406, the parliament entered on the rolls an item that first required chancery clerks to attend to their duties diligently and not demand 'excessive regard' for their work, and then went on to say 'q'ils ne soient du conseil de nulluy encountre le Roy'.[58] This did not prohibit all service in private bureaucracies, but its effect was the same; the Percies had been supporters of the house of Lancaster in 1399, but by their own choice they had turned against Henry IV and brought about the downfall of themselves and the chancery clerks associated with them. The lesson would have made other clerks nervous and hesitant to build such close bonds. If clerks continued to serve anyone other than the king, they kept it quiet: no mention of such service appears on the rolls for the rest of the reign.

When Henry V came to the throne, he also took strong measures. In confirming the chancery's officers (i.e., when he regranted them their posts), the king included a clause stating that each officer received his royal annuity 'so that he be not retained by anyone else'.[59] Notably, two of the officers so chided were John Rome and John Scarburgh. And the magnates could not complain about Henry's action. When he forbade chancery officers to serve in private bureaucracies, he included his own among them: John Sprynthorpe was dismissed from the chancellorship of the duchy and county palatine on 4 April 1413, just two weeks after Henry V became king. Never again would a royal chancery clerk hold those offices.[60] Nor does it seem that many chancery clerks held lesser positions in the duchy and county palatine. John Mapilton alone survived Henry's purge of the Lancastrian chanceries, and he was the attorney for the duchy in the royal chancery – an office that could probably be held only by a chancery clerk.[61]

The king may have other reasons for dismissing royal clerks from his private bureaucracies, as well. Henry V had never been close to the royal chancery or its clerks during the reign of his father and he may have viewed both it and them with suspicion: except for his own period of prominence (1410–11), the chancery had been controlled by Archbishop Arundel for much of the latter part of Henry IV's reign. And it does seem that chancery clerks were singled out in the duchy, for elsewhere personnel did continue under Henry V: John Leventhorpe retained the powerful office of receiver-general, for example.[62] On the other hand, it was common enough for a new king to put his own men in positions of importance – Henry IV had chosen William Burgoyne over John Wakeryng to fill the duchy's chancellorship at the beginning of his reign.

Moreover, the clerks did not suffer any indignities in the royal chancery which Henry viewed as their proper place. Wakeryng himself was promoted by Henry V to the privy seal and later endowed with the bishopric of Norwich, but Wakeryng was a man of both high ability and piety, characteristics for which the king had great respect. Henry V also employed John Stopyndon in the chancery at Rouen from at least 1421 and, briefly, as the royal secretary toward the end of his reign.[63] Stopyndon's connections to the *royal* chancery at the time were tenuous at best, however. In November, 1420, he was nominated for a pension from the bishop of Exeter as a clerk of chancery – whether this meant the English or the Norman chancery is not made clear; but he would become keeper of the hanaper of the English chancery in 1426 and later keeper of the rolls there.[64]

The reasons for John Mapilton's durability probably turned on his longer acquaintance with the new king. In 1404, Mapilton had success-fully represented the prince in a chancery case and, although this is the only recorded tie between the two men during Henry IV's reign, later events suggest that the chancery clerk may have been in Prince Henry's service; certainly Henry V showed great trust in Mapilton once he had become king.[65] In 1414, Henry chose Mapilton to draw up the great charter of his Hereford inheritance and incorporate it into the duchy.[66] In that same year, according to J.H. Wylie, he became the chancellor of the dowager queen, Joan of Navarre, though his appointment is not mentioned in the household accounts published by A.R. Myers and a John Launet is called her secretary in the French rolls of Henry V.[67] However, if Mapilton did serve as the queen's chancellor, this might give some insight into the sequestration of her estates in 1419: in 1421, it was Mapilton who established the king's right to seize the Bohun estates of the countess of Stafford.[68] In any case, Mapilton was a useful tool of the king and, to Henry, his affiliation to the chancery may have been of secondary importance.

After the death of Henry V, there is evidence that some royal chancery clerks again found private employment. William Godyng acted as the receiver of the lordship of Burwell for the duke of Bedford in the 1430s; several *deputy* chancellors in the duchy of Lancaster were clerks of the royal chancery in the 1440s; and Robert Fenne served as a receiver of the Stafford family in the county of Rutland in the 1450s.[69] And there are a few other, less certain, examples of the same sort. Three points should be noticed here. First, the men serving in these positions were not masters, or even important clerks of the lower forms, while they held these posts. Second, most of these offices could be performed by deputy, and even if the clerks chose to fulfill them personally, they were not serving as important councillors. And finally, these men were laymen whereas all those mentioned above were clergymen.[70] The period 1390–1413, when some chancery clerks found so much work outside their office and became deeply embroiled in the factional politics of the time, was an aberration in the history of the office. Its end was symptomatic of changes in the social climate during the reigns of Henry IV and Henry V.

The parliamentary ruling of 1406 had forbidden chancery clerks to serve any insurgent lord and thereby inhibited all private service for a number of years when it was very difficult to ascertain who might be a potential rebel. Additionally, the ordinances of chancery, first issued in 1388 and then reissued by Henry V, directed that all chancery clerks (except the two clerks of the crown) were to be clergymen, just at the time many noblemen were beginning to employ laymen.[71] Together, these two factors kept chancery personnel out of the market in the early fifteenth century – the period when many noblemen appear to have reorganized their own administrations. The rise of the educated layman (especially those trained at the inns of chancery and court), the widespread demand for university graduates (among whom few were chancery clerks), and the residual effects of the rabid anticlericalism of the late fourteenth century (which had been aimed particularly at those absentee and pluralist clerks among whom chancery clerks numbered themselves) combined with the chancery's prohibitions to insure that few positions would be available when the clerks of chancery did begin to seek them in the minority of Henry VI. Prior to the reign of Richard II, chancery clerks had been members of a relatively small company of highly-trained administrators; after the reign of Henry VI, they formed a very small proportion of a large group. Society had outgrown whatever small reliance it had put on the clerks of chancery.

NOTES

1   T.F. Tout, *Chapters in the Administrative History of Mediaeval England*, 6 vols. (Manchester: 1920–33), 4:51.
2   *CPR 1388–91*, 508. The names of chancery clerks in this essay are spelled according to the consistent signatures found on chancery documents.
3   *CPR 1370–74*, 266, 428; *CPR 1381–85*, 535.
4   *CPR 1388–91*, 363. I use the term 'general attorneys' to avoid confusion. Anyone leaving the country or otherwise unable to watch over his or her affairs could appoint one or more persons – a great lord might have more than twenty – to be general attorneys, hence, this office was not restricted to chancery clerks nor are general attorneys to be confused with attorneys-general (in the sense that Rawcliffe used it, see below) or with attorneys hired to act in specific actions (though a general attorney might also do this kind of work).
5   G.A. Holmes, *The Estates of the Higher Nobility in Fourteenth Century England* (Cambridge: 1957), 63; PRO C.219/9/1.
6   *CPR 1391–96*, 500, 638; *CPR 1396–99*, 33, 186, 349; *Anglo-Norman Letters and Petitions*, ed. M.D. Legge (Oxford: 1941), 59; Holmes, 130–31.
7   *CPR 1396–99*, 266. Since Mortimer was still alive in 1397, it is unclear why the king was involved in what was, after all, a private arrangement; perhaps Overton, like Scarburgh, was

insuring his good fortune. Chancery clerks often had their private papers enrolled: enrollment cost them nothing and the protection it afforded was priceless.

8 *Ibid.*, 4, 39.
9 *Ibid.*, 422. John Rome of Yorkshire was a mainpernor with John Scarburgh in 1379, he became a notary public by apostolic authority in 1389: *CPR 1377–81*, 315; *CPL*, 4:320.
10 *CCR 1381–85*, 335; *CCR 1392–96*, 232. Prior to its enrolment, all parties to a legal instrument had to affirm its contents before a chancery clerk or some other officer of the crown empowered to receive such acknowledgements.
11 *CPR 1391–96*, 355.
12 *CCR 1396–99*, 123–24.
13 *Ibid.*, 564; see also *RP*, 5:317.
14 *CPR 1391–96*, 117, 718; *CPR 1396–99*, 34, 185, 349, 451. For the purpose or this essay, a clerk is considered to have attained the rank of master when he first received attorneys on his own authority, sat as a receiver of petitions to parliament, acted as a commander or examiner of writs – all duties theoretically restricted to masters – or else was called a master in a contemporary document. Additionally, a man appointed to be keeper of the rolls or clerk of parliament – offices that entitled him to be a receiver of petitions to parliament – will be considered a master from the date of his grant of office.
15 *CPR 1391–96*, 472; *CPR 1396–99*, 334; *CCR 1392–96*, 321, 330, 400, 419, 481, etc.
16 *CPR 1391–96*, 477; *CPR 1396–99*, 519, 520; *CCR 1396–99*, 73, 248, 256, 268. Gaunstede was also from Yorkshire: *CCR 1385–88*, 488.
17 Billyngford: *CPR 1385–88*, 56; *CCR 1377–81*, 305, 411; *CCR 1389–92*, 319; *CPR 1396–99*, 555. Maupas: *CCR 1385–89*, 112; *CPR 1391–96*, 475; *CPR 1396–99*, 204, 554. Chitterne: *CCR 1377–81*, 129; *CPR 1381–85*, 131, 433; *CPR 1385–88*, 320; *CPR 1391–96*, 699, 700. In each case there are further references tying the clerks to the noblemen.
18 Carole Rawcliffe, 'Baronial Councils in the Later Middle Ages' in C.D. Ross, *Patronage, Pedigree and Power in Late-Medieval England* (Gloucester: 1979), 87–108, especially 90–94.
19 In each case, the nobleman was out of or leaving England and this probably explains why the clerks were 'permanent' members of the council learned but not estate staff as Rawcliffe thought normal.
20 Robert Somerville, *History of the Duchy of Lancaster: 1265–1603* (London: 1953), 56–57, 127; *John of Gaunt's Register, 1379–83*, ed. Eleanor C. Lodge and Robert Somerville, 2 vols. (Camden, 3rd series, vol 56 & 57: 1937), 1:39,207; 2:412; J.F. Baldwin, 'The Chancery of the Duchy of Lancaster' *BIHR* (1926–27), 4:135. Henry Grosmont had employed Henry Haydok from the royal chancery as his chancellor in the county palatine.
21 *Gaunt's Register, 1379–83*, 1:248; Somerville, 61, 475.
22 *RP*, 3:184, 203, 215, etc.; *CPR 1391–96*, 468. See C.L. Kingsford's biography of Scarle: *DNB*, 17:888.
23 Gaunt's earlier register does not mention any chancery clerks in his service: *John of Gaunt's Register, 1372–76*, ed. Sydney Armitage-Smith, 2 vols. (Camden Society, 3rd series, vols. 20 & 21: 1911).
24 Barton apparently retired from the royal chancery to his prebend at Salisbury in the mid-1390s: Kathleen Edwards, *The English Secular Cathedrals in the Middle Ages* (Manchester: 1949), 81–82, 361–62.
25 Somerville, 366, 388, 476. Wakeryng became a master between 18 October and 12 December 1394: *CPR 1391–96*, 498, 510.
26 Somerville, 477 & n.; PRO C.219/9/1, 3, 8, 13. Lilleston, an Oxfordshireman, had been in chancery since at least 1384: *CCR 1381–85*, 440. For Gaunstede see Malcolm Richardson, 'The Influence of Henry V on the Development of Chancery English' (unpubl. Ph.D. diss., University of Tennessee, 1978), 131.
27 Somerville, 477 & n. Richard II presented Aghton to two benefices and Hugh Bavant, another royal chancery clerk nominated Aghton to be one of his general attorneys in 1398: *CPR 1396–99*, 212, 277, 375.

28   The towns of Farington, Clitheroe, and Brockholes are in Lancashire, and that of Malpas is in Cheshire. As was noted above, however, Maupas claimed to be from Yorkshire, thus showing the dangers of assuming that surnames are toponyms. Stanley was the kinsman of Sir John Stanley, a Lancashire supporter of the crown: Tout, *Chapters*, 4:51. See also Michael J. Bennett, *Community, Class and Careerism; Cheshire and Lancashire Society in the Age of Sir Gawain and the Green Knight* (Cambridge: 1983), 151–55.

29   In 1394, Faryngton was appointed keeper of the rolls in Ireland, and, in 1398, he was made treasurer there: *CPR 1391–96*, 34; *CPR 1396–99*, 283, 409, 410, 411. Thomas Stanley served as treasurer and victualler of Calais, 1395–97: *CPR 1391–96*, 620.

30   Somerville, 64–65.

31   Bennett, 205–6; see also 151–52; B. Wilkinson, *The Chancery Under Edward III* (Manchester: 1929). 179; Tout, 3:447; G.P. Cuttino, 'King's Clerks and the Community of the Realm' *Speculum*, 29:404. I am thankful to Dr. Bennett for conversations we had on this subject at Kalamazoo, and I want to emphasize that I do agree that these chancery clerks were capable bureaucrats and that *most* of the time the vast *majority* of them were not influenced by politics.

32   See J.L. Grassi, 'Royal Clerks form the Archdiocese of York in the Fourteenth Century,' *Northern History* (1970), 5:12–33; A.H. Thompson, 'The Registers of the Archdeaconry of Richmond, 1361–1442,' *Yorkshire Archaeological Journal* (1919), 25:129–268.

33   A.L. Brown, 'The Reign of Henry IV' in *Fifteenth Century England*, ed. S.B. Chrimes, C. Ross, and R.A. Griffiths. (Manchester: 1972), 1–28.

34   *RP*, 3:417,456. After he resigned as chancellor, the king granted Scarle the archdeaconry of Lincoln: *CPR 1399–1401*, 547.

35   Somerville, 132–33 & n.; *Expeditions to Prussia and the Holy Land made by Henry Earl of Derby 1390–1, 1392–3, being the Accounts kept by His Treasurer during two years*, ed. Lucy T. Smith. (Camden Society, old series, vol. 52: 1894), xci–xcvii.

36   Somerville, 69 & n.

37   *Ibid.*, 140 n., 154–57, 388–89.

38   *Ibid.*, 476.

39   *CPR 1401–5*, 120, 136. Thomas was the kinsman of Sir John Stanley, K.G., see above.

40   *CPR 1405–8*, 93; *CCR 1377–81*, 324.

41   Somerville, 456, 477 & n.

42   *CPR 1391–96*, 510, 713; *CPR 1396–99*, 70, 414, 418.

43   *CCR 1392–96*, 311; *CPR 1396–99*, 315. Mapilton was a Yorkshireman, but he could plausibly have been a relative of Thomas Mapleton, an auditor of John of Gaunt: *Gaunt's Register, 1372–76*. Bolton's origins are obscure, though he may have been from Lancashire: *CCR 1399–1402*, 501.

44   See J.L. Kirby, *Henry IV of England* (London: 1970), 116, 258; *CSL 1399–1422*, xii; A.B. Emden, *A Biographical Register of the University of Oxford to A.D. 1500*, 3 vols. (Oxford: 1957–59), 1:294–96.

45   PRO C.219/9/10; *CCR 1399–1402*, 528; *CPR 1405–8*, 138. See also, A.J. Otway-Ruthven, *The King's Secretary and the Signet Office in the XV Century* (Cambridge: 1939), 181–82.

46   Emden, *Oxford*, 2:1075–76.

47   PRO C.269/9; C.253/9/19, 24, 41.

48   *CPR 1408–13*, 150–51. In the 1907 biography of Humphrey, Vickers does not mention Hertilpole's service. John Farwell, however, was mentioned as the master and governor of John of Lancaster, and his duty was to educate the future duke of Bedford: E.C. Williams, *My Lord of Bedford* (London: 1963), 3.

49   *CPR 1408–13*, 269. See also *CPL*, 6:225 and the index where the relationship between the two men was hopelessly garbled by the editor.

50   *CCR 1399–1402*, 7. *CPR 1399–1401*, 207. Rome was in fact one of those who received the grant with the countess.

51   *CPR 1399–1401*, 227.

52   *CPR 1399–1401*, 24; *CPR 1401–5*, 218, 390; *CCR 1399–1402*, 515.

53 CPR 1401–5, 390. Roudon lived until at least 1411, for in that year he and John Chitterne alienated some property to Abingdon abbey, Berkshire, to provide for services for John Legh, a deceased colleague of both men in the chancery: CPR 1408–13, 347.
54 CPR 1401–5, 38.
55 Ibid., 212–13.
56 PRO C.219/10/3. In 1405, he had received royal licence to accept papal provisions: CPR 1405–8, 2.
57 CPR 1408–13, 452.
58 RP, 3:588. Overton may have returned to the chancery after his pardon. His signature appears on a summons in 1419 and, in 1420, he and Thomas Haseley, a clerk of the crown in chancery, were commissioned to arrest some canons of St. Mary's, Merton: PRO C.219/12/3; CPR 1416–22, 321.
59 The clerk of parliament, the underclerk of parliament, and the two clerks of the crown in chancery all had the clause in their re-appointments; the royal notary in parliament did not: CPR 1413–16, 13, 89, 151, 157, 171. Neither the keeper of the rolls nor the keeper of the hanaper received an *inspeximus* of his patent of office, and apparently none was needed.
60 Somerville, 389–90. Somerville was incorrect in assuming Walter Shiryngton, chancellor of the duchy and county palatine 1431–49, was a clerk of chancery. Shiryngton was a clerk of the signet: Somerville, 194; Otway-Ruthven, 182–83.
61 Somerville, 456.
62 Ibid., 176–77.
63 CNR, 2:405, 449; Otway-Ruthven, 68, 171–72.
64 CCR 1419–22, 130. Stopyndon had been involved with Henry's expedition by 1418 and had been granted property in Harfleur in 1420: CNR, 1:719; 2:339. Keeper of the hanaper, keeper of the rolls: CPR 1422–29, 379; CPR 1436–41, 245.
65 CPR 1401–5, 478.
66 Somerville, 177, 456. Like his father, Henry V wanted to keep his personal estates separate from those of the crown.
67 J.H. Wylie, *History of England Under Henry the Fourth*, 4 vols. (London: 1884–98), 2:284; A.R. Myers, 'The Captivity of a Royal Witch: the Household Accounts of Queen Joan of Navarre, 1419–21,' BJRL (1940), 24:263–84; 26:82–100; CFrR, 579. Wylie mistakenly indexed Simon Gaunstede as keeper of the privy seal and chancellor of the duchy of Lancaster during the reign of Henry V: J.H. Wylie, *The Reign of Henry the Fifth*, 3 vols. (Cambridge: 1914–29), 2:501; Wylie, *Henry the Fourth*, 4:442.
68 Somerville, 179–80. Myers believed that the queen was deprived of her estate and dowry for largely financial reasons and that the charges of sorcery against her were only a ruse: Myers, 274.
69 CPR 1429–36, 507; Somerville, 477–78; Carole Rawcliffe, *The Staffords, Earls of Stafford and Dukes of Buckingham 1394–1521* (Cambridge: 1978), 205. The deputy chancellors at Lancaster were John Dedwode (1439–40), Henry Gairstang (1442–43), and William Garnetz (1448–51); their signatures all appear on chancery instruments. Dedwode (1430–36): PRO C.219/14/2, 15/1; Gairstang (1441–51): PRO C.253/32; Garnetz (1446–50): PRO C.219/15/4, 16/1.
70 Godyng, for example, called himself a Southwark gentleman in 1429, first signed a chancery writ the following year, and never did anything that might make one suspect he was a master of chancery: CCR 1422–29, 338; PRO C.219/14/2.
71 For a collated transcription of the known copies of the ordinances see Wilkinson, 217–23.

Index